Crystal Magick

"Diamonds are a girl's best friend" is a phrase we are all familiar with. And yes, I agree they are... but I would have to rephrase to read "Crystals are everyone's best friend!"

It is no coincidence that diamonds are so sought after. Not because they are expensive but because they are the highest frequency stone of the crystal kingdom. It is the ultimate crystal to bring balance back into the body. And let's face it; we all need rebalancing at one time or another.

Life is a challenge at the best of times, and crystals are the perfect aid to help us back on track. They listen to us, accept us, help us and never answer back!

If you have never held a crystal, you are truly missing out on one of nature's gifts to us. They are beauty and unconditional love personified. You only need to look into the depths of a crystal to be drawn into another world.

All Rights Reserved.

Except for short extracts for credited quotation or review, the contents of this book may not be reproduced in any form, without the written permission of the author. All sources for copyrighted images and materials have given permission and have been acknowledged, with thanks.

©2019 Cover design Gaile Griffin Peers and Tamsin German.
©2019 Cover photography by Esperanza Isabel German

©2019 Tamsin German

Tamsin German asserts her moral rights

A CIP Catalogue record of this book is available from the British Library

Paperback Edition ISBN 978-0-9954758-2-3

eBook ISBN 978-0-9954758-3-0

FIRST PAPERBACK EDITION

First published in Great Britain in 2019
by Light My Way Publishing Avon Dassett, Southam UK

www.TamsinGerman.com

Crystal Magick

An Easy to follow Guide to Choosing and Using Crystals.

By

Tamsin German

I dedicate this book to all those beautiful souls who are already "awake" or are "awakening".

May this book guide you and assist you on your path...

Blessed Be xx

Preface

Crystals can be bought just about anywhere, and many of you no doubt have been drawn to buy a few. They are tactile and pretty to look at. Most often they are bought and placed on a shelf, and soon forgotten about, where they gather dust. True or not? I know most of you will have to agree that yes, it's true.

Have you ever wondered why you were drawn to buy them? Yes, they are pretty, but the reason is because you needed them. Crystals have incredible healing abilities and will always attract us in our times of need.

They work on our energy that flows through our body. When this energy gets out of sync, our body will find ways to heal itself. Headaches, pains, aches, etc. are all ways the body is letting us know it needs help. At such times we may be drawn to go outside, as nature is very healing, or, if we happen to pass by a store that sells crystals, we may be drawn into the store just to absorb some healing energy from the crystals.

Crystals are simple to use and very effective at healing our body and bringing it back into balance energetically. What have you got to lose?

Tamsin xx

Contents

Preface 5
Contents 7
My Journey of Discovery 15
What are Crystals? 17
Crystal Shapes 19
Quartz Forms 25
Choosing Crystals 31
Crystals and The Zodiac 33
Cleansing Your Crystals 35
Charging Crystals for Specific Magickal Workings 37
Storing Your Crystals 40
Dedicating and Programming Your Crystal 42
A Little Bit More About Crystals! 45
How Do They Work on The Body? 46
Ways of Using Crystals 52
    Beauty 52
    Jewellery etc 56
    Gridding rooms etc 58
    Gridding the body to heal the chakras 60
The Major Chakras of The Body 62
Crystal Layouts for Healing 65
    Aura Cleanser 65
    Chakra Balancer Spread 68
    Powerful Chakra and Aura Cleanser 70
    Energising and cleansing spread for chakras and aura. ... 73
    Harmonising Spread 75
    Hematite Shield of Protection 78
    The Seal of Solomon Spread 81
    General balance spread 81
    The Emotion Buster Spread 82
    The Recuperation Spread 83
    Chair Spread 85
    Grounding Chair Spread 86

Magickal Correspondences to enhance Crystal Healing 87
   Monday 88
   Tuesday 88
   Wednesday 89
   Thursday 89
   Friday 90
   Saturday 90
   Sunday 91
Meditation 92
Crystal Essences 95
   Direct method: 96
   Indirect method: 97
   Crystal recipes 97
   Common complaints 98
Crystal list 99
   Adamite 100
   Agate 101
      Blue Lace Agate 102
      Dendritic Agate 103
      Moss Agate 103
   Alexandrite 105
   Amazonite 106
   Amber 107
   Amethyst 108
      Black Amethyst 109
   Ametrine 110
   Angelite 111
   Apatite 112
   Aquamarine 113
   Aragonite 114
   Aventurine 115
   Cleaning method: 115
      Blue Aventurine 116
      Green Aventurine 116
   Azurite 117
   Azurite with Malachite 118
   Beryl 119
   Bloodstone 120
   Calcite 121

- Black Calcite 122
- Blue Calcite 122
- Clear Calcite 122
- Gold Calcite 123
- Green Calcite 123
- Orange Calcite 124
- Pink Calcite (Mangano Calcite) 124
- Red Calcite 125
- Yellow Calcite 125

Carnelian 126
Celestite 127
Chalcedony 128
- Blue Chalcedony 129

Charoite 130
Chiastolite 131
Chrysanthemum Stone 132
Chrysocolla 133
Chrysoprase 134
Chrysotile (Chrysotite) 135
Citrine 136
Danburite 137
Diamond 138
Herkimer Diamond 139
Emerald 140
Fluorite 141
- Blue Fluorite 142
- Clear Fluorite 142
- Green Fluorite 143
- Purple Fluorite 143
- Yellow Fluorite 144

Galena 145
Garnet 146
Hematite 147
Howlite 148
Iolite 149
Iron Pyrite (Fools Gold) 150
Jade 151
- Blue/Blue-Green Jade 152
- Brown Jade 152
- Lavender Jade 153

  Orange Jade 153
  Red Jade 153
  White Jade 154
  Yellow Jade 154
Jasper 155
  Blue Jasper 156
  Brown Jasper and Picture Jasper 156
  Dalmatian Jasper 157
  Flamingo Jasper 158
  Green Jasper 158
  Red Jasper and Brecciated Jasper 159
  Mookaite (Jasper) 159
  Yellow Jasper 160
Jet 161
Kunzite 162
  Clear Kunzite 163
  Green Kunzite (Hiddenite) 163
  Lilac Kunzite 164
  Yellow Kunzite 164
Kyanite 165
  Black Kyanite 165
  Blue Kyanite 166
Labradorite 167
  Yellow Labradorite 168
Lapis Lazuli 169
Larimar (Dolphin Stone, Blue Pectolite) 170
Lepidolite 171
Magnesite 172
Malachite 173
Marcasite 174
Moldavite 175
Moonstone 177
Muscovite (Mica) 178
Obsidian 179
  Apache Tear 180
  Black Obsidian 180
  Mahogany Obsidian 181
  Rainbow Obsidian 181
  Snowflake Obsidian 182
Onyx 183

Opal	184
Peridot (Chrysolite, Olivine)	185
Petrified Wood	186
Pietersite (Tempest Stone)	187
Prehnite	188
Preseli Bluestone	189
Quartz	191
Aqua Aura Quartz	192
Blue Quartz (Dumortierite)	193
Green Quartz	194
Harlequin Quartz	194
Natural Rainbow	195
Phantom Quartz	195
Rose Quartz	196
Rutilated Quartz (Angel Hair Quartz)	197
Smoky Quartz	197
Snow Quartz	198
Tangerine Quartz	199
Tourmalinated Quartz	199
Rhodochrosite	200
Rhodonite	201
Rhyolite	202
Ruby	203
Ruby in Zoisite (Anyolite)	203
Sapphire	204
Blue Sapphire	204
Green Sapphire	205
Pink Sapphire	205
Purple Sapphire	205
Yellow Sapphire	206
Cleaning method:	206
Sardonyx	207
Selenite (Satin Spa, Desert Rose)	208
Orange Brown Selenite	209
Blue Selenite	209
Desert Rose Selenite	209
Fishtail Selenite	210
Green Selenite	210
Seraphinite (Serafina)	211
Serpentine	212

- Smithsonite 213
- Sodalite 214
- Spinel 215
    - Black Spinel 215
    - Brown Spinel 215
    - Colourless Spinel 216
    - Green Spinel 216
    - Orange Spinel 216
    - Red Spinel 217
    - Violet Spinel 217
    - Yellow Spinel 217
- Stillbite 218
- Sugilite 219
- Sunstone 220
- Tanzanite 221
- Tektite 222
- Tiger's Eye 223
    - Blue Tiger's Eye (Hawk's Eye) 224
    - Gold Tiger's Eye 225
    - Red Tiger's Eye 225
- Tiger's Iron 226
- Topaz 227
    - Blue Topaz 227
    - Clear Topaz 228
    - Golden Topaz 228
    - Pink Topaz 228
- Tourmaline 229
    - Black Tourmaline (Schorl) 229
    - Blue Tourmaline (Indicolite) 230
    - Brown Tourmaline (Dravide) 231
    - Green Tourmaline (Verdelite) 231
    - Pink Tourmaline 232
    - Purple-Violet Tourmaline 232
    - Red Tourmaline (Rubellite) 233
    - Watermelon Tourmaline 233
    - Yellow Tourmaline 234
- Turquoise 235
- Unakite 236
- Variscite 237
- Zircon 238

    Brown Zircon 238
    Green Zircon 239
    Orange Zircon 239
    Red Zircon 239
    Yellow Zircon 240
  Zoisite 241
A quick reference guide for common ailments: 242
A quick guide for common magickal uses: 306
Conclusion 308
Index 309

Tamsin German

My Journey of Discovery

I was drawn to crystals in my twenties. I was fascinated by them, loved the look and feel of them. It's quite odd when I look back because I had no idea why! They were more than just a pretty stone to me, they made me feel better. People no doubt thought I was a little odd especially my friends as they were not really like me. They all fitted into society, but I have to say I never did. I shone above the rest even though I'd try very hard to blend into the background. When you are growing up you try very hard to be like all the rest of the kids. Unless of course you are the queen bee – then you want to set the standards and shine as brightly as possible. I never wanted to, but looking back I did. Now I have no problems about standing out... well with purple and blonde hair I can hardly blend, can I?!!?

I can't remember when I bought my first crystal exactly, but I do know it was after I went to a healing circle. I went to receive some healing because I suffered from eczema at the time. I was so amazed at the healing I received that I went on to study many different types of healing. They didn't use crystals at the healing, but they talked about them, after the healing session was done, and recommended that I get some. My first crystal was a quartz....it was the first of many I would buy.

I do remember being unsure of which crystal was right for me. Everyone told me one would stand out more than the rest and, when I picked it up, I would know it was the right one. That was exactly how it was! But I have to add I was, and still am, very sensitive to energies and knew without a doubt it was the right one. On top of that advantage, I'm also psychic and gifted with clairvoyance (the gift of seeing guidance in the form of pictures or symbols), clairaudience (the gift of hearing guidance), claircognisance (the gift of knowing) and clairsentience (the gift of feeling things, usually energies). So yes, I had a bit of help, even though at the time I wasn't really aware of these gifts.

In fact, I loved crystals so much that I went on to become a crystal healer. Their healing powers still amaze me to this day and no doubt will continue until it's time for me to "go home" as they say!

That's really the main reason for writing this book. I want you all to be able to experience the gift of healing in all its forms that crystals can provide.

The book has been set out in a simple format to help you confidently choose the right crystals and be able to put them to the best use.

Tamsin German

What are Crystals?

A crystal is a solid material whose constituents (atoms, molecules, ions) form in a highly ordered way forming a crystal lattice (structure) which extends in all directions. The way a crystal microscopically grows is used to identify the type of crystal.

Crystals grow forming one of seven possible geometric forms: hexagons, parallelograms, rectangles, rhomboids, squares, trapeziums or triangles.

These shapes lock together to form the crystal shape. For example, a hexagonal geometric shape will form a hexagonal crystal, while a square shape will form cubic crystals etc. Crystals come in all shapes and forms and some can only be identified by their internal structure, and not by their external appearance. Luckily by the time a crystal has reached a retailer the identification has been done!

Crystals come in many different shapes, but their internal structure is based on these seven basic forms. Each crystal will grow in this set pattern to form its external shape. Temperature; pressure; chemical conditions and the amount of space available are just some of the things that can affect their growth. Crystals were formed as the planet itself formed. Some crystals were subjected to enormous pressure, some dripped into being, others were laid down in layers and some grew in chambers.

All these different forces affect the properties of crystals and the way the crystals function. However, the crystal was formed, they all have the ability to absorb, store, focus and emit energy, especially on the aura (the energy that surrounds our body).

The colour of a crystal is caused by the minerals that form it. The most common are chromium, iron, manganese, titanium and copper. It is chromium that forms the intense red of ruby and the green of emeralds. Iron is responsible for the red, blue and yellow in garnet, spinel sapphire, peridot and chrysoberyl. While copper forms the blue and green of turquoise and malachite, and manganese the pink of rhodonite.

Tamsin German

Crystal Shapes

Crystals come in different forms, either rough, tumbled, natural formation or artificially shaped.

Crystal balls/spheres: These spheres send energy in all directions and are the most unified of all the shapes. They contain no rough edges and therefore facilitate smooth communication in group gatherings. Crystal balls can be used to purify and fill gaps in the aura when either worn or held. Small balls when worn as jewellery can be used to ameliorate degenerative diseases. Larger balls can be used for scrying into the future and/or past. Quartz balls are the most often used for this, but other semi-transparent crystals can be used.

Crystal bowls: These are formed from chunks of crystal into a bowl shape. The bowl is then used to produce a sound by running a mallet around the edge. They are used for healing, meditation and cleansing other crystals.

Crystal clusters/beds: The terminations (points) grow in close proximity to one another and share a common base. There may be as few as two points or many hundreds. Each individual point will have its own unique energy pattern, but all will be in harmony with each other. The points will emit energy in a sporadic pattern and constantly recharge each other. Clusters usually consist of single points but may contain some double points. Clusters are great for purifying the air. Place them in a room after an argument has occurred to clear the negative energy. Clusters also promote group harmony so are useful in families, businesses and social gatherings. Quartz or amethyst beds are a good way to cleanse other crystals and jewellery. You can place the crystals that require cleaning on the bed of terminations and leave overnight.

Crystal wands: These can be naturally formed or polished. Wands are traditionally used as healing tools by Shamans, healers and metaphysical workers. Wands focus energy tightly around the tip. Wands can be programmed before using to increase their potency. These should be used with respect as they are powerful healing tools. It is important to allow universal energy to enter through you when using a wand: allow it through the crown chakra and down into the hand holding the wand. Point the tip to the area and use your intent to draw off energy, or to increase energy in the area.

Vogel wands have a very precise vibratory signature. They have been polished to have indented facets, with specific angles down the sides of the wand to create a very specific healing tool. They have one thin faceted end and one fatter faceted end. The fatter end is the female end, and this draws pranic energy which is amplified as it spirals through the facets. The thinner, longer end is the male, and this transmits energy out in a laser beam. Vogels can be used to connect the chakras, remove entities and clear negativity. They can detect and clear blockages of energy in and around the body. Vogels need to be programmed before use and used with caution.

Naturally occurring quartz wands are called **laser points/quartz wands**. These are a long slender quartz that tapers towards a single termination, with small facets. The sides can be slightly curved. These are extremely powerful tools that need to be used with caution. Never randomly point the tip to anyone as you can do damage to their aura. Always use with respect and intent. They focus, concentrate and accelerate energy into a tight beam at the tip, like a laser. Useful for psychic surgery and for working deep within the body. These wands can be used to detach entities, remove cords and clear negativity of all kinds from the **Double termination (point)**: These have terminations at both ends. They usually grow in clay beds, and in rare cases, in clusters. These make powerful healing tools because they draw in, hold and release energy from both ends. They both ground and raise the vibrations in the body at the same time. physical and spiritual bodies.

Egg shaped crystals: These are as their name implies, an egg shape. Held sideways between the thumb and finger they can be used to scan the aura for any imbalances. Cold areas indicate a sluggish energy or blockage, warm or tingly areas indicate clear areas. The small end can be used in reflexology, zone therapy, acupressure and shiatsu. They are a very comfortable shape to hold during meditation.

Elestial: These have many natural terminations which fold over a multi-layered crystal. Their gentle energies remove fear, blockages and balance the polarities. Useful to use when experiencing many changes as their comforting energies will help sustain you through any emotional burdens. They can be used to view karma in past lives and help you understand your spiritual progress.

Geodes: Geodes look like a piece of rock on the outside but, when these rocks are cut open, they display a multitude of terminations on the inside. They are one of the most beautiful forms of crystal found in its natural state. These forms absorb, cleanse and amplify energy. They are useful for protection, aid spiritual growth and can break addictions and aid overindulgent personalities.

Layered crystals: Layered or plate-like crystals, such as Lepidolite, can work on several levels at the same time. The energy spreads out through the layers and can assist in getting to the bottom of things.

Natural formations: These are stones that come in their natural form, straight from Mother Earth so to speak. They come in a variety of shapes according to how they grow.

Occlusions: These are cloudy spots or patches in the crystal. They are formed by a deposit of another mineral. Quartz are the most common for having occlusions. An occlusion radiates the energy of the mineral and will be amplified by the crystal surrounding it.

Obelisk shaped crystal: This is a tapering four-sided shaft with a pyramid apex or point. They help connect to the ancient cultures of Egypt and stimulate the marking of time.

Phantom crystal: A phantom crystal is recognised by having a smaller ghost like appearance within a larger crystal. Phantoms have absorbed learning over many eons of time. They help us put the past into perspective and point us towards the future to allow our growth to continue. Very good to use during times of stagnation.

Polished Quartz: Sometimes quartz will be machine cut and polished to form either a single or double terminated piece. The inherent qualities of the quartz will be the same, but it is personal choice whether the polishing process affects the healing quality of the finished piece.

Pyramid shaped crystals: Pyramids have four sides on a base, tapering to an apex or point. They focus the energy through their apex and can charge and preserve objects. This beam of energy in the apex is focused and amplified due to the structure of the pyramid. Place on chakras to draw off negative energies and blockages.

Rough/raw chunks: These are partially tumbled to remove any sharp edges but remain near to their true form. Some healers prefer to use crystals in this form because they feel they are not traumatised by being polished. They are not so "pretty" to look at because polishing brings out the true colours of the crystal, but it really is down to personal taste. I use both rough and tumbled in healing. Some crystals are not safe to use in their rough state such as malachite.

Seer stone: These are naturally water polished stones, that are cut to reveal an inner world. They are used for scrying as they can show past, present and future. You can programme them to take you back to a specific time frame to access their knowledge.

Single termination (point): These occur where a single point has broken off from the base. They are usually six-faceted with a jagged, irregular base. Sometimes the base may be smooth if it has been polished. Single points are very versatile to use in meditation, healing, grid work and cleansing. Energy will flow from the point end. To draw energy off direct the point away from the body; to energise direct the point towards the body.

Square crystal: Squares consolidate energy within. They are good for grounding and setting intentions. Either naturally occurring or polished.

Tabular crystals: These have two wide sides and two narrow sides, resulting in a flattish looking crystal. They can be either single or double terminated. The energy moves freely through the crystal. "Tabbies" as I call them remove confusion, misunderstanding and misinterpretation, and are good to help communication on all levels; including to other realms. In healing they can be used to link two points to bring perfect balance. Useful to enhance telepathy and to activate other crystals. Tabbies amplify the energy of other crystals.

Tumbled (polished) stones: These are tumbled to form a highly polished crystal. They are smooth to the touch. You can get naturally tumbled stones which have been polished by water moving them such as river tumbled. These are in their true natural form. They are smooth to the touch but may have smooth grooves etc in them. These are among my favourite style of crystal!

Quartz Forms

I have included quartz shapes as a separate chapter because they can come in many different forms, each form containing its own unique properties, as well as the inherent properties of quartz itself.

Abundance Quartz: This form consists of one long quartz point with many small points around its base. It's used to attract abundance and wealth into your life. Place in the wealth corner of the house or your business (the point at the farthest rear left of the front door). Or on your altar when you are casting a spell to draw abundance into your life.

Barnacle Quartz: Barnacle quartz has small crystals covering some of the main larger crystal. These are useful for meditation on family, community or group matters. They provide a cohesive group energy when working towards a common goal.

Bridge Quartz: This occurs when one crystal grows out of the side of another. Bridges bring things together and this is what these are used for. They can join the inner and outer worlds, higher self and ego or help you connect to another. Good to use when trying to convey ideas to others: such as in public speaking.

Cathedral Quartz: These contain the wisdom of the ages, they are libraries of light. All that has occurred on Earth has been stored in these quartzes. The larger the generator the more knowledge stored. The main crystal body appears to be composed of various points, giving it a convoluted appearance. These multiple terminations will have at least one apex. The knowledge is accessed through meditation. They give one access to the Akashic records, and when placed on the site of pain, will ease it. These can be programmed to bring about a better world.

Channelling Quartz: These have one face on the apex that is seven sided, with a triangular face on the opposite side. These help to bring down information from the universe and other higher sources and then help us to assimilate the information. They can be used in trance channelling, but you should be experienced in such matters before you use them for this.

Cross Quartz: In this formation one crystal grows at a right angle to another, usually larger crystal. These are used to help spiritual study and growth. They can be used to remove energy implants. Use on any chakra and it will clear and activate it.

Diamond Window Quartz: One of the faces on the apex of the crystal displays a diamond shape. Gazing into the diamond will take you deep into yourself or enable you to gain insight into another. Some diamonds are large and connected from the base to the apex. Diamonds provide a doorway into other realities and a deep connection of the self.

Etched Quartz: These look like they have hieroglyphs etched onto the surface. They are for personal use in meditation to access ancient wisdom from civilizations of old, and to reawaken inherent skills and healing abilities. Useful for past life work; seeing where a dis-ease started or where destructive emotional patterns began.

Generator Quartz: Generators have six facets or faces that meet equally in a sharp point. These crystals draw in energy equally on each facet and are powerful tools to optimise healing; aid focus and clarity. These act as earth energy batteries allowing us to access and use the electromagnetic energy of the earth's aura. Use to recharge your energies when feeling tired, ill or injured. They can either be a single generator or a cluster of generators. Clusters can be used to bring harmony into group situations, and each point can be programmed for different people. They are wonderful to use in group healings.

Isis (Goddess) Quartz: This has one dominant five-sided face. It is said to represent the five elements of earth, fire, water, wind and storm. This sacred pentagon formed by the five sides stimulates our connection to the Divine. Use to heal anything that is broken: physical, emotional, mental or spiritual. Good for empaths as it ameliorates over-identification with the suffering of others. Helps us get in touch with our feeling side, taking us deep into our heart centre. Beneficial for anyone who is facing transition to the next world: place by their bed.

Life Path Quartz: These are long thin, clear quartz with one or more completely smooth sides which teach us to follow our soul and not our ego. Accessing our life purpose, they guide us to go with the flow and follow our bliss or spiritual destiny.

Record Keeper Quartz: These have clearly etched pyramid shapes on the sides of the main body and/or face of the quartz. These triangles point up to the apex. The triangles can be sunken or raised on the surface. The raised are more common than the sunken. There can be one or several triangles showing. They are portals for spiritual wisdom and will show us what has gone before. They show us perfect harmony of mind, body and spirit. The triangles can be placed to the third eye or rubbed during meditation to open them to the knowledge you seek. Care and respect must be used when working with these crystals. They are good for inner work and can help propel us forward removing obstacles in our path. Other crystals can be record keepers, but quartz is the most commonly found.

Sceptre Quartz: These have a central rod around one end of which another crystal has formed. They appear to have a larger bulbous end. They can be a reversed sceptre where the bulbous end can be the smaller end. Also used for accessing ancient knowledge and to channel higher vibrations. Sceptres are excellent healing tools because they direct energy to the core of the problem dissolving the dis-ease out through all the subtle bodies. They help us "walk the talk" aligning our actions to our ideals and empower us so we can control changes in our life. Fertility and balancing the male and female energies can also be helped. Reversed sceptres free the mind from false illusions and can bring inner calm.

Self-Healed Quartz: These have the normal termination at one end but the other end where it has broken off from the main base has small terminations where it has begun to grow again. These are master teachers that help us accept our difficult pathways and show us how much we have grown from the experiences. Excellent to use in healing, they reveal parts of our inner self that need to be accepted. Useful for healing wounds from surgery or trauma and for mending broken bones.

Soulmate and **Tantric Twin Quartz**: These both exhibit the same shape where two crystals grow from a common base and are joined along one side. Soulmate quartz draw our soulmate to us, although this may not necessarily be a sexual partner. Soulmate quartz are great for all kinds of relationships, and the closer in size the two crystal points the more harmonious the relationship. These crystals show us how to be separate but united in an equal relationship. A tantric twin has two identical crystals aligned side by side on the same base. These help us to truly know and accept our self and assists when two people are working together as equals.

Time Link Quartz: Also known as portal quartz, these consist of a parallelogram that creates a seventh face on the apex of a crystal. When you look at the face of the crystal the parallelogram can be on either the left or right. These formations teach us that time is an illusion that we have created to organise our experience here on earth. A left-inclined parallelogram takes us into the past to explore other lives and other dimensions; while a right-inclined parallelogram takes you to possible futures. Some time-links display both. A pair of time-links are a powerful tool to work on both right and left-brain hemispheres, healing disorders on both sides of the body. A left inclined time-link works on the right side of the body and a right inclined the left side. Right inclined time-links will assist in emotional healing and intuitive work, while left inclined time-links will activate beings with knowledge of technologies and sciences that could prove useful in our evolution.

Transmitter Quartz: Transmitters have two seven sided faces on their apex, with two triangular faces between them. These can be used to transmit long distance healing or thought patterns. They are also useful for linking to higher vibrations to open intuition, gather wisdom and connect to higher dimensions.

Trans-Channeling Quartz: This is a combination of a channelling and transmitter. It has three seven sided faces on the apex, with triangles between each. These are used to access universal knowledge to benefit humankind.

Trigonic Quartz: These are among the rarest quartz forms around. They have a triangle etched into the face as in the record keepers but the triangle points down away from the apex. They contain knowledge of other realms, especially the realms beyond death. Not only can they be used to see the deep past of humanity, but they are keys to the future as well. They teach us to remain open to the flow of the possible future, to remain in a state of grateful anticipation of whatever comes. Trigonics are said to come to those who are able to work with them. I was blessed with one which came to me in a very curious way... I met a wonderful lady on an Atlantean workshop. The workshop itself was rather dull and we spent more time chatting than listening! I was studying crystals at the time and the lady I met was a therapist who had worked with crystals for years. She invited me to her house to see her collection of crystals. When I got there, she told me she had to offer a crystal for me to buy if I felt inclined. As soon as I saw it, I knew I had to have it. She told me she had the bought the crystal 30 years earlier and had carried it around with her and had never used it as she knew it was not for her! I had no idea it was so special and neither did she, it was four months later that I saw the inverted triangle and become curious as to what it meant. I still have it today and it sits on my altar.

Tamsin German

Choosing Crystals

There is an abundance of crystals on the market to buy, which can make choosing the right one a bit daunting. There are many ways to choose. Looking through the crystals listed farther down can give you a good starting point. Choose a crystal that covers the imbalance/s that you are trying to heal. There may well be more than one, so compile a short list of those that interest you. Then go to a good crystal shop and look and hold each one of the crystals on your list. You will be drawn to some but not to others.

Sometimes a crystal will shine brighter than the rest or it will create a tingling sensation when held. This is the crystal's way of getting your attention!

You can buy crystals online but make sure they have a return service in case you don't like the crystal. I like to handle my crystals because I find that some will resonate while others will feel wrong! Buying from a picture can also be misleading as the pictures are usually a lot prettier than the actual crystal. This will not affect its healing power, but you may be disappointed when you see it. Remember it is not the look of a crystal that counts but how it feels to you! I remember having a lovely moldavite crystal pendant that I loved but every time I wore it, kids especially, would comment about how it looked like a bogie!

Using your intuition can also be a fun way to choose. Just ask the crystals which one is right for you and be drawn to the right one. With crystals you can't make a mistake because even if they don't heal the problem you wanted them to, there will be a reason why you were drawn to it.

At some time, we might be gifted a crystal by someone. These are always special and should be treasured.

You can also choose a crystal for someone else by asking

the right crystal to show itself. A crystal will always make itself known to you.

If you are still unsure which crystal is right for you, your birth stone can be used as a guide. This will connect you to your zodiac sign and earth energies.

Tamsin German

Crystals and The Zodiac

Capricorn Dec 22nd - Jan 19th Amber, Aragonite, Azurite, Carnelian, Fluorite, Galena, Garnet, Green & Black Tourmaline, Jet, Labradorite, Magnetite, Malachite, Onyx, Peridot, Quartz, Ruby, Smoky Quartz, Turquoise.

Aquarius Jan 20th - Feb 18th Amethyst, Amber, Angelite, Aquamarine, Atacamite, Blue Celestite, Blue Obsidian, Boji Stone, Chrysoprase, Fluorite, Labradorite, Magnetite, Moonstone.

Pisces Feb 19th - March 20th Amethyst, Aquamarine, Beryl, Bloodstone, Blue Lace Agate, Calcite, Chrysoprase, Fluorite, Labradorite, Moonstone, Smithsonite, Sunstone, Turquoise.

Aries March 21st - April 19th Amethyst, Aquamarine, Aventurine, Bloodstone, Carnelian, Citrine, Diamond, Fire Agate, Garnet, Jadeite, Jasper, Kunzite, Magnetite, Orange Spinel, Pink Tourmaline, Ruby, Topaz.

Taurus April 20th - May 20th Aquamarine, Azurite, Black Spinel, Boji Stone, Diamond, Emerald, Kyanite, Kunzite, Lapis Lazuli, Malachite, Rhodonite, Rose Quartz, Sapphire, Selenite, Tiger's Eye, Topaz, Tourmaline, Variscite.

Gemini May 21th - June 20th Agate, Apatite, Apophyllite, Aquamarine, Blue Spinel, Calcite, Chrysocolla, Chrysoprase, Citrine, Dendritic Agate, Green Obsidian, Green Tourmaline, Sapphire, Serpentine, Tourmalined and Rutilated Quartz, Tiger's Eye, Topaz, Tourmaline, Ulexite, Variscite, Zoisite.

Cancer June 21st - July 22nd Amber, Beryl, Brown Spinel, Calcite, Carnelian, Chalcedony, Dendritic Agate, Emerald, Fire Agate, Moonstone, Moss Agate, Opal, Pearl, Pink Tourmaline, Rhodonite, Ruby.

Crystal Magick

Leo July 23rd - Aug 22nd Amber, Boji Stone, Carnelian, Cat's or Tiger's Eye, Chrysocolla, Citrine, Danburite, Emerald, Fire Agate, Garnet, Golden Beryl, Green & Pink Tourmaline, Kunzite, Larimar, Muscovite, Onyx, Orange Calcite, Petalite, Pyrolusite, Quartz, Red Obsidian, Rhodochrosite, Ruby, Topaz, Turquoise, Yellow Spinel.

Virgo Aug 23rd - Sept 22nd Amazonite, Amber, Blue Topaz, Carnelian, Chrysocolla, Citrine, Dioptase, Garnet, Magnetite, Moonstone, Moss Agate, Okenite, Opal, Peridot, Purple Obsidian, Rubellite, Rutilated Quartz, Sapphire, Sardonyx, Smithsonite, Sodalite, Sugilite.

Libra Sept 23rd - Oct 22nd Ametrine, Apophyllite, Aquamarine, Aventurine, Bloodstone, Chiastolite, Chrysolite, Emerald, Green Spinel, Green Tourmaline, Jade, Kunzite, Lapis Lazuli, Lepidolite, Mahogany Obsidian, Moonstone, Opal, Peridot, Prehnite, Sapphire, Sunstone, Topaz.

Scorpio Oct 23rd - Nov 21st Apache Tear, Aquamarine, Beryl, Boji Stone, Charoite, Dioptase, Emerald, Garnet, Green Tourmaline, Herkimer Diamond, Hiddenite, Kunzite, Malachite, Moonstone, Obsidian, Red Spinel, Rhodochrosite, Ruby, Topaz, Turquoise, Variscite.

Sagittarius Nov 22nd - Dec 21st Amethyst, Azurite, Blue Lace Agate, Chalcedony, Charoite, Dark Blue Spinel, Dioptase, Garnet, Gold Sheen Obsidian, Labradorite, Lapis Lazuli, Malachite, Okenite, Pink Tourmaline, Ruby, Smoky Quartz, Snowflake Obsidian, Sodalite, Spinel, Sugilite, Topaz, Turquoise, Wulfenite.

Cleansing Your Crystals

Crystal shops have lovely energies when you walk into them, even for those not sensitive. You may feel uplifted when you enter a shop. This is because the crystals will have been busy clearing and absorbing any negative energy that is expelled by the people who enter the shop.

This is why when you have bought a crystal it will need to be cleansed before you start to use it. There are different methods to do this. All are effective so choose one that suits you best.

- Crystals can be placed under running water such as a tap to wash all the negativity away. As you hold them under the water, hold the intention that the water is cleansing them. Imagine the crystal/s releasing any negative energy and it being carried off down the plug hole. Hold them back under the water again and imagine the crystal/s being filled with golden light. Dry the crystal/s and place out in the sun for a minimum of one hour to energise it again. Or place in moonlight overnight.

- Immerse the crystal/s in a bowl of saltwater. Fill a bowl with water and place a tablespoon of rock salt in the water, swirl to dissolve it. Make sure the crystal is not friable (water soluble) or you will slowly be dissolving it away! Leave the crystal/s for an hour with the intention set that the salty water will cleanse them. (**Friable crystals**: Amber, Azurite, Calcite, Dioptase, Kyanite, Selenite, Sulphur, Zeolite, cannot be cleaned this way.)

- Immerse the crystals in the sea, again holding the intention to cleanse the negative energy away. Hold the crystals tightly as they have been known to 'jump' out of your hand never to be seen again!

- Smudging with an incense stick. Hold the crystal in the smoke and hold the intention of the smoke cleansing the negative energy away. Place in the sun for a minimum of one hour or overnight in the moonlight.

- Place on either a quartz or amethyst bed. This is a natural flat piece of crystal with lots of terminations to it. Leave the crystals overnight and they will be cleansed by the morning. This is also the best method to cleanse any friable crystals and crystal jewellery. I always pop my jewellery on a quartz bed each night while I sleep so it will be ready to wear the next morning.

- Place your crystal in a small bowl and cover completely with either salt or brown rice. Leave overnight for the energies to be absorbed into the rice or salt. Gently clear any remaining particles off the crystal and throw the rice or salt away. Never try to reuse the salt or rice because it will be full of negative energy! Some crystals are self-cleaning such as Azeztulite, Citrine, Kyanite and Selenite. I would just rinse them to clear any dust or brush the dust off when you think they need it.

Tamsin German

Charging Crystals for Specific Magickal Workings

Magick work often involves working with the elements of nature: air, earth, fire and water. So, it is best to use at least one of the elements to charge your crystals. Some of the elements have particular qualities which can be used to enhance any spell work. Air is the power of movement and intelligence. Earth represents the energy of nurturing, abundance, welcoming and home. Fire is the creator and destroyer. Water is cleansing and contains the essence of love. Choose the most appropriate for the spell you are working.

- Water energy: Leave the crystal under cool running water for a few minutes.

- Earth energy: Bury your crystal in the ground for a few hours so it can absorb the earth energies which are strength, magnetism, attraction and to banish negativity.

- Power energy: Put your crystal outside in a thunderstorm to absorb power (strength) energy.

- Air energy: Hold your crystal in the smoke of a burning incense stick (Sage or Sandalwood are good all-purpose incense sticks to use). Air energy is good for communication, intellect and understanding.

- Fire energy: Pass the crystal briefly through the flame of a candle. Fire energy is good for purification spells.

Crystal Magick

- You can rub your crystal with any herbs that are in tune with what your spell work is for.

- A charging ritual can be used that combines all four elements.

You will need:

A candle
An incense stick (sage or sandalwood are good)
A small bowl of water
A small clay or wooden bowl containing some soil
A bottle of essential oil (lavender, frankincense, sandalwood or sage are good choices)

1. Arrange the items in a circle. If you know the directions, then place the items as follows:

North: Bowl of earth
East: Incense stick
South: Candle
West: Bowl of water
Place the essential oil in the centre.

2. Light the candle to represent the fire element. Then, using the candle flame, light the incense to represent the air element.

3. Hold your crystal and sprinkle some of the water on it, whilst saying the words "I charge you with the power of water"

4. Sprinkle a little of the essential oil over the crystal while visualising energy passing from you into the crystal.

5. Next pass the crystal through the candle flame, whilst saying "I charge you with the power of fire"

6. Pass the crystal through the incense smoke, whilst saying "I charge you with the power of air"

7. Now place the crystal in the bowl of earth, whilst saying, "I charge you with the power of earth"

The crystal is now ready to be used or you can do this ritual in advance and store the crystal in a piece of silk cloth or bag.

Crystals can be used in magick in whatever way you wish, just use your intuition to guide you. Before using them, you need to set the intention into the stone for the purpose you want it for. This is done by simply sitting quietly whilst holding the stone and stating what you want the stone to do. Imagine the words entering into the stone. Once you feel the words have been "heard" you can use it as part of your magick work.

Storing Your Crystals

Storing crystals is a very personal thing. I like mine scattered around the house in bowls or grouped to spread their energies, rather than stored away. But if you have small children then this may not be an option. Crystals vary in hardness and this can influence how you store them. The hardness of a crystal is determined by its resistance to scratching when another substance is drawn across it. A substance can only be scratched by a substance that is harder. The hardness of minerals is measured on a decimal scale known as the Mohs Scale. 10 being Diamond and 1 being Talc. When storing your crystals avoid placing in air-tight plastic or polythene bags. These can have a detrimental effect on the crystals vibrations and in some cases can cause fading.

If you want to wrap your crystals to help prevent scratching, then the best material to use is silk. It is a natural non-abrasive material that is believed to be the best insulator to prevent the crystals losing their charge. Wrap crystals individually especially if they are on the softer side of the Mohs Scale. Try to avoid placing in extremes of temperature of heat and cold, as this could cause damage. Avoid direct sunlight as some crystals will fade if left for too long or are photosensitive.

Some crystals require extra attention. Opal for example is made up of 10% water and should never be kept near heat sources, which will dry them out and cause cracking in the stone. Equally they should never be placed in dry places as this will cause them to lose their colour. Store Opals in a small container of water. Pearls contain 2% water, and like Opals should not be kept near heat sources.

Also avoid contact with acidic liquids such as vinegar or red wine as this will cause them to dissolve.

Mohs Scale examples

CRYSTAL	HARDNESS
Amber, Gypsum	2
Calcite, Jet	3
Fluorite, Malachite, Pearl	4
Apatite, Lapis Lazuli, Obsidian, Opal, Turquoise	5
Agate, Carnelian, Garnet, Hematite, Jade, Jasper, Labradorite, Moonstone, Pyrite	6
Onyx, Peridot, Quartz, Tiger's Eye, Tourmaline	7
Emerald, Topaz	8
Ruby, Sapphire	9
Diamond	10

Dedicating and Programming Your Crystal

Crystals should be dedicated and programmed before you use them. The purpose of a dedication is to help anyone who comes within your energy field to gain from the experience; while programming is for specific purposes.

I like to use the following dedication on all crystals that I buy. I hold the crystal in my palm and say the words "I dedicate this crystal to bring love, light, healing and abundance to all who come near me". I hold the crystal and imagine the words going into it. This is just my personal favourite but feel free to find a dedication that feels right for you.

Programming a crystal is for you to help clear whatever troubles you. If you have a long-standing illness that you want to heal, you can programme your crystal for that specific healing. Emotional hang-ups and mental conditioning can also be helped by programming your crystal. The fact that you are 'verbalising' your wish to clear an area of your life that is giving you problems is the first step to helping you heal yourself.

Sit quietly, holding your crystal in your hands. Feel its shape. Look at it from every angle. Notice any marks on it. Now look at the colour of it. Start to see it in all its beauty. As you do this you will start to form a connection with it. Now, when the connection feels right, ask your crystal to help you with whatever you wish to heal.

A simple, "Please crystal can you bring me back into balance so that I may experience complete joyful health", will suffice; or you can be more specific about voicing what help you need.

The choice of wording is for you to decide. Just remember to be clear about what you need. Sit for a few moments sending the intention of your healing wishes into the crystal. Once you feel it has taken the intention, then bless and thank your crystal. Now it is ready to help heal you! Carry your crystal with you every day and know that its energies are working to bring balance back into your life.

If you want to programme multiple things into your crystal, then you will need to connect a little deeper with the crystal. You can do this during meditation. I like to sit holding my crystal and to make the connection by observing the colour of it. I see if there are any inclusions or marks on it. I then place it on my heart and imagine the crystal growing very large until it stands before me. I imagine myself walking around the outside of it until I find the door which lets me enter inside the crystal. I ask at the door if I may enter. I have never been refused entry yet! (But I know some who have. In these cases, I would just sit with the stone and try to open the door another day).

Inside it is cooler and the walls are like the crystal, shiny and cold to the touch. There is usually a pathway into an inner room. Chairs or sofas may be present, or on occasions it appears more like a kitchen! The deva is usually sitting, waiting for me, or I may be drawn on toward a programming room first. Either way is ok. Once in the programming room, there may appear various screens – each one acting as a computer for you to programme what you want.

For example: If the crystal is citrine, you may wish to use one screen to programme more wealth into your life; more self-esteem on another screen and to help clear depression on another.

You may experience a different interior but however it appears it will make sense to you! After you have placed your personal programmes into the crystal, return to the first room and talk to the deva (see below for a further description) if you wish; if not, just walk out of the crystal the way you came in. Imagine it shrinking in size until you feel it on your heart and bring your attention back to the present. Hold the crystal and thank it for its help and use it daily to bring the healing help requested.

Most of all enjoy each day as it presents itself to you.

Tamsin German

A Little Bit More About Crystals!

Crystals contain an elemental deva inside them. These devas are the spirit protectors of the crystals. When you sit quietly with your crystal you may be lucky enough to make contact with the deva inside. When I programme my crystals, I often get to meet them and have a little chat. Devas can reveal other uses for the crystal that are not found in books. This was what happened to me while I was taking my crystal course. I would quietly meditate with my chosen crystals and learn a wealth of information that no book contained. I have always trusted this guidance as it has always turned out to be true.

The devas are lovely, lively spirits and are from the fairy realm. I find they normally appear in the same coloured clothing as the crystal and with a similar personality. Yellow for a citrine crystal for example and a lively energy because citrine is great for boosting us up. Devas look after the crystals and ensure that their energies help us as they should. Devas like to be treated with respect, so always remember to thank your crystals for their healing energy. Crystals can become your best friend. They are always there for us in times of need, they give us guidance, they rebalance our energy and they don't answer back! What more could you want in a best friend!!

How Do They Work on The Body?

To understand how crystals work on the body we have to understand how the body works. When we think of the body, we tend to think of it in terms of a physical structure. Muscles, organs, bones, etc. But we need to look deeper... and I mean even deeper than the smallest cell!

We were taught at school that our cells are composed of protons, electrons and neurones and that these are the smallest particles that exist. However, this theory is rather old school because quantum physicists have discovered that there are smaller particles, which are so small that they have no form, but are an un-measurable amount of energy! To put it in simple terms we are just a large mass of energy. Each different structure of the body: eyes, muscles, organs, etc. are formed of a different density of energy. The density of energy depends on the frequency at which it vibrates. So each part of the body will vibrate at a specific frequency to form that part of the body and keep it functioning at its optimum frequency to produce health in that area. The kidneys will vibrate at a specific frequency which will differ from the skin, for example.

The energy that the body is made up of has no boundary from the edge of the body, even though to the naked eye we finish at the skin. The energy continues out from the skin and forms an electromagnetic field which is also known as the aura. This aura continues out several feet before it begins to thin out. There is no "end" to it and it links to everything around it. So, when you hear spiritual gurus say "We are all one," you can now begin to understand what they mean. We are only interested in the physical body and the aura for the purposes of this book.

Our auras consist of seven layers which connect to different aspects of the body.

Our first layer deals directly with the physical body. It's like a blueprint of our physical body. This layer is the etheric body.

The second layer is the emotional body and deals with our emotions.

The third layer is the mental body and deals with our mental chatter. These three layers deal with the physical body. The bridging body, known as the astral body, is the fourth layer which connects our physical and spiritual bodies together.

The next three layers are our spiritual bodies. The fifth layer is the etheric template which holds our perfect physical body in a template form, a bit like a photographic negative; the sixth layer is the celestial body which deals with our spiritual emotions and the final seventh layer being the ketheric template which deals with our spiritual mental aspects. Understanding of these levels is not needed for healing to occur but it may be of interest to some of you! These seven layers make up our aura.

Our aura is like a vibrating field that collects all the energy that we need to live and brings it into the body via specific energy points called chakras. There are seven main chakras which link directly to the endocrine system in the body. The endocrine system consists of seven ductless glands which control the functioning of the body via hormones. When the endocrine glands are functioning in perfect harmony, we have health; when not, then dis-ease occurs. The flow of energy between the aura, chakras and endocrine glands keep us functioning as a human being.

The first or Base chakra is located at the base of the spine. It links to the adrenal glands in the endocrine system. This chakra works directly with controlling all solid parts such as the skeletal structure, bones, teeth, nails and also the anus, rectum, colon, prostate, blood and building of the cells. It governs survival and our basic instincts.

The second chakra or Sacral chakra is located behind the navel. It is linked to the reproductive organs in women and men. This chakra works directly with controlling the reproductive organs, bladder, kidneys, spleen, mammary glands, bowels, fluid functions and potency. It governs our emotions.

The third or Solar Plexus chakra is located at the base of the sternum. Linked to the pancreas in the endocrine system, this chakra works directly with controlling the digestive system, muscles, liver, gall bladder, stomach, autonomic nervous system and lower back. It governs our personal power, the ego.

The fourth or Heart chakra is located in the centre of the chest. It is linked to the thymus gland of the endocrine system. This chakra works directly with the heart, rib cage, lungs, circulation, skin and upper back. It governs relationships with our self and others.

The fifth or Throat chakra is located in the base of the throat. It is linked to the thyroid gland of the endocrine system. This chakra works directly with the throat, ears, teeth, jaw, neck, head, airways, upper lungs, arms, nerves and muscles of upper body and vocal apparatus. It governs creative expression and communication.

The sixth or Third Eye chakra is located between the eyebrows. Linked to the pituitary gland of the endocrine system, this chakra works directly with the left eye, nose, ears, sinuses, left brain hemisphere and parts of the nervous system. It governs intuition and connection to the higher spiritual forces.

The seventh or Crown chakra is located at the top of the head. It is linked to the pineal gland of the endocrine system. This chakra works directly with the right eye, right brain hemisphere and the central nervous system. It governs our spiritual connection and is the main spiritual centre.

This is the simplified version of how the body works from an energetic point of view. Now comes the bit about crystals...they also vibrate! Yes, they vibrate at specific frequencies which gently brings the body's energy back into balance. They are able to conduct an electric current called piezo electricity. When placed on or near the body, their vibrations link to our vibrations. This connection occurs in the aura and works its way into the body by the chakra system; which in turn links to the endocrine glands. So, the healing occurs first in the aura, then the chakras and finally through into the physical body via the endocrine system.

Crystals were placed here on our planet as a natural form of healing, but their knowledge has been lost over the years. However, people are becoming more aware of the natural forms of healing available, especially as allopathic medicine brings so many debilitating side effects. These old healing forms are coming back into fashion as we all seek more natural ways to help heal ourselves.

Crystals are one of the easiest forms of natural healing around. Their effects are gentle but powerful in their results. There are no side effects and they can be used on children. They can work to bring balance on all levels – mental, emotional, physical and spiritual. These stones heal holistically, as all levels need to be in balance for perfect health. When placed near us, they vibrate our subtle energies and dissolve dis-ease in the body.

Our emotions can have a powerful effect on the body. When we are happy everyone knows it, even when no words are spoken! We smile and radiate a happy light energy which people will feel on an energetic level. Being near a happy person rubs off on us. It makes us smile and feel happy. However, the reverse is also true. Unhappy people make us feel sad and heavy when they are around. We all go through a range of emotions every day, which will have an effect upon our health and the health of others.

Challenges are part and parcel of life, we all experience bad days. Losing a job; breaking up from a partnership or marriage; losing a loved one; can create lots of unhappy emotions and sometimes it can be very hard to deal with these emotions.

Unhappy thoughts create a very heavy energy which hangs around the body and causes blockages in our natural flow of energy through the aura and into the chakra system. This blockage, when left, can eventually cause ill health in the body. Crystals are a great way to help us deal with difficult times because they will resonate with our emotional part of the aura and help to clear any blockages in it.

Crystals can also work the same way on our mental chatter. When our brains can't shut down and we find we are constantly stressing about work, money, kids, etc. crystals work directly with our mental layer in the aura. For those walking their spiritual path they can be used to work directly with the spiritual layer of the aura.

Crystals can be used not only to rebalance the body on all levels, but they can show us why we have the illness. Many are great at getting to the root cause of an illness and showing us that insight. This is an important factor because we can learn from the mistakes that caused the dis-ease in the first place. They are also a great aid when the dis-ease has a past-life link.

Many people suffer the symptoms of past life dis-eases, but, because it is "past life", no root cause will be found.

As a healer I have found many instances of this.

The medical profession is mystified while seeing the pain suffered by their patient. Healing and crystal healing are two of the best ways to clear this type of dis-ease. Many crystals can be used to help clear past-life traumas. They show us the underlying cause from our past life, so we can work to clear it from our present life. They connect to the trauma of a past life related illness by connecting to the part of the aura relevant to that time. Healing will occur at that level to release the energy blockage. Once it is cleared then the balancing effect will move down through the aura until the physical body is healed.

Factors such as the environment in which we live can have an impact upon our health. All electrical devices emit radiation which can impact our health. This electromagnetic smog can cause dis-ease within the body. Televisions, mobile phones, computers and microwaves are among the worst offenders for giving off electrical radiations. Other environmental effects come from geopathic stress which is created by underground water, power line, and negative Ley lines. These emit subtle electrical emanations which can run through the earth and affect us and any buildings; causing illness and dis-ease. Another factor that is now considered a very real illness is Sick Building Syndrome. The symptoms of headaches, nausea, dizziness, breathing difficulties and general fatigue are caused through poor ventilation, air pollution and negative geopathic stresses running under a building. Crystals are a perfect way to help combat these environmental factors without going to the expense of moving or changing jobs!

Ways of Using Crystals

Beauty

Crystals can be added to beauty products to enhance their properties, such as cleansers, toners and moisturisers. Pop a crystal in the container with the product and use as normal. Remember to remove from the container once it is empty! Or use a flat stone to work the cleanser or moisturiser into the skin. Oils for the body can also be enhanced by the addition of crystals.

Crystals can be used to massage the body with or without oil. Smooth rounded stones are ideal to use as they are easy to hold. Simply move the stone across the area of the body you want to massage in a smooth circle. Apply as much pressure as is comfortable for you, or the person you are massaging. All areas of the body can be worked either by you or a partner. This form of massage is very relaxing when applied gently with awareness of sensitive areas, such as bony areas. The following list gives a few examples of good crystal to use for massage:

Agate. Gives feelings of being protected. It helps the metabolism of the connective tissue. "Lace" agates help with waste disposal of the connective tissue and aids the arteries and intestines.

Agatised Coral. This helps reduce deep rooted tension.

Alabaster (orange). Loosens stiff muscles and strengthens the tissues. Stabilising stone if you are suffering any psychological conditions.

Amazonite. This mood balancing stone is good for joint problems, caused by stress, rheumatism, infections, liver conditions etc.

Amethyst. If you need to draw out emotional states such as grief or sadness, then this is the stone. It works at a deeper level to release emotions and bring inner peace. Particularly good for the skin and nerves.

Anthophyllite. Use around the ears to help tinnitus and other ear complaints. Also good for the kidneys.

Aquamarine. Good for tired or aching eyes. Used regularly around the eyes can help prevent cross-eyedness and will regulate near or far sightedness.

Aventurine. Useful for heart conditions because it encourages relaxation and reduces stress and nervousness. Effective for infections, sunburn and sunstroke; use very gentle strokes.

Banded Amethyst. Good for sufferers of chronic fatigue. Use around the head area to relieve tension headaches.

Bloodstone. Strengthens the body's defences and eases infections.

Blue Banded Chalcedony. Use to activate the lymph glands, kidneys and bladder. Lowers blood pressure.

Blue Calcite. Massage the jaw for teeth problems. Good for the bones, colon, connective tissue, lymph and skin.

Blue Quartz. A cooling calming stone that helps nervousness, lowers blood pressure, soothes pain and reduces tension.

Blue Tiger's Eye. A grounding stone, good for hormonal balance. Eases restlessness, nervousness, shivering, and pain and is good in crisis situations.

Dalmatian Jasper. This has a strengthening and balancing effect.

Dumortierite. This "take it easy" stone helps cramps, headaches, nervousness, pain, nausea and motion sickness.

Fluorite. Eases chronic tension, helps mobility and postural problems. Good for skin, tissue, bones and joints.

Girasol Quartz. Use around the eyes to strengthen vision.

Hematite. Use for power and vitality. Improves blood circulation.

Jasper (Brecciated or Red). Good for weakness and exhaustion. Activates the circulation and energises the body.

Jet. Use around the jaw to ease bruxism (grinding or clenching of the teeth). Over the stomach to improve digestion and the intestines. Also good for joints, spine, mouth and skin.

Kabamba Jasper. Good for clearing the skin. It opens the pores and encourages perspiration.

Labradorite. Useful for people who are sensitive to the cold. Reduces blood pressure and eases rheumatic conditions.

Lapis Lazuli. A cooling throat stone, good for sore throats and calming the nerves.

Magnesite. Deeply relaxing and helps with pain and cramps of all kinds.

Mookaite. Vitalising and relaxing at the same time. Use to encourage blood purification and strengthen the spleen, liver and immune system.

Moss Agate. Relieves heavy, depressed feelings from the body. Activates the lymph flow, mucus membranes and the respiratory tract.

Onyx Marble. Use in cases of intense mental strain. Good for the spine, inter-vertebral discs, meniscus and joints. Orange Calcite Revitalises the body. Good for the abdomen, skin, joints and bones.

Petrified Wood. Grounding, relaxing and fortifying on the digestion; use where overweight is an issue.

Quartz. This cools, refreshes and revitalises the body. A good wake up stone!

Rhodonite. Very good for the muscles, connective tissues and circulation. Helps scars and heart conditions.

Rhyolite. Balances activity and rest and improves sleep. Useful to activate digestion and excretion.

Selenite. Mentally calming this stone tightens tissues and eases pain.

Serpentine. Strongly relaxing; use to help nervousness and unease. Alleviates cardiac arrhythmias, kidney, stomach and menstrual disorders.

Smoky Quartz. Eases pain caused by stress and tension. Good for headaches, neck and back problems.

Snowflake Obsidian. Mentally motivating. Use for blood circulation dysfunctions and chronically cold hands and feet.

Sodalite. This cooling stone can ease heat sensitivity, reduce fever and blood pressure and help sore throats.

Tiger's Eye. Brings calmness when life gets too hectic. Good for grounding and helping one feel whole again.

Jewellery etc

Stones when shaped and polished become very decorative and are used to enhance pieces of jewellery. This is one of the easiest ways to bring their healing power into your everyday life.

Men and women alike can wear crystal jewellery. They can be fashioned into intricate pieces mounted in silver or gold, or they can simply be a pendent hanging from a string. Buy according to your taste and budget!

I would love to be dripping in Diamonds, not because of their value but because they are the highest frequency crystal and bring powerful healing benefits. However, Herkimer Diamonds are almost as good but cost far less. So, my advice would be to decide what crystal you wish to work with and see if it's possible to buy a piece of jewellery with the crystal mounted in it. If it's too expensive then try for a pendent in the crystal. There are always various options available. However, if it's still out of your price range then opt for another crystal which will have similar properties.

Crystals set in rings symbolise eternity, because the ring shape has no beginning and no end. On your wedding finger a ring can also affect your career. Try wearing Amber if you are hoping for a rise in salary. Or wear a ring on your index finger for luck. Try Rose Quartz for luck in love or Turquoise for luck in travel.

Crystal bracelets work well at infusing the whole body with healing because they touch the pulse points. Any blue crystals or an Amethyst bracelet helps with recovery after illness.

Wear a crystal pendant around the throat to help with communication issues. Blue Lace Agate would be good here. Or on a longer chain over the heart area to help you to attune to your own feelings. Rose Quartz or Ruby would be good choices here.

Earrings inlaid with crystals will aid you to hear and understand the world around you more clearly. Celestite would be good to increase your intuition, enabling you to "hear" your inner voice.

Wearing as jewellery means you only have to put it on in the morning and not think about it until you take it off at night. Nothing could be simpler. The jewellery will be at work all day clearing any blocks and absorbing any negative energy, so it will need cleansing each night. The easiest way is to buy an Amethyst or quartz bed (flat pieces of crystal with lots of terminations) to lay the jewellery on at night. Gold and silver jewellery that doesn't have any crystals can also be cleansed this way because they will absorb negative energies as they are a naturally occurring metal.

If you are not a jewellery type person then just popping a crystal in your pocket will work just as well.

These touchstones can bring you a boost of reassurance and support when you need it. Here are a few examples but feel free to choose your own crystal!

Amethyst protects, heals and encourages fidelity.

Celestite is a heavenly stone that will enable you to be more receptive to magickal and angelic guidance.

Citrine soothes away anxiety.

Jasper encourages passion.

Pyrite deflects bad luck, helping to prevent accidents.

Rose Quartz promotes love.

Tiger's Eye instils courage.

Turquoise protects travellers.

Or women can pop them in their bras! Just remember it's there when you take your bra off! I have broken lots of crystals this way because my house has tiled floors... My solution to my forgetfulness was to pop said crystals into a small silk purse and pop that in my bra. This way when I forget about them when undressing they land safely in their purse and, so far, none have broken. If you feel drawn to use the crystals on specific parts of the body and want to keep them there during the day then Sellotape does come in handy! Or use any method that works for you.

Crystal charms can be used in rooms to inspire a positive energy and also look pretty! Carvings of Buddhas bring luck. Hold a small one to boost your luck or place a larger one by a doorway and touch it when you enter or leave the room for an extra boost! Elephant shaped charms increase your fortune (provided they are not placed facing a door, in which case your luck will leave your home). Hanging clear Quartz by windows helps to focus the energy of the sun and moon into a room.

Gridding rooms etc

Placing crystals by your bed, or on the floor around it (one by each bed leg), can help our healing process and aid restful sleep. We are more receptive to their energies while asleep because the body naturally goes into a healing mode. Rose Quartz is very soothing to have near us, as it is nurturing especially if we feel in need of love in our life. Amethyst helps aid sleep with its protective energies. Some crystals can be used to boost our immune system while we sleep such as Chrysocolla, Chrysoprase, Green Tourmaline, Malachite and Moss Agate. This is a great idea when you feel under the weather. I have several different crystals by my bed and even place them under my pillow if I feel a need to. Gridding a bed is especially good if you have Ley lines running under your house. Dendritic Agate and Aragonite can be placed at each leg of the bed to help clear any negative energy the Ley lines may be causing.

Gridding can be used for space clearing; protection; charging or any specific healing use. It involves placing crystals around a room, or the whole house. Black Tourmaline is good for protection from negative influences; to clear electromagnetic smog and geopathic stress. Selenite is another protective stone and also helps invoke the angels to come near to us. Sardonyx, when placed at each corner of the house or room, will help guard us against crime. A piece placed outside the front door will deter robbers. When gridding crystals, they should be cleansed and programmed first before you place them. This way you have set the intention of how you want them to help you. Quartz points can be used in each corner of a room. Point the termination towards the corners of the room for protection. The terminations of the quartz points can also be used to raise, amplify or enhance the energy by pointing in a clockwise rotation or an anti-clockwise rotation to ground or diminish the energies. Small quartz points work best for this type of gridding.

Once you have placed your crystal/s of choice you may like to form a golden circle of light to enhance their energies in the room. This is simply done by standing in the centre of the room and visualising a golden light coming out of your right hand or holding a crystal wand or other specific crystal point and forming a circle connecting the crystals. Grid-ding crystals in your sitting room or meditation area can clear the environment of any negativity. Geodes are especially good for this. Geodes are formed with crystals on the inside of a rock. They are usually cut in half to expose the crystal centre. They work by drawing in negative energy and transmuting it in to positive energy. They are highly decorative and functional at the same time. Geodes can be placed according to Feng Shui to help draw in love, wealth, protection, etc.

Small crystal grids can be made by arranging crystals in any pattern that you like. The grid normally has a central stone which is surrounded by other stones in either a symmetrical pattern or asymmetrical depending on your preference.

For example, if you choose to do a love grid you would choose stones that have love as one of their properties, such as rose quartz. An example would be to place a ruby in the centre surrounded by 3 rose quartz. The stones would be held while your intent was programmed into them. Then you could place them by your bed. Other grids may contain 50 stones of various types. It really depends on how creative you want to get. There are no set rules to creating a grid. Just pick your stones to match your intent and then get creative. The grid can be changed weekly, if desired, or left for months.

Some ideas for grids could be for love, luck, money, healing or protection. Some people add a photograph under the central stone if they are making a grid to heal a loved one. This could be either human or animal.

Gridding the body to heal the chakras

When we feel out of sorts; ill; depressed; or low on energy it is often because the energy flow through the body has become disrupted – out of tune with your spiritual self. Crystals can be used on and around the body during relaxation and/or meditation; to act as tuning forks to rebalance the energy centres (chakras) by adjusting their frequency to what they should be. You can simply place them by your chair while watching TV; hold them in your hand; or hold them against a specific part of the body. If you want to relax laying down, you can place crystals on your body.

Each chakra can be worked on individually each day; or you can work them a few at a time; or all at the same time.

To amplify the healing energies around the body hold your chosen crystal and imagine gold energy passing up from the Earth through your feet, up through your body, into your heart;

then out along your arms and through your hands, to be focused through the crystal you are holding. Direct it towards the afflicted area on the body, rubbing the crystal over the area to focus the energy there.

Massaging the afflicted area is another way to focus the energy. Smooth tumbled stones are best for this. Spheres or eggs are ideal but any crystal large enough to hold comfortably can be used. Oil (examples: Almond, Coconut) can be rubbed on the area to be massaged first to make it easier to move the crystal over the surface. Then gently rub the area in any way that feels good.

Wands can be used to clear the energy around the body. Clear quartz is particularly good for this. Hold the wand and set the intention that it clears the aura of any blocked or negative energy. Then simply hold it a few centimetres from the body with the point directed at the body. Start at the crown of the head and work your way down through the chakras. You may pause longer at some than others. This can be done daily if you feel the need.

The Major Chakras of The Body

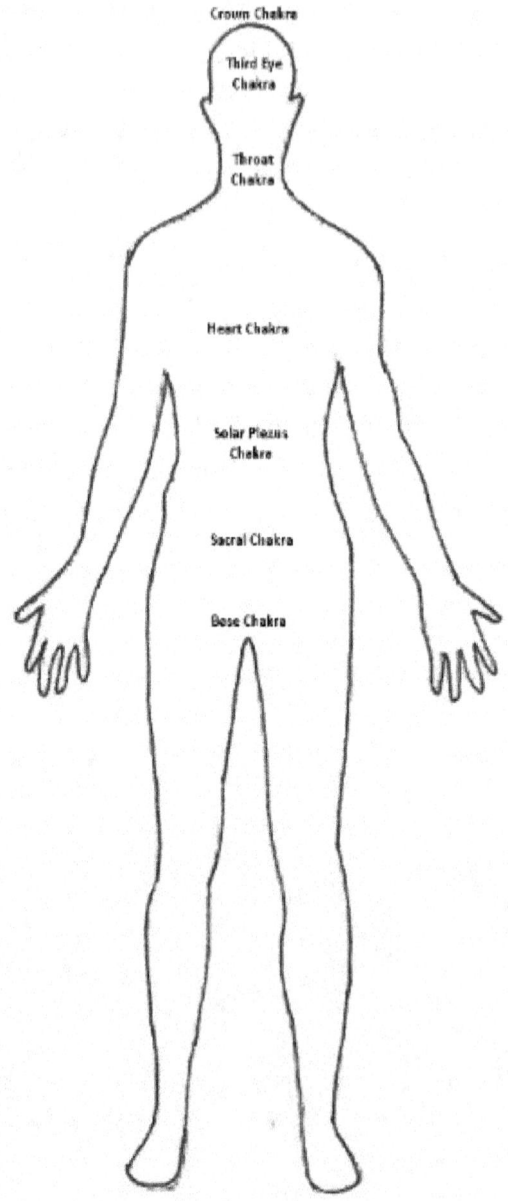

You can place them according to their colours:

Red, brown and black crystals – Base (Root) Chakra: Place on the groin area, or one crystal at the top of each leg. These earthy coloured crystals will stimulate the base chakra and help improve fertility and sex drive; ease menstrual problems, blood disorders, frigidity and inhibition and can help with increasing courage. Examples are: Garnet, Hematite, Jet, Obsidian, Red Jasper, and Ruby.

Orange crystals – Sacral Chakra: Place on top of the belly button. Orange crystals stimulate the sex organs (ovaries, testes), the womb and the base of the spine. They can help to increase our energy; improve lactation; dispel inhibitions and repressions and ease kidney problems. Orange crystals would work extremely well with a navel piercing. Examples are: Carnelian, Citrine, Yellow Jasper and Tiger's Eye.

Yellow crystals – Solar Plexus Chakra: Place at the base of the sternum. This is where the rib cage meets in the middle of the chest. Yellow crystals (which include turquoise, due to its yellow veins) stimulate the stomach. They help with digestion and ease food allergies; liver problems and muscles cramps. Examples are: Agate, Amber (light coloured), Citrine (light coloured), and Turquoise.

Green or pink crystals – Heart Chakra: Place in the centre of the chest between the breasts. Pink and green crystals balance and ease problems of the heart. Use to treat emotional problems such as stress, anger and depression. Examples are: Aventurine, Jade, Malachite, Rose Quartz and Watermelon Tourmaline.

Pale blue crystals – Throat Chakra: Place in the indentation at the base of the throat. They can also help with glandular problems; bronchial problems; teeth and gums diseases and conditions affecting the alimentary canal. Examples are: Blue

Lace Agate, Blue Chalcedony and Celestite

Indigo blue crystals – Third Eye Chakra: Nose and throat. Also good for headaches, including sinus pain; agitation and stress; to boost concentration and mental awareness. Examples are: Azurite, Lapis Lazuli, and Sodalite.

Purple or white crystals – Crown Chakra: Place next to the top of the head. These increase our sense of well-being; improve self-esteem and dispel mental anguish and depression. Examples are: Purple- Amethyst, Fluorite, Sugilite; white – Clear Quartz, Diamond (or Herkimer Diamond) and Zircon.

You can also use them according to their healing properties. Placing a specific crystal directly over the site of dis-ease such as Orthoclase on the lung area to heal a lung condition. Many crystals have multiple uses on different chakras.

If you feel drawn to place a crystal on a chakra that isn't usually used on that chakra, then go with your intuition. I'm always using crystals on chakras that they aren't usually used, but it always has a good result!

The colour of a crystal can also be used to help energise, calm or soothe the body. Red crystals energise and enliven. Green crystals soothe and blue crystals calm the body. Crystals can also be used according to colour association.

The following list is a guide to some colour associations:

White: Blank slate (any purpose), innocence, pure spirit.
Black: Grounding, protection, strength.
Gold: Money, success.
Silver: Intuition, money, psychic ability.
Blue: Dream work, healing, peace.
Green: Fertility, growth, money, success.
Orange: Gaining energy, memory, success.
Purple: Intuition, mental focus, psychic energy, spirituality.
Red: Life, love, power, romance, sex.
Yellow: Luck, success.

Crystal Layouts for Healing

The following are some layouts to enhance healing of the body:

Aura Cleanser

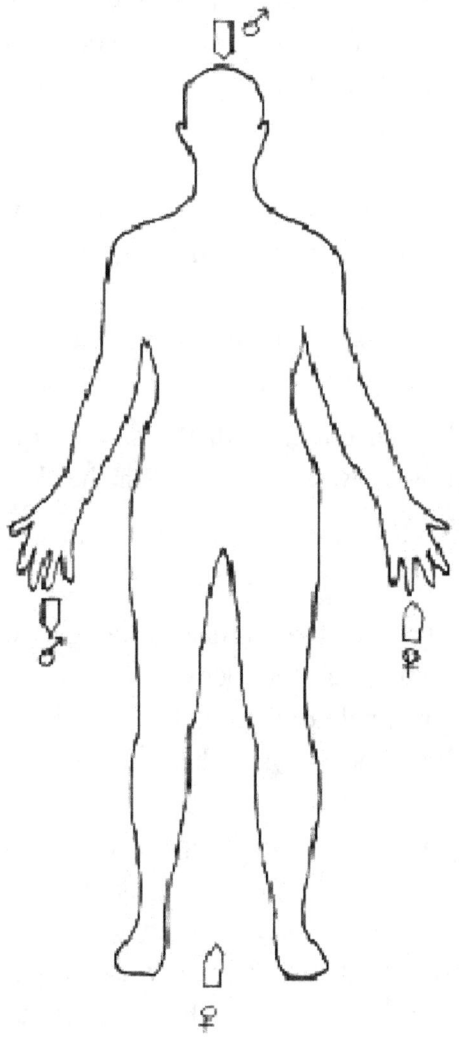

You need:

2 female single termination clear quartz's
2 male single termination clear quartz's

Good for using:

After any type of surgery.

When stressed, worrying, having negative thoughts or when others negative thoughts are affecting you.

Make a "thought" connection for the intention of the crystal to assist in any of the above imbalances. You do this by simply holding the crystals and asking them to heal any imbalance caused by surgery or stress etc (state which is most applicable to you).

Hold the crystals until you intuitively feel that they have heard your intention. Then place them as directed below:

- Lie on the floor (on a mat) or on a bed. Play some soft relaxing music.
- Place 1 male quartz with the single termination pointing down towards the top of the head.
- The second male quartz is placed in the right hand pointing down towards your feet.
- The female quartz is placed below your feet pointing up towards your body.
- The other female quartz is placed in the left hand pointing up to the top of the head.

Visualise a light coming from the crystal at your head and direct that light to the crystal in your right hand. Continue taking this light to the crystal at your feet. Feel the light flowing from one crystal to the other. At first you may find this hard but just use your imagination, intention is all that is needed to do this. Now continue this light into the crystal in your left hand and then up to the crystal at the top of your head. Feel this circle of light surrounding your body. Now visualise a light from the crystal at the top of your head connecting to the one at your feet. Then a light connecting the right and left crystals together. This has now created a cleansing shield around you. Imagine this light surrounding the whole body and clearing out any imbalances that there are. Lie and relax in these healing energies for a minimum of 20 minutes.

When you feel you want to come out of the healing, release the crystals in each hand. Rub the hands gently together as you bring your consciousness back. Thank the crystals for their help and place them to one side to be cleansed in whatever method you like.

Drink a glass of water to help ground the energies into the body.

Chakra Balancer Spread

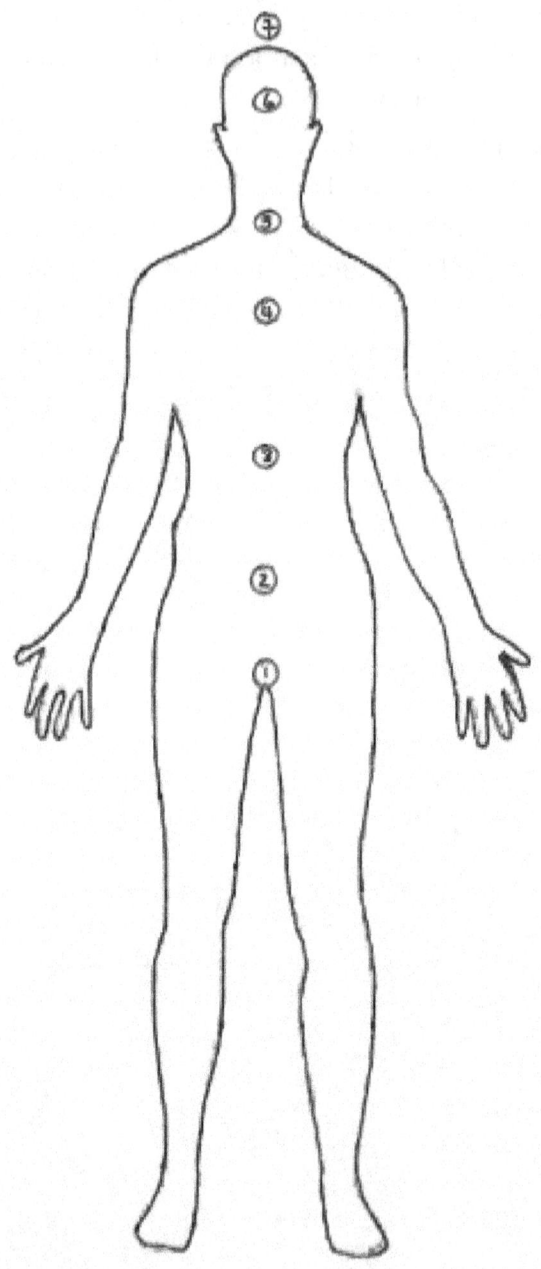

You need:

    7 crystals, one for each chakra

Good for using:

    Daily for energising

    Daily for well being

Hold the crystal for the Base Chakra and ask it to balance it. Repeat with the other crystals for each Chakra. Once all 7 have been given your intention, lie down in a comfortable place and put the crystals on the appropriate chakras.

Relax for a minimum of 20 minutes. When the relaxation has finished put the crystals to one side of you and then allow your awareness to come back. Drink a glass of water to help integrate any energy changes that have occurred during the healing. Remember to cleanse the crystals so they are ready for use again.

Crystal Magick

Powerful Chakra and Aura Cleanser

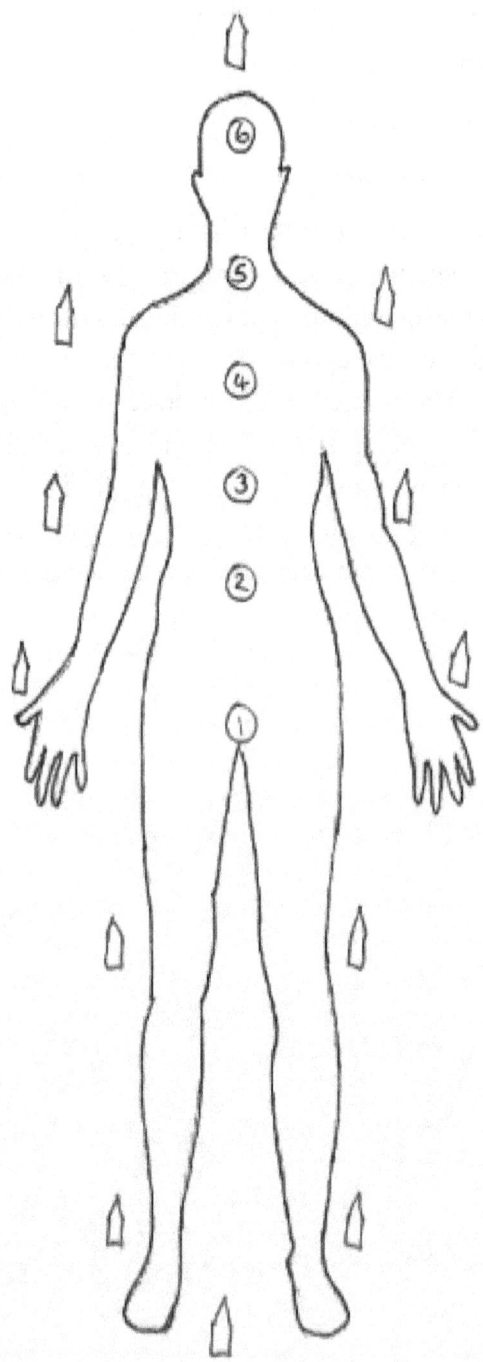

You need:

    12 single termination clear quartz's
    7 chakra crystals

Good for using:

    In times of extreme stress

    When dealing with grief

    When dealing with emotional loss

    When dealing with debilitating illness

This is a powerful cleanser for the aura and chakras. It is what you might term as a heavy-duty cleanser! The intention is given to each of the chakra crystals to bring balance to the matching chakra. Then hold (if possible) or place in your lap and place your hands-on top of the 12 quartz crystals and ask them to heal and rebalance the aura and chakras. Sit on either the floor or your bed and place the crystals as follows:

- Place 1 quartz at the bottom of your feet, termination pointing up.
- 1 quartz to your right and left in line with your ankles, knees, hips. Place a few inches away from the body. Terminations pointing up towards the head.
- Now lie back carefully and place 1 quartz to your right and left in line with your elbows and shoulders. Terminations pointing up towards the head.
- 1 quartz at the top of the head. Termination pointing up.
- 1 crystal on each chakra as appropriate.

Relax and visualise all the quartz's joining together so a stream of light flows around the body in a clockwise direction. Now visualise all the chakra crystals joining their light together from the base crystal up to the crown. This light then joins the light flowing around the body in a clockwise direction. Enjoy the energies flowing around you and imagine them clearing out all the emotions that you no longer need. If you feel emotions surfacing release these, don't suppress them.

When you have finished the relaxation, gently remove the chakra crystals and place to one side. Relax for a minimum of 20 minutes, but longer is advised for better results. If you begin to feel dizzy at any point remove the crystals and come out of the healing. You can try again the next day or use the chakra balancer spread for a few times before attempting this spread. Bring your awareness back slowly. You may need to rub your hands together to bring you fully back and sit on the bed for a few minutes to feel grounded again.

A large glass of water and something to eat will help ground you properly, after this deep cleansing layout.

Energising and cleansing spread for chakras and aura.

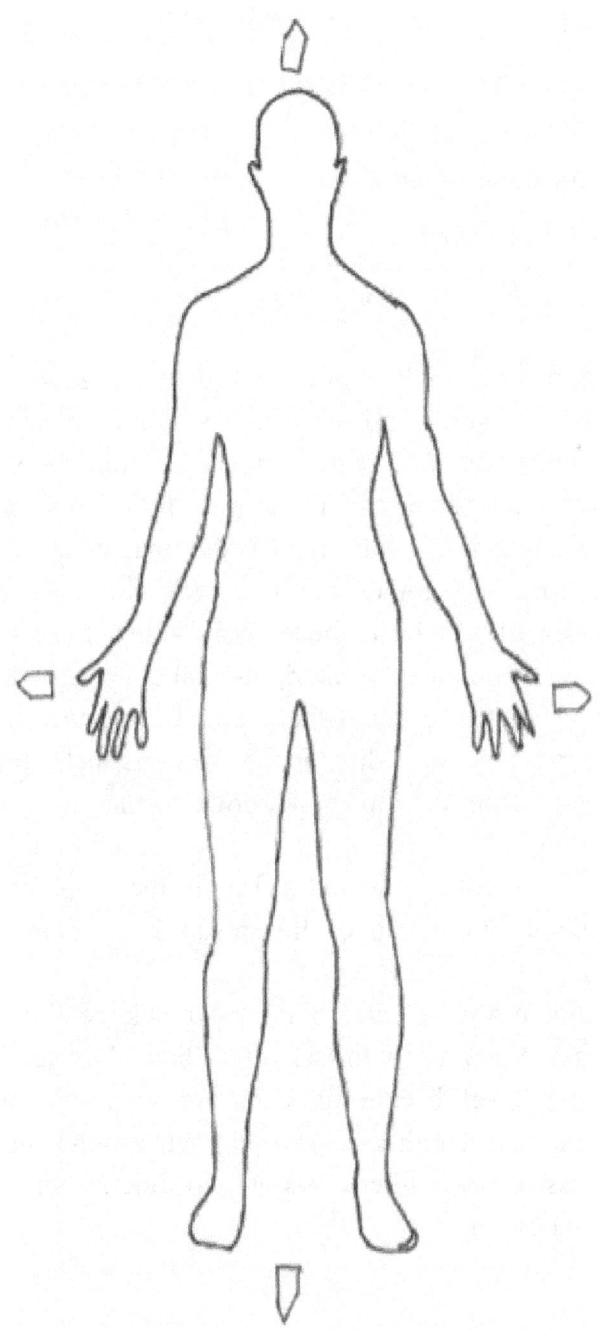

You need:

    4 single termination clear quartz crystals

Good for using:

    To draw out negativity

    To draw out tension

    To draw out toxins

    On mental, emotional and physical bodies

Set your intention in the four crystals by holding them. Lie in a comfortable position and place four single terminated quartz crystals one at the head pointing up away from the body. One to each side of the body pointing away from it and one at the feet pointing down away from the body. Imagine there is a light extending from the top crystal in a clockwise circle. It moves from the top of the head to the left-hand side of the body, down to your feet; continues to the right-hand side of the body and connects back to the top of the head. Feel the flow of energy moving in a clockwise direction. When this feels strong then send energy from the top crystal down to the feet crystal and from the right-hand side of the body to the left-hand side. So, you have a circular flow and a flow in the shape of a cross. Enjoy the healing effects of this spread for a minimum of 20 minutes.

When you want to end the healing, break the circle of light by moving the crystals at the side of the body. Lay quietly while you bring yourself back to full consciousness. Rub your hands together and bend your legs. This will help ground you. Have a large glass of water afterwards and sit quietly until you feel fully grounded again.

Harmonising Spread

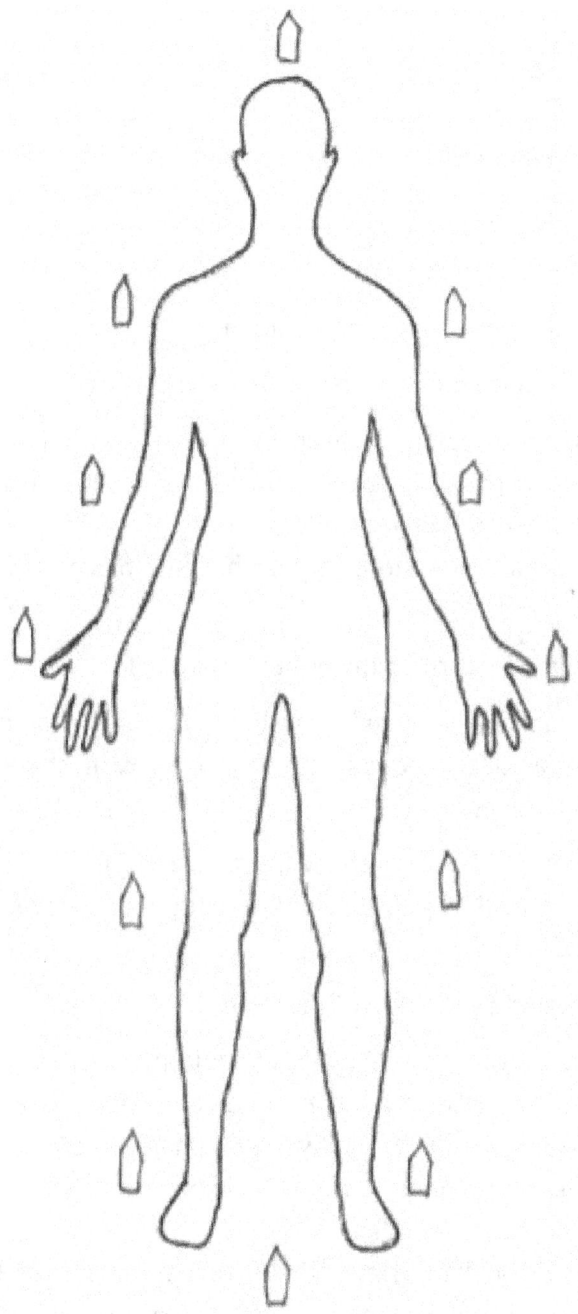

You need:

12 single termination clear quartz's

Good for using:

In times of extreme mental stress

To help obesity

To help ease depression

To help ease arthritis

To aid conscious enlightenment

To balance and harmonise the whole body

This is a powerful cleanser for the whole body. Hold (if possible) or place in your lap the 12 crystals and place your hands on top and set your intention.

Sit on either the floor or your bed and place the crystals as follows:

- Place 1 quartz at the bottom of your feet.

- 1quartz to your right and 1 to your left in line with your ankles, knees and hips. Place a few inches away from the body.

- Now lie back carefully and place 1 quartz to your right and 1 to your left in line with your elbows and shoulders.

- 1 quartz at the top of the head.

Relax and visualise all the quartz's joining together so a stream of light flows around the body in a clockwise direction. Enjoy the energies flowing around you and imagine them clearing out what you no longer need. If you feel emotions surfacing, release them; don't suppress them.

When you have finished the relaxation gently break the circle of light my moving some of the crystals away from you. Bring your awareness back slowly. You may need to rub your hands together to bring you fully back and sit on the bed for a few minutes to feel grounded again.

Relax for a minimum of 20 minutes but longer is advised for better results.

Hematite Shield of Protection

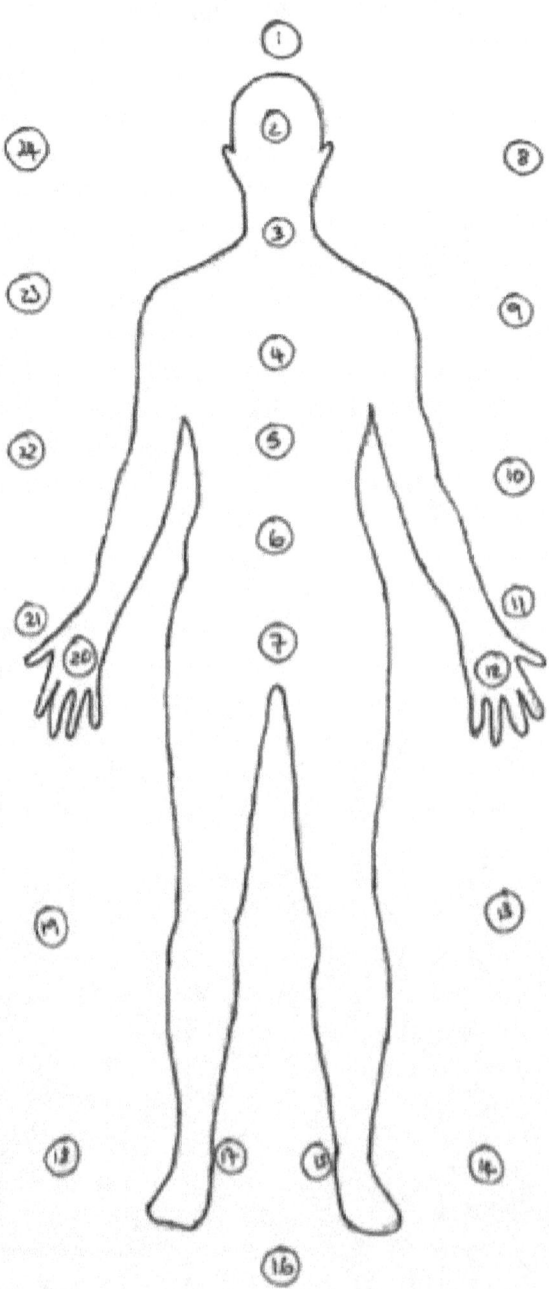

You need:

24 small hematite crystals

Good for using:

When you are being psychically attacked

When you are feeling vulnerable

When other's negativity affects you

When you are being influenced by others and are not able to control their effect.

This is a very powerful protective shield. It is extremely effective when we are in need of protection from external influences. Set the intention for the crystals to form a protective shield around you.

Place the hematite as follows:

- 1 at the bottom of the feet.
- 1 at each heel of the foot (touching it).
- 1 at each ankle a few inches out from the body.
- 1 at each knee a few inches out from the body.
- 1 at each hip a few inches out from the body.
- 1 at each elbow a few inches out from the body.
- 1 at each shoulder a few inches out from the body.
- 1 at each ear a few inches out from the body.
- 1 at the top of the head.
- 1 on the base, sacral, solar plexus, heart, throat and third eye chakras.
- Hold one in each palm.

Send light from the left hand through the crystal and into all the crystals surrounding the body. Feel the energy flowing in a clockwise direction around the body. Now feel light from the crystal in the right hand flowing out and into the base chakra and working its way up through the other chakras until it joins the top crystal. Now the light is flowing all around and through the body.

This powerful light is forming a shield to encompass the aura and physical body. Feel all the stress, tension and negativity leaving the body. Feel your energies getting stronger and know that you are completely protected in your shield.

Take note how you feel in this protective shield. Hold this thought, so that when you need to recall the shield you will be able to imagine it surrounding you even when it isn't. You may need to do this a few times to be able to recall it when you are out and about. The intention will be enough for you to draw the energies to you at any time you feel the need.

When you want to come out of the relaxation remove the crystals from the chakras and break the circle of light by pushing some of the surrounding crystals away from the body. Bring your awareness back slowly and repeat to yourself that you are surrounded by a circle of light that you can call in anytime you feel in need of protection.

This powerful shield can be used daily if needed.

Drink a large glass of water to help integrate the hematite energies into the body.

It's helpful to carry a hematite with you so you can call on its protective shield when you are out and about.

Anytime you feel in need of protection hold the crystal and call forth its help.

The Seal of Solomon Spread

You need:

    1 Rose Quartz
    6 double or single terminated clear Quartz.

Good for using:

    To relieve stress.

Place a rose quartz on the heart chakra, then the six quartz in a circle around the Rose Quartz in a star shape. With single terminated Quartz, place terminations pointing out. Relax for 10 minutes if using the single terminated Quartz; then point the terminations into the heart centre and relax for a further 10 minutes. If using double terminated relax for 20 minutes, as the crystals won't need turning as they are dual polarity.

General balance spread

You need:
    1 Amethyst
    1 Labradorite
    1 Rose Quartz
    1 Tiger's Eye

Good for using:
    For general balance

    For relaxation

    To energise the body when feeling tired

Place the Amethyst on the forehead, between the eyebrows. This is the Third Eye Chakra and will help energise the mind: giving you clearer thought processes and helping to link you to your spiritual self.

    Place the Labradorite on the hollow of the throat. This will stimulate the Throat Chakra and help with any pent-up emotions or words that have been repressed. Now place the Rose Quartz on the Heart Centre. This will bring feelings of love to this centre. It will also calm any emotions. Lastly place the Tiger's Eye on the pubic bone. This is the Base Chakra and will help to ground us; strengthen the aura and energise the body. Relax with eyes closed for a minimum of 20 minutes.

The Emotion Buster Spread

What you need:

> 8 Clear Quartz single terminations
> 1 Amazonite
> 1 Turquoise

Good for using:

> To release emotions after very stressful events

This is the layout to use if you receive distressing news or are going through a very emotional time. The formation using the Amazonite will help the body to release the stress associated with the event/s and Turquoise will absorb the negative emotions.

Position the Amazonite just below the belly button. Place four Quartz points in an "X" around it. The terminations should be pointing inwards to balance the emotional energies.

Now place the Turquoise on the heart centre, with four Quartz points facing outwards, in an "X" around it. These will help to release the emotional distress and absorb it to clear it from the body.

Tamsin German

The Recuperation Spread

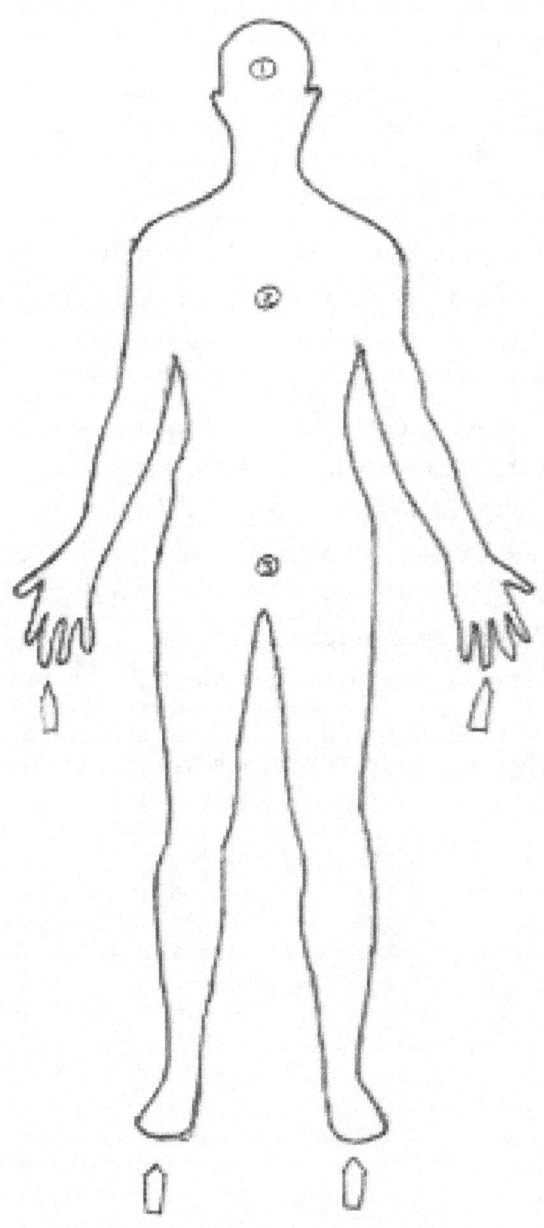

What you need:

- 4 single termination Clear Quartz
- 1 Carnelian
- 1 Rhodonite
- 1 Topaz

Good for using:

After recovery from a long illness.

First place the four Quartz points by each foot and each hand. The point should face inwards to send the healing energy into the body. Place the Carnelian on the pubic bone to enhance the energy levels and restore physical balance.

The Rhodonite helps to balance the energies and should be placed on the Heart Centre. Topaz is used on the Third Eye Chakra to help regenerate the body's defences.

Relaxation music is recommended as it will enhance the relaxation of the body. After illness the physical and spiritual bodies will be in need of rebalancing.

The deeper the relaxation the better the result of the healing spread.

Relax for at least one hour. This will be very beneficial for the body's natural healing system. Much repair is done while the body is in a sleep like state or very relaxed.

Chair Spread

Crystals can be placed around the legs of a chair, in a circle, if you find lying down uncomfortable.

You need:

> 4 single terminated clear quartz crystals
> 1 crystal of choice

Good for using:

> To energise the body
>
> To rebalance the body
>
> To harmonise the body

As with the spreads above hold the crystals to set your intention in them. Then place the quartz around the legs of the chair, with the terminations pointing in towards the chair. Hold the crystal of choice in your hands. Visualise a circle of light connecting the four crystals in a circular clockwise flow around the base of the chair. Imagine this light rising upwards around the body, until you are surrounded by a column of light.

Relax for a minimum of 20 minutes. When you feel you want to come out of the relaxation, imagine the light flow slowing and gradually falling back to the floor and then stopping.

Rub your hands together to help ground the energies into the body. Have a glass of water to help integrate the energies.

Grounding Chair Spread

You need:

> 4 single terminated clear quartz crystals
> 1 grounding crystal of choice (tiger's eye, hematite, black obsidian, black tourmaline, red jasper etc)

Good for using:

> To ground
>
> When feeling spaced out
>
> When your head feels floaty and concentration is difficult

Hold the crystals to set your intention for them to ground you. Then place the quartz around the legs of the chair, with the terminations pointing out away from the chair. Hold the crystal of choice in your hands. Visualise a circle of light connecting the four crystals in a circular clockwise flow around the base of the chair. Imagine this light rising upwards around the body, until a column of light surrounds you. Next, imagine roots growing out of the soles of your feet down into the floor. Let them continue their journey downwards into the earth until you feel they have grown deep enough. Feel the connection with the earth. Let your roots anchor you firmly. Continue to relax, enjoying your deep connection with Mother Earth. When you feel you want to come out of the relaxation, draw your roots back up and see the circular light slowing until it stops. Stay sitting until you feel your awareness has totally returned. Drink a glass of water and rest for a few hours. All these spreads can be adjusted in any way that you feel is right for you. Using crystals is using your intuition! You may feel that you need to add more crystals or reduce the number, these are here as a guideline to get you started.

Magickal Correspondences to enhance Crystal Healing

Crystals can be integrated into any magickal ritual or ceremony. The simplest way to utilise their potential is to place them on your altar. Choose crystals according to which spell or ritual you are performing to add an extra boost of power. Amethyst is good to use on the altar when you are meditating. Carnelian, one can be placed in each of the four directions (north, east, south and west) to add a protective energy over any workings you are doing. Citrine can be used when doing prosperity spells. Rose Quartz, when love spells are being performed.

These are just some examples; more are listed further on. Use your intuition and place what feels right for you. The stones can be changed daily or weekly to suit your mood. Other factors can be taken into account when using crystals to heal. The days of the week; ruling planet; colours; herbs; oils; etc. can be corresponded to bring greater potential to any magickal work or healing you are doing. Individual correspondences can be used, or all of them together.

Choose the day which represents the healing you are looking for, then add any other correspondences to enhance your healing. Coloured cloth or coloured paper may be used to correspond to the day. Herbs or oils may be added to your meditation or worn on the body. The following list gives some correspondences that are useful to use on your altar, in your meditation or as part of magickal working. The correspondences may vary if you follow specific pathways within the craft, these are a few ideas:

Monday

Ruling planet: The Moon.

Colours: Grey, lavender, pearl, white or silver.

Herbs and oils: Gardenia, Jasmine, Lemon balm, Lotus.

Crystals: Carnelian.

Chakra: Root (Base) Chakra.

Best for workings of: Emotional matters, including reconciliations; rituals and spells involving astrology; children; dreams and astral travel; divination; family; feminine issues; fertility; healing; household activities; imagination; intuition; magic; new age pursuits; messages; peace; psychic development; purification and protection; theft and voyages.

Tuesday

Ruling planet: Mars.

Colours: Red, pink or orange.

Herbs and oils: Clove, Nutmeg, Sage.

Crystals: Amethyst, Lepidolite.

Chakra: Sacral Chakra.

Best for workings of: Rituals and spells for aggression; banishing negativity; boosting confidence; beginnings; business; combat; confrontation; courage; energy; gardening; movement; muscular activity; military honour; passion; partnership; personal struggles; physical challenges; revenge; sex; stimulation; surgery and will power.

Wednesday

Ruling planet: Mercury.

Colours: Purple or yellow.

Herbs and oils: Caraway, Dill, Fennel, Lavender, Peppermint.

Crystals: Agate, Aventurine, Lapis Lazuli.

Chakra: Solar Plexus Chakra.

Best for workings of: Rituals or spells associated with accounting; astrology; communication; computers; correspondence; editing; education; business transactions; employment; healing; hiring; journalists; information granting; learning; languages; legal appointments; music; phone calls; signing contracts; pursuits of knowledge by studying; short distance travel; writing and wisdom.

Thursday

Ruling planet: Jupiter.

Colours: Dark blue, purple or metallic colours.

Herbs and oils: Cumin, Frankincense, Ginger.

Crystals: Garnet, Red Jasper, Ruby.

Chakra: Heart Chakra.

Best for workings of: Rituals or spells for attracting luck; business; career; charity; college; doctors, education, expansion, forecasting, fidelity, happiness, foreign interests, health; healing animals; agriculture; holidays; gambling; long distance travel; legal matters; publishing; reading; male fertility; prosperity; self-improvement and wealth.

Friday

Ruling planet: Venus.

Colours: Pink or white.

Herbs and oils: Mint, Rose Absolute, Ylang Ylang.

Crystals: Rhodonite, Rose Quartz.

Chakra: Throat Chakra.

Best for workings of: Rituals and spells for love and relationships; romance and partnership; affection; alliances; architects; artists; amusement; beauty; chiropractors; designers; engineers; enjoyment; friendships; gardening; gifts; money; marriage and social life.

Saturday

Ruling planet: Saturn.

Colours: Black, brown or grey.

Herbs and oils: Comfrey, Patchouli.

Crystals: Jet, Obsidian, Onyx.

Chakra: Third Eye (Brow) Chakra.

Best for workings of: Rituals and spells for ambition; amulets; banishing and ridding old energies; binding spells; justice; karma; obstacles; major changes; protection; separation; tests; obligations and responsibility.

Sunday

Ruling planet: The Sun.

Colours: Amber, gold, orange or yellow.

Herbs and oils: Frankincense, Rosemary, Sandalwood.

Crystals: Amber, Sunstone.

Chakra: Crown Chakra.

Best for workings of: Rituals and spells for ambition; authority figures; banishing; attracting healing energies; career; children; crops; drama; fame; fun; goals; health; law; masculine issues; personal finances; promotion; protection; selling; speculating; truth in all matters; strength; spirituality and success.

Meditation

Meditation is known to be good for us; even before we add crystals to the scenario. We all live very hectic busy lives. Few take the time to simply be "in the moment", but we should, because we all need quiet time! Meditation can be a time to connect with our inner most feelings and process what is going on in our life. Crystals help to enhance this and can take us into a deep state of relaxation much quicker. Kyanite, Snowflake Obsidian, Serpentine and Turquoise are all good for enhancing meditation. We can either lie down or sit to meditate and place the crystals around us in a circle. A minimum of three crystals should be used to form this circle, using up to as many as you feel is right for you. These will help you relax into the meditation faster and help you go deeper. It is when you are in this deeply relaxed state that you can "hear" what you need to hear. This can be guidance from our higher self, the angels or from spirit guides. The hearing may come in many forms...pictures, symbols, feelings, colours, words, voices or even just a knowing of what we need to do. Extra crystals can be held during meditation if we are working with specific crystals. There are no set rules on how to meditate, you just need to make sure of the following basics:

- Turn your phone off or put it on silent!
- Turn the TV off.
- Wear comfortable clothing so that you can relax.
- Make sure you are warm or you will fidget and find it hard to unwind.
- Choose a comfortable chair or mat (if lying down).
- Have a glass of water as sometimes when the throat chakra opens it can make us cough.

- Make sure you are in a comfortable position and can relax.

- Ensure that anything you know needs to be done, is sorted before you start.

- Play some soft music in the background.

- Place your circle of chosen crystals around your space. Select any other crystals you may want to use. You can simply hold the other crystals or lay them on the body over the chakras or where dis-ease is present.

- Start to breathe in through the nose and out through the nose. Place your hands on your tummy and feel the breath from here. This will ensure your breath is coming from the diaphragm and not from chest, ensuring a deep cleansing breath rather than a shallow one. It is very good for the body to breathe deeply as it clears out all the stale air and brings in more oxygen on the following breath.

- Breathe consciously in and out. Now on the 'in' breath, breathe in the feelings of peace. Feel or imagine that peace filling the body. You can just imagine the word being breathed in – go with whatever feels natural to you. If it feels difficult at first, just persevere. Soon it will become easier.

- Now when you breathe out, breathe out any tension in the body. You can imagine the word or just feel the tension leaving you.

- Continue to breathe in "peace" and out "tension". Do this for as long as feels natural for the body to begin to relax. You will soon start to feel the muscles relax in the body. The more you practice the faster you will feel the body responding. You can even clench each set of muscles and then relax them. Start with the feet. Tense them, then as you breathe out tension from the body, relax them. Then tense the legs and repeat the action. Then clench the buttocks, stomach, hands, arms, shoulders, jaw, eyes and repeat to each set of muscles. By the time you get to the eyes you will be very relaxed!

• If any mental chatter enters your mind just let it gently float away. Don't stress about the mental chatter just imagine putting it in a bucket and letting it go.

• Continue to relax and quiet the mind.

• Now concentrate on any feelings that come over you, any words, pictures, symbols, etc. You can even ask your crystals if there is anything they want to impart to you. Just be in the moment and be observant if possible. If however you find that you have fallen asleep don't despair as your body needed sleep and whatever the crystal or higher guidance wanted you to know will still have gone into you on a subconscious level.

• You can remain in this state for a minimum of 30 minutes. This type of meditation can be practiced as often as you like. Every day would be ideal but if you can only manage 2-3 times a week then choose the same days each week. Make it become a ritual and you are more likely to continue with it.

Crystal Essences

Crystal gem essences can be made from water infused with crystal energy and charged by the sun or moon. They will help restore physical and emotional health and promote spiritual growth.

Crystal essences can be taken over a prolonged period of time to treat ongoing conditions.

Most crystals can be used directly in water but there are some exceptions. Some crystals will leach out metals and minerals into the water, which cannot be processed by the body. Tumbled stones are better to use because they can be cleaned better and have less chance of any bacteria growing on the crystal. If in doubt whether a stone can be used directly in water always play safe and use the indirect method.

Do not place the following crystals directly in water as they are toxic, use indirect method:

- Amazonite,
- Atacamite,
- Auricalcite,
- Azurite,
- Bronchantite,
- Chalcantite,
- Chalcopyrite,
- Cinnabar,
- Conicalcite,
- Chrysocolla,
- Cuprite,
- Dioptase,
- Galena,
- Galenite,
- Garnierite,
- Gem Silica,
- Lapis Lazuli,
- Marcasite,
- Malachite,
- Opyrite,
- Mohawkite,
- Psiomelan,
- Realgar,
- Smithsonite,
- Stibnite,
- Vanadanite,
- Wulfenite.

Crystal Magick

What you will need:

- A small bowl or jar
- Water (Distilled or mineral)
- A crystal of choice (cleansed, charged and programmed)
- Brandy or vodka
- A dark glass jar for storage

There are two ways of making essences, the direct method and the indirect method. The indirect method is used for crystals which cannot be placed directly in the water due to their toxic nature. If you are unsure of whether a crystal is toxic or not always err on the side of caution and use the indirect method.

Direct method:

- Place your crystal in the glass bowl and fill with water until the crystal is covered.

- Decide which light you wish to use – either sun or moon light. Sunlight infusing will need a minimum of 4 hours, while moonlight infusing will need to be left until sunrise and is best made on the new or full moon. New moons are good for new beginnings, while full moons are good for clearing things away.

- Decant the water into the glass storage jar until half full. Top up with brandy or vodka. The crystal can also be placed in the storage jar for a more potent remedy.

- Label your remedy, noting when it was made, the light source used and what it is for.

- Store in a cool, dark place. It can keep for up to 3 years.

Indirect method:

Place your crystal in a small glass. Place this glass inside the glass bowl. Fill the glass bowl with water until ¾ of the way up the glass containing the crystal. Ensure no water touches the crystal.

Follow as before except DO NOT ADD the crystal to the storage jar. The water in the glass bowl will absorb the crystal energies even when not in direct contact.

Crystal recipes

Agate: Use to help maintain general health and insomnia.
Amber: Use to ease muscular strain and for memory problems.
Amethyst: Use to treat alcoholism and to boost the immune system.
Aventurine: Use for eczema and sunburn. Use to clear negative emotions such as excessive pride or rigidity.
Beryl: Use to boost confidence and self –esteem, also good for throat infections.
Bloodstone: Use for circulatory problems, insecurity or attention-seeking tendencies.
Dark Blue Tourmaline: Use for eye and brain complaints.
Kunzite: Use for depression.
Malachite: Use for PMS (pre-menstrual tension).
Onyx: Use to strengthen bones and soothe an impatient nature.
Opal: Use to treat eye complaints.
Quartz: Use when you need protection from negative influences, and to help general health and well-being.
Tiger's Eye: Use to treat eye conditions and to combat fear of success.
Yellow Sapphire: Use to remove toxins from the body.

Common complaints

Anxiety: Amethyst; Rose Quartz; Moonstone.

Arthritis: Carnelian; Garnet; Hematite.

Asthma: Amethyst; Iron Pyrite; Tiger's Eye.

Constipation: Citrine; Jasper.

Depression: Garnet; Jade; Lapis Lazuli; Moss Agate; Sunstone.

Digestive problems: Carnelian; Citrine; Clear Quartz; Iron Pyrite; Labradorite.

Fatigue: Aventurine; Carnelian; Sunstone.

Fertility: Carnelian; Garnet; Moonstone; Rose Quartz.

Headaches: Clear Quartz; Hematite; Lapis Lazuli; Rose Quartz.

Immune system boost: Aventurine; Bloodstone; Clear Quartz; Lapis Lazuli.

Improve circulation: Bloodstone; Hematite.

Improve concentration: Carnelian; Clear Quartz; Red Jasper.

Insomnia: Amethyst; Hematite; Lapis Lazuli.

Stress relief: Lapis Lazuli; Smoky Quartz; Rose Quartz.

Tamsin German

Crystal list

Adamite

Colours: Yellow

Cleaning method: All.

This stone of creativity will enhance metaphysical gifts. For people ruled by their emotions this crystal creates emotional equilibrium and a calm space in which to process any raging emotions without them affecting your inner serenity.

Links the Solar Plexus, Heart and Throat Chakras together with the Universal Mind to give clarity and inner strength in emotional times. It attracts more joy into one's life. Being a creative stone, it helps you move forward in life with confidence and activates entrepreneurial skills. It helps you see new avenues for growth in both your business and personal life.

Physically it supports the lungs, heart, throat and the endocrine glands. Beneficial for SAD (seasonal affective disorder), PMS and chronic fatigue.

Magickal uses: Spells for prosperity and attracting a new job. Use when you need to be steadfast in anything.

Agate

Colours: Clear, milky white, grey, blue, brown, green or pink with bands running through the crystal. Other colours are available, but these are artificially coloured.

Cleaning method: All.

This is a good grounding stone. If you feel that your head is in the clouds and you find it difficult to stay focused, then this will help to bring you back down to earth. It is a very calming stone, helping to protect and stabilise your energies. Bringing balance to the emotional, physical and intellectual areas, it can be used where a lot of emotional trauma is being experienced. Agate harmonises our ying and yang, the male and female energies. It soothes and calms us, working slowly, but, as it does so, it brings with it great strength and courage. It will bring to the surface any hidden information about why we are experiencing imbalance in our life.

Agate aids self-confidence, self-analysis and acceptance of the self. Dis-ease preventing well-being is brought to our attention: clearing emotional bitterness in the heart; emotional trauma and dissolving internal tensions. It raises consciousness and encourages one to speak your truth. It also enhances creativity.

Agate stabilises the aura, eliminating and transforming negative energies, making it a powerful cleanser of emotional and physical levels. Place it on the heart chakra to heal emotional dis-ease that prevents acceptance of love. Place on the abdomen to stimulate the digestive process and relieve gastritis.

Physically agate is healing to the eyes, stomach and uterus; cleansing the lymphatic system and the pancreas. It also strengthens the blood vessels and heals skin disorders.

Magickal uses: Use in spells to clear a heavy mood or in an amulet to guard against the evil eye. Also for bravery, strength and longevity.

Agates come in different forms but they will all have the above properties as well those listed below.

Blue Lace Agate

Colour: Pale blue with darker blue and white bands running through.

Cleaning method: All.

Blue lace agate is a gentle, calming stone that engenders tranquillity and brings peace of mind. It activates and heals the Throat Chakra and encourages you to speak truthfully.

Easing the 'harsh edge' off communication in difficult times, it enhances public speaking, and smooths discussions.

Blue lace agate is a healing and nurturing stone, dissolving old patterns of repression and allowing a new mode of expression.

It is an inspiring stone that can assist inner attunement and has been used to perform miracles. The calming energies can be used to cool anger. It assists in flight, grace, reaching higher spiritual planes, and communicating with angels.

Physically, it has been used to aid arthritis; headaches; digestive issues and bones. It is a powerful throat-healer. By clearing blocked self-expression, it releases shoulder and neck tension.

It is good for thyroid deficiency; throat and lymph infections. Lowers fevers and removes blockages of the nervous system. Helpful on the capillaries and the pancreas.

Magickal uses: Use in spells involving clear communication or where you need to induce calm, peace and happiness.

Dendritic Agate

Colour: Clear, brown and /or green with fern-like markings.

Cleaning method: All.

Dentritic agate is known as the stone of plenty, bringing abundance to all areas of our life. It has a strong connection with the plant kingdom and can be used to keep plants healthy. It brings stability in times of confusion and helps us find the way through the challenges. Having a strong connection to the earth it can be used to ground us and is useful at clearing negative black Ley Lines and Geopathic stress.

Physically, it heals dis-ease caused by our chakras being out of balance, opening the chakras and aligning them. The branch like markings in dendritic agate work with the branching nerves and blood vessels of the body and are good for conditions such as neuralgia and can reverse capillary damage in the circulatory system. Good for problems of the skeletal system and helping to align it. It can be used to relieve pain.

Magickal uses: In prosperity spells or any Earth work.

Moss Agate

Colour: Green, blue, red, yellow or brown, with a moss like appearance to the markings.

Cleaning method: All. BUT avoid strong sun as it may fade the colour.

This is a stabilising stone strongly connected to nature. It refreshes the soul and helps you see the beauty around you. Helpful to reduce any sensitivity to the weather and to pollutants. Otherwise known as the 'Midwives stone' it helps with the birthing process by lessening pain and ensuring a good delivery. Moss agate is a stone of new beginnings; it releases blockages. A stone of abundance and wealth, helping you to access your intuition as well as your more practical side. It improves self-esteem and will enhance more positive personality traits. A balancing stone that releases fear and deep-seated stress, helping one to get along with others more easily. Inspiring new ideas after a period of stagnation, it encourages self-expression and communication. Moss agate will give insights into why one is unhappy with life or depressed. It is an 'optimistic' stone.

Physically moss agate will speed up recovery after illness. It will cleanse the circulatory and elimination systems and encourages the flow of lymph. It is anti-inflammatory and will boost the immune system. Helpful for depression; hypoglycaemia; dehydration and infections such as colds and flu.

Magickal uses: Spells for long life, fertility, happiness and riches.

Alexandrite

Colour: Green, blue-green in sunlight. Red, red-purple in artificial light.

Cleaning method: All.

A stone of longevity that brings about joyful inner transformation. Worn over the heart it is said to bring luck in love. It shows us both sides of the picture, linking the heart to the mind so we can view things from a dispassionate viewpoint.

This stone will strengthen will power, self-respect and self-worth. It harmonises male and female energies.

Physically it aids the nervous system; glandular system; soothes inflammations and muscular tension.

Magickal uses: Can be used as a substitute for pearl. Good for spells to help self-esteem or to bring more joy into your life, to draw luck, love and good fortune.

Amazonite

Colour: Bluey green with veins running through it.

Cleaning method: All.

This is one of the best crystals to calm and soothe emotional aggravation. Soothing to the nerves it dispels irritating and negative energy. Soothes all of the chakras; especially the heart, thymus and throat chakra. Enhancing our communication concerning love.

It balances our male and female energies bringing clarity and aligning the aura as it goes. A stone of good health, helping you to manifest and maintain universal love. Thought to enhance intuition, psychic powers, creativity and intellect.

Physically good for the nervous system because it dissipates any energy blocks. It is high in calcium and aids calcium assimilation. Protects against tooth decay, osteoporosis and diminishes calcium deposits within the body. It also helps to dispel muscular spasms.

Magickal uses: For spells to enhance confidence and inner strength, or to promote feelings of calm and balance. Also use to attract money, luck and success.

Amber

Colour: Golden brown or yellow resin. It is usually opaque or transparent and can have insects or vegetation inside.

Cleaning method: Do not clean with water.

This is one of the best tonic stones for the body. It allows the body to heal by absorbing negative energy and transmuting it into positive energy. It will draw dis-ease and negative energy out of the body and replace it with positive energy.

Amber is also a very powerful chakra cleanser. It emits bright, soothing, sunny energy, to calm nerves and enliven the disposition, helping when you wish to manifest things into your life. Stimulating to the intellect, it opens the crown chakra. Enhancing decisiveness and strengthening the memory.

Amber aligns ethereal energies to the physical, mental and emotional bodies and balances the aura. It is therefore a good stone when you are stressed. It cleanses the environment where placed and is good to purify rooms for birthing and re-birthing.

Purifies the body, mind and spirit.

Physically it treats goitres; throat problems; eyes; kidneys; bladder; liver; gall bladder; alleviates joint problems and strengthens the mucous membranes.

Magickal uses: For spells concerning bringing balance, mental harmony, feelings of calm or confidence into your life; draw business success or to stimulate the flow of money.

Amethyst

Colour: Dark purple to pale lilac. Usually transparent but can have white bands running through it.

Cleaning method: All.

The stone of sobriety; said to help heal alcoholism, compulsive behaviours and addictions of all kinds. It is a very spiritual stone with a high vibration. When worked with, or worn, it will raise your vibrations. Its serenity enhances higher states of consciousness and is excellent for meditation.

Amethyst balances the mental, emotional and spiritual bodies, clearing and stabilising the aura. A stone of protection against psychic attack. Enhancing stability, strength, calmness, invigoration, balance, courage, inner strength and peace. Helps you find your path in life. Also reputed to be beneficial when dealing with legal problems, and money issues, which can lead to prosperity and abundance. Dispelling anger, rage, fear and anxiety, amethyst is a calming stone.

Physically it can help with arthritis; hearing disorders; strengthening the skeleton; nervous system; endocrine system; chronic fatigue; fibromyalgia; digestive tract; heart; stomach; skin and teeth.

Magickal uses: As a protection against thieves and sorcerers. Use in an amulet or carry in your pocket. In spells to enhance psychic abilities; bring clarity; help dream recall or when seeking the truth of a situation in yourself or others. Draws business success.

The following amethysts will have the above properties as well as the extra ones listed below.

Black Amethyst

Colour: Very dark purple.

Cleaning method: All.

This amethyst is heavily included with hematite which gives it its dark almost black appearance. This is a very protective and grounding stone due to the hematite included in it. A very good stone for replenishing your energies especially for healers who feel drained after using their healing abilities.

Good for emotional grounding, they work to very deep levels and will blast through any blockages. Environmentally cleansing, these stones will remove radiation build up from the body; computers and TV's; etc. Good meditation stone and will aid psychic abilities. An emotional balancer.

Physically can help addictions; anger; cancer; eczema; fibromyalgia; headaches; boosts the immune system; insomnia; stress and tinnitus.

Magickal uses: Spells for protection.

Ametrine

Colour: Purple and yellow. This transparent stone is a combination of amethyst and citrine.

Cleaning method: All.

This powerful combination counters long standing illness and shows us insight into why dis-ease is present. Helpful when astral travelling it provides protection while we do.

Ametrine relieves psychic attack and helps clear tension from the head area to bring in more calm. Helps open our third eye chakra and can aid mental clarity. Good for concentration, it assists us to think things through, bringing creative solutions to any problems. It connects our intellect to our higher self. Releases negative emotional programmes, to bring about positive transformation and understanding of causes of emotional stress within. Promoting optimism and well-being that is undisturbed by external influences.

Physically, it is a powerful blood cleanser that clears toxins from the body. It energises the body and strengthens the immune system, regenerating the physical body.

Stabilising our DNA/RNA and can be used to heal chronic fatigue syndrome (CFS); depression; gastric upsets and ulcers; fatigue; tension headaches and any stress related dis-ease. Useful for conditions affecting the autonomic nervous system and where the body needs to be oxygenated more.

Magickal uses: For spells of protection.

Angelite

Colour: Blue and white with veins. Opaque.

Cleaning method: All.

Angelite facilitates connection with the angelic realm. It enhances telepathy and helps astral travel. A new age stone of awareness, representing peace and oneness. A stone for healers because it heightens perception and deepens attunement.

Helps us speak our truth and be more compassionate and accepting of how things are, especially that which cannot be changed.

Relieves psychological pain and counteracts cruelty. A stone of peace and tranquillity, deepening our connection with universal knowledge. Use to raise your awareness and open psychic channelling.

Physically, if applied to the feet, will unblock the meridians. It resonates with the Throat Chakra clearing inflammations, sore throats and balances the thyroid and parathyroids. Angelite has diuretic properties as it works to balance the fluid levels in the body. It can repair blood vessels and tissues and will cool the pain of sunburn.

Magickal uses: For spells bringing peace and tranquillity into your life.

Apatite

Colour: Blue, green, grey, brown (red brown), white, purple, violet or yellow, either opaque or transparent.

Cleaning method: All.

Apatite connects to a higher level of spiritual guidance and eliminates negativity. Extremely useful for expanding knowledge. Increases motivation, builds up energy reserves, it helps to raise Kundalini energy, inner clarity creating a sense of oneness with the higher self, assisting in reaching deeper states of meditation. Helps us to be more open and socially at ease. It harmonises, balances and brings together the physical, intellectual, emotional, and spiritual bodies. Apatite helps inspire the development of clairvoyance, clairaudience and clairsentience. It can help to access past-lives having an impact on your current life. It balances the male and female (yin-yang) energies and stimulates creativity and intellect. Clears confusion and helps us access information to be used personally and for the collective good. Helping to ease sorrow, anger and apathy, it reduces irritability and overcomes exhaustion. Clears frustration and endorses guiltless passion.

Physically, it helps hyperactive and autistic children. Heals bones and will encourage the formation of new cells. Aids calcium absorption and helps cartilage, bones, teeth, motor skills, and hypertension. Thought to ameliorate arthritis, joint problems and rickets. Suppresses hunger, raises the metabolic rate, Apatite is healing to the glands, meridians and organs. Use with other crystals to enhance their healing powers.

Magickal uses: For creativity, insight, intuition or service to others spells. It can be used in conjunction with other crystal to help the results of a spell.

Aquamarine

Colour: Greeny-blue clear or opaque crystal.

Cleaning method: All.

Aquamarine has the calming, soothing energy of the sea. This is the stone of courage that reduces stress, fears and quietens the mind. It is tranquilising, uplifting and encourages openness and innocence. It enhances creativity, communication, self-awareness, confidence and purpose. It invokes tolerance of others. Aquamarine encourages taking responsibility of the self and breaks old self-defeating patterns. It clarifies perception and clears up confusion and is good when feeling overwhelmed by one's life. It brings closure where needed; sharpens intuition and opens one up to clairvoyance. A good meditation stone that shields the aura and aligns the chakras. It clears the Throat Chakra bringing communication from higher levels. Good on the throat, spleen and Heart Chakra. Use for protection on journeys, especially those who travel on water. It has an effect on the etheric and mental levels. Aquamarine helps stabilise and harmonise unsettled surroundings and helps one attune to nature.

Physically recommended as a purifier of the throat it helps sore throats and swollen glands. Harmonises the pituitary and thyroid by regulating hormones. A tonic for the body and also helps eyes; jaw; teeth and stomach. It is detoxifying and calms an overactive immune system (helpful for autoimmune diseases and hay fever).

Magickal uses: Spells to enhance psychic powers, inner peace, inspiration, balance, clear thinking or confidence. Can be used in love spells to draw affectionate feelings from others.

Aragonite

Colour: Blue, brown, white, yellow, gold or green.

Cleaning method: All.

Aragonite is an earth healer and grounding stone. It transforms Geopathic Stress and clears blocked Ley Lines. With its ability to centre and ground physical energies, it is useful in times of stress. It gently takes you back into childhood or beyond, to explore the past. Psychologically it teaches patience and acceptance, combats over-sensitivity, encourages discipline and reliability, and develops a pragmatic approach to life. Mentally it aids concentration and brings flexibility and tolerance to the mind. Emotionally it combats anger and emotional stress, providing strength and support.

Physically it makes you feel comfortable and well within your own body. Spiritually it stabilises spiritual development; restores balance and prepares for meditation by raising your vibrations and bringing energy into the physical body. It strengthens the immune system and regulates processes that are proceeding too fast. It helps Raynaud's disease and chills. Aids calcium absorption, heals bones, and restores elasticity to discs. It also ameliorates pain and stops night-twitches and muscle spasms.

Magickal uses: Spells for healing Mother Earth.

Aventurine

Colour: Brown, green, blue, peach and red. Opaque with shiny speckles.

Cleaning method: All.

Enhances our creativity, imagination, intellect and mental clarity. A stone of prosperity, bringing career success. Brings a sense of calm, balance and enhances happiness. It helps one to see alternatives and potentials in all situations, giving a positive outlook, motivation, courage and inner strength. Said to bring luck, especially in games of chance. Aventurine brings friendship into one's life and enhances leadership and decisiveness. Its protective energies are good against vampirism of your energies (when someone draws energy from you without your consent or knowledge). Balances male and female energies, and mental, emotional, physical and auric bodies. It has a strong connection to the Devic realm and can be used to guard against Geopathic Stress.

Physically treats lungs, heart, adrenal glands, muscles and the urogenital system. Helps relieve stammers and severe neuroses bringing understanding of what lies behind the condition. Beneficial for blood and the circulatory system; headaches; general health and sleep disorders. Aventurine is associated with the Heart Chakra.

Magickal uses: Spells to enhance creativity and originality; healing emotional pain; prosperity; and when seeking the truth. Use as an all-round good luck stone.

Aventurine comes in blue, green, red and peach. They all have the same abilities as above and blue and green have the following extra properties as well.

Blue Aventurine

Colour: Blue with shiny speckles.

Cleaning method: All.

Excellent mental healer.

Magickal uses: Spells to heal emotional pain and mental stress.

Green Aventurine

Colour: Green with shiny speckles.

Cleaning method: All.

Brings harmony and healing to the heart. Dissolves negative emotions and thoughts. An all-round healer that brings emotional calm and wellbeing. It settles nausea and is useful in malignant conditions.

Magickal uses: Spells to enhance prosperity and to heal emotional pain.

Azurite

Colour: Deep blue.

Cleaning method: All.

Azurite brings clear understanding and expands the mind. Helps to release long-standing communication blocks; and helps you to let go of long-standing programmed belief-systems aiding you to move forward into the unknown without fear. Emotionally this is a good stone to clear stress and worry, grief and sadness, allowing in more 'light'. It transmutes fear and phobias and brings the understanding of why they occurred in the first place.

Physically, Azurite treats arthritis and joint problems; aligns the spine; clears throat problems and works at a cellular level to restore any damage to the brain. It can be used to heal kidney, gallbladder and liver problems. Useful for the spleen; thyroid; bones; teeth and skin. A stone for detoxification of the body. Azurite has a special affinity with the mind and mental processes.

Magickal uses: Spells to help you move forward in life and in healing spells.

Azurite with Malachite

Colour: deep blue and green.

Cleaning method: all.

These crystals combine the properties of both malachite and azurite. They are powerful energy conductors and help to open the third eye. Helps with visualisation and spiritual vision. Emotionally it clears ancient blocks and present day thought patterns that no longer serve you and brings a deep level of healing.

Physically azurite and malachite help with healing muscle cramps.

Magickal uses: Spells to help you move forward in life.

Beryl

Colour: Blue, golden, green, pink, white or yellow.

Cleaning method: All.

Beryl is the best stone to help you shed unnecessary baggage. It teaches you how to only do that what you need to do. It shows you your potential and deals with stress.

The crown and solar plexus chakras can be opened and activated with beryl. Good for helping us find courage and calming the mind. Discourages over thinking and shows us a new positive view to life. Use to reawaken love in those who have been together for many years and have become jaded.

Physically beryl strengthens the lungs and circulatory system. It helps the body eliminate toxins and pollutants. Used to treat the heart, liver, spine and stomach. Made into an elixir it can be used to treat throat infections.

Magickal uses: Spells for marital harmony; attracting good luck; good fortune; psychic awareness; protection when travelling; dispel fear or to guard against gossip.

Bloodstone

Colour: Red and green flecked stone.

Cleaning method: All.

Bloodstone is a healing stone for Base, Sacral, Solar Plexus and the Heart Chakra It is the stone associated with courage; abundance; purification and good fortune. Helping one to accept the turmoil associated with change. Overcome anxiety, depression and melancholy when working with bloodstone. Balancing the mental, emotional and physical bodies, it brings harmony, adaptability and strength. It renews relationships and helps your love life. Bloodstone helps with the decision-making processes and helps in attuning to the spiritual realms. Provides vitality, boosts talent, organisational abilities and charitable instincts.

Physically, bloodstone can help to cure psychosomatic illness (one with more emotional roots than physical) and pains. Purifies the blood and detoxifies the organs, especially liver, kidneys, bladder and spleen, by neutralising the toxins and eliminating them.

It is helpful in cases of Leukaemia; failing eyesight, lung congestion and rashes.

Magickal uses: Spells to draw success and victory; enhance strength; to calm and sooth an overactive mind; to ground the body; to increase wealth and prosperity; to assist in legal matters and business and to increase crop yields.

Calcite

Colour: Blue, brown, clear, grey, green, orange, pink, red and yellow. A translucent stone with a waxy and sometimes banded appearance.

Cleaning method: All except water-based ones.

Calcite is a powerful energy-cleanser and amplifier. It removes negative energy from the environment simply by being in a room. It removes stagnant energy from the body. It accelerates spiritual development and aids channelling, psychic abilities and astral travelling. It is a stone of motivation, combating laziness. Calcite calms the mind and teaches discernment.

Boosting the memory, it is good to use when studying. A good mental healer, dissolving rigid beliefs and old programmes and restoring balance. It alleviates emotional stress and replaces it with serenity. Calcite is a stabilising stone, which helps one to trust in one's own abilities. Aids willpower and the ability to overcome setbacks.

Physically calcite cleanses the organs, aids elimination and helps constipation. Assists calcium uptake in bones; dissolves calcifications; strengthens the skeleton and joints and stimulates blood clotting and tissue healing. It strengthens the immune system and comes in an array of colours each of which has the above properties as well as others associated with their colour.

Magickal uses: Good for purifying spells to clear negative energy from the body and enhances the power of any spells cast.

Black Calcite

Colour: Black or dark brown.

Cleaning method: All except water-based ones.

Used to go back to past lives, it can help unlock the past to deal with anything affecting the current life. Helps the soul to return to the body after trauma or stress. Helpful to alleviate depression and when you are having fearful thoughts at night.

Magickal uses: Good for purifying spells to clear negative energy from the body, and good for protection spells.

Blue Calcite

Colour: Blue.

Cleaning method: All except water-based ones.

A gentle calming stone, helpful when recuperation is needed. Aids communication, especially where there is dissent. It can absorb energy, filter it and return it to benefit the sender. Gently soothes the nerves, lifts anxieties and releases any emotional stress. It lowers blood pressure and dissolves pain on all levels.

Magickal uses: Good for purifying spells to clear negative energy from the body and is good for spells where communication is blocked by traumas or emotional stress.

Clear Calcite

Colour: Clear translucent stone.

Cleaning method: All except water-based ones.

This is a powerful detoxifier. It is a 'cure-all' stone that clears and aligns all the chakras. It heals at a deep soul level.

Magickal uses: Good for purifying spells to clear negative body energy.

Gold Calcite

Colour: Honey.

Cleaning method: All except water-based ones.

This is a great meditation stone. It helps one attain a connection with higher planes, making us more mentally alert.

It is particularly good for the sacral and crown chakras.

Magickal uses: Good for purifying spells to clear negative energy from the body or to assist when one is trying to enhance psychic abilities.

Green Calcite

Colour: Green.

Cleaning method: All except water-based ones.

A good mental healer, as it dissolves rigid beliefs and old programmes and then restores balance to the mind.

It helps to clear away anything that no longer serves us.

It is a powerful immune booster, which absorbs negative energy and clears the body of bacterial infections.

Helpful with arthritis; constrictions of the ligaments or muscles and with the realignment of bones.

The green ray is cooling to fevers, burns and inflammations as well as soothing any anger-generated dis-ease.

Magickal uses: Good for purifying spells to clear negative energy from the body; for spells to clear mental confusion and in prosperity spells.

Orange Calcite

Colour: Orange.

Cleaning method: All except water-based ones.

This is a great energising and cleansing stone, which can be used on any of the lower chakras. Helps to balance the emotions, clear fear, and overcome depression. It is useful for the reproductive system; gallbladder; intestinal disorders (IBS) and helps to clear mucus from the body.

Magickal uses: Good for purifying spells to clear negative energy from the body, especially good when depression is present.

Pink Calcite (Mangano Calcite)

Colour: Pale pink with or without white banding.

Cleaning method: All except water-based ones.

This has connections with the angelic realms and is a good heart stone. It helps us to forgive and release fear and grief from the heart centre. Brings unconditional love, aiding our self-worth and self-acceptance. Helps to prevent nightmares. It is good to use when one has suffered a trauma of any kind. Healing to nervous conditions: it lifts tension and anxiety.

Magickal uses: Good for purifying spells to clear negative energy from the body; to open the heart to be able to receive and give love freely and in love spells.

Red Calcite

Colour: Red.

Cleaning method: All except water-based ones.

A Base Chakra stone that is both energising and healing. Increases one's energy; uplifts the emotions; aids willpower and opens the heart chakra. It clears fear and helps one to understand its origin. Clears blocked energy that is preventing your stepping forward in life. It clears constipation; heals hip and lower limb problems and loosens the joints.

Magickal uses: Good for purifying spells to clear negative energy from the body, especially when this is holding us back from moving forward in life.

Yellow Calcite

Colour: yellow.

Cleaning method: all except water-based ones.

An uplifting stone that is good at eliminating that which is holding us down. It stimulates the will. Is good for relaxation and meditation. Stimulating the higher mind. Use on the Crown and Solar Plexus Chakras.

Magickal uses: Good for purifying spells to clear negative energy from the body, especially if caused by excess worry.

Carnelian

Colour: Red, orange, pink or brown translucent.

Cleaning method: All.

An inspirational stone of creativity, individuality and courage. It is a member of the agate family and, as such, has protective energies. Protecting against envy; jealousy; fear and rage. Stimulates analytical precision and awakens one's inherent talents; inquisitiveness and initiative. It is good at dispelling apathy; indolence and passivity. It can aid memory, including recall of past lives. Assists one in finding the right mate. In addition, it can help with manifestation of one's desires, and brings good luck. Carnelian can help ease or remove sorrows from the emotional body. Increases personal power, energy and compassion. Helps stabilise energies in the home. It is sometimes called the 'actors' stone'. Carnelian is associated with the Root and Sacral Chakras.

Physically carnelian has been used to heal open sores; colds; pollen allergies; rheumatism; kidney stones and other kidney problems; gall stones and neuralgia. It rejuvenates tissues and cells and is useful in aiding disorders of the spine, spleen and pancreas.

Magickal uses: Spells to give courage and eloquence when speaking publicly; for peace; harmony and protection and when needing strength and determination. Health spells for depression.

Celestite

Colour: Blue, yellow, white or red. Transparent crystal.

Cleaning method: All.

This is the stone of balance, alignment and deep peace. It heals the aura and reveals the truth: teaching us to trust the infinite wisdom of the divine. Its calming energies cool fiery emotions. It sharpens the mind, disperses worry and promotes mental clarity. It aids fluent communication.

Physically this healing stone dissolves pain and brings in an abundance of love. It can be used to treat the eyes and ears, to eliminate toxins and to soothe tense muscles. It is good for any throat problems.

Magickal uses: Spells to keep worries and fears at bay and for healing headaches.

Chalcedony

Colour: White, blue, pink, red, greyish. Transparent or opaque

Cleaning method: All.

This is a nurturing and optimistic stone promoting brotherhood. Enhancing group stability so is good when groups of people are working together. Chalcedony helps thought transmission and enhances telepathy. Good for absorbing and dissipating negative energy, so place in a room where you spend a lot of time. It brings the mind, body, emotions and spirit into harmony and balance. Removes hostility and transforms melancholy into joy. Chalcedony eases self-doubt and aids constructive inward reflection. Opening the mind to new ideas and helping acceptance of these new ideas and situations. It imparts mental flexibility and verbal dexterity, so is useful when learning new languages. Improves the memory.

Physically, Chalcedony is a powerful cleanser for open sores. It fosters one's maternal instinct and increases lactation. It improves mineral assimilation and combats mineral build-up in the veins. It is thought to lessen the effects of dementia and senility. It increases one's energy levels; heals the eyes; gallbladder; bones; spleen and blood and aids circulation. It aids the regeneration of mucus membranes and helps disorders caused by weather sensitivity (glaucoma). It boosts the immune system, stimulates lymph and banishes edema. It has an anti-inflammatory effect, lowers temperature and blood pressure. It heals the lungs from the effects of smoking.

Magickal uses: Spells to protect from drowning; banish fear and hysteria; prevent psychic attack; enhance strength and spells used to prevent and/or cure melancholy.

Chalcedony has all the properties previously noted. Specific colours have others – as follows.

Blue Chalcedony

Colour: Blue.

Cleaning method: All.

This creative stone opens the mind to new ideas and helps us assimilate new situations. A stone of communication assisting our listening skills and is useful when learning new languages because it helps our memory. An optimistic stone.

Physically blue chalcedony ameliorates dis-ease caused by weather sensitivity or pressure such as glaucoma. It enhances the immune system and stimulates the flow of lymph, good for edema. It regenerates the mucus membranes, lowers temperature and blood pressure and has an anti-inflammatory effect. Heals the lungs and is good for clearing the respiratory system of the effects of smoking.

Magickal uses: Spells to protect from drowning and spells used to prevent and/or cure melancholy and open our mind to new ideas.

Charoite

Colour: Purple mottled or veined stone.

Cleaning method: All.

This is a stone of transformation. Stimulating our inner vision and enhancing our spiritual development. It connects the heart and crown chakras and links us to the higher levels. Charoite facilitates the acceptance of others. Releases fear and puts everything into proper perspective. Showing us how things really are. It is a good stone for releasing worry and dissolving stress: bringing with it a sense of relaxation. It can help one overcome compulsions and obsessions. Mentally, charoite is a stimulating stone and physically, an energising stone. Good for transmuting negativity.

Physically, Charoite is good with problems of exhaustion; blood pressure; eyes; heart; reversing liver damage due to alcohol; and cramps, aches, and pains. It helps insomnia and can help enhance our dreams. Good for cases of autism and for bi-polar disorders.

Magickal uses: Spells to clear nightmares and to release and let go of fears, anxieties and worries.

Chiastolite

Colour: Brown, grey, rose, reddish brown, olive green with a distinctive cross in the centre of the crystal.

Cleaning method: All.

Powerful protective stone that wards off ill wishes and curses. Dispelling negative thoughts and feelings and transmuting conflict into harmony. Being a creative stone, it helps with problem solving and change. Chiastolite can help out of body travel and helps those making the transition beyond death. It helps us face reality, dissolving illusions and fear. Particularly helpful at clearing the fear where feelings of "going mad" are felt. Releases worn out patterns; clears feelings of guilt and helps to stabilise the emotions. It shows us our soul's purpose.

Physically, Chiastolite balances the immune system and repairs chromosome damage. It lessens fevers and staunches the flow of blood. Good for over acidification in the body and helps gout and rheumatism. Stimulates milk in lactating mothers.

Magickal uses: Protection spells.

Chrysanthemum Stone

Colour: Brown, grey with white.

Cleaning method: All.

This gentle stone harmonises any environment with its calming energies. It helps us to enjoy being centred in the moment and encourages us to blossom. It inspires and energises us to fulfil our dreams, bringing our endeavours to fruition. Bringing out our inner child so we can enjoy our self-development on our spiritual path. Helps us overcome ignorance; bigotry; narrow-mindedness; jealousy and self-righteousness and shows us how to love the world more. Counteracts superficiality and guards against distractions. This stabilising stone eliminates animosity and resentment.

Physically good for treating eyes; skin and skeleton. Also useful for clearing toxins and dissolving growths.

Magickal uses: For spells to draw earth energies in and encourage joy and laughter. The brown colour is particularly good for this.

Chrysocolla

Colour: Green, blue or turquoise, opaque crystal with inclusions, and sometimes bands.

Cleaning method: All.

Used in the home, chrysocolla absorbs negative energy. This tranquil stone is great for meditation and helping us accept constant change in our life. Invoking inner strength; clearing; calming and aligning the chakras with the divine. A good stone to have around if a relationship has become rocky. Its gentle presence heals the environment and the people involved. Place at the Solar Plexus to clear guilt and destructive emotional programmes. Use at the Heart Chakra to heal heartache and the Throat Chakra to improve communication. At the Third Eye Chakra it opens psychic vision. Chrysocolla imparts confidence and encourages self-awareness, enhancing personal power. This creative stone provides motivation where lacking; promotes speaking one's truth and reduces mental tensions. A stone to help overcome phobias.

Physically chrysocolla treats arthritis; blood disorders; bone diseases; digestive tract problems; lung problems and muscle spasms and cramps. Detoxifies the liver, intestines and kidneys. Chrysocolla re-oxygenates the blood and works at a cellular level in the lungs to improve lung capacity. Regenerates the pancreas and regulates insulin. The cooling action of chrysocolla will heal infections of the throat and tonsils; soothe burns; lower blood pressure; relieve arthritis; strengthen the thyroid and treat PMS. Will dissolve miasmas.

Magickal uses: Spells to invoke inner strength; soothe emotions and bring inner peace.

Chrysoprase

Colour: Lemon, apple green opaque, often flecked.

Cleaning method: All.

This is a very balancing and energising stone and will bring the male and female (yin/yang) energies into balance. Aligns the Chakras, especially the Heart Chakra and brings in universal energy to the physical body. It helps with co-dependency. Chrysoprase is a good stone for deep meditation. Gives one personal insights into the self to help self-love. Chyroprase dissolves the ego and shows us any self-defeating patterns and heals the inner child. A stone of forgiveness and compassion, opposing judgementalism. Encourages fidelity in both business and personal affairs. Good for stimulating speech and enhancing one's mental dexterity.

Physically chrysoprase helps with the assimilation of vitamin C. Useful for the heart; liver; reproductive organs; detoxifying; clearing nightmares; claustrophobia; removing heavy metals from the cells; gout; eye problems; balancing hormones and fungal infections.

Magickal uses: Spells to banish greed; envy; selfishness; tension and stress.

Chrysotile (Chrysotite)

Colour: Yellow and green.

Cleaning method: All.

This Shamanic stone can be used to connect to your power animal and connect to its wisdom. Use it to clear away the debris of the past so you can integrate and connect with your authentic self. A stone of integrity and self-honesty, showing where we seek to control others and steering us to let go and follow our destiny. Can bring us our desires but you need to be aware of what this will involve before you seek it!

Physically it will work on the etheric blueprint to heal cellular memory, correcting blocks and imbalances to prevent dis-ease from occurring.

Magickal uses: Spells to connect with our power animal; to bring inner peace and to amplify thoughts.

Citrine

Colour: Yellow to yellowish brown, transparent.

Cleaning method: Self-cleaning.

Known as the 'wealth' stone because it is said to promote success and abundance, especially in business and commerce. Citrine is purported to bring good fortune, sometimes in very unexpected ways. Enhances mental clarity; confidence; self-esteem; motivation; happiness and will-power. A good protective stone and a powerful cleanser of the chakras: clearing and aligning the aura with the physical body. It is warming, energising and creative in its energies and is one of the few crystals that doesn't need to be cleansed, because it doesn't hold onto negativity. It is a stone of joy.

It alleviates depression and self-doubt and diminishes irrational mood swings due to its effect on mental clarity. Improves and encourages self-expression and helps overcome difficulty in verbalising thoughts and feelings. Brings about an inner calm so one's own wisdom can be found releasing negative traits, fears and feelings. It also releases the past; fear of responsibility and can help stop anger. It is associated with the Solar Plexus Chakra.

Physically, citrine is said to aid digestion and helps eliminate nightmares that disturb one's sleep. Balances the emotions; helps CFS (chronic fatigue syndrome); depression; phobias; spleen; reverses degenerative diseases; pancreas; clears kidney and bladder infections; blood and circulation; thyroid gland; constipation; cellulite and the eyes.

Magickal uses: Spells to help problem solving; boost confidence; obtain mental and emotional clarity; protection when travelling and to attract success and abundance.

Danburite

Colour: Pink, white, lilac or yellow, with striations, usually clear.

Cleaning method: All.

This high vibration stone works with the Heart Chakra and helps link to the angelic realms. Danburite helps link us to our inner wisdom and is a great meditation stone providing a calming serene energy. Facilitating deep change within, so we can leave the past behind and move smoothly ahead to the future. Useful as a karmic cleanser it will clear past life diseases that have left an energetic imprint in the form of a miasm. Very comforting by the bedside for those dying, as it enables a conscious spiritual transition to take place. Danburite activates the Third Eye, Crown Chakra and Higher Chakras. Aids lucid dreaming and can clear the aura. Brings patience and helps the soul on through its pathway in life, bringing peace of mind as it goes. Pink Danburite is particularly good at opening the heart and encouraging self-love.

Physically, Danburite is a very powerful healing stone, clearing allergies and chronic conditions. It heals the liver and gallbladder and has a strong detoxifying action. Good for muscular and motor functions, it can also aid weight gain where needed.

Magickal uses: Spells for healing, bringing inner peace and to help connect to the angelic realms.

Diamond

Colour: Clear, white, blue, brown, yellow or pink. Transparent when cut and polished.

Cleaning method: All.

Diamond is an energy amplifier, increasing the energy of anything with which it comes into contact (so is especially useful when used with other crystals). A stone of abundance and wealth. Excellent at clearing electromagnetic stress and protecting against phone radiation. Diamonds cut through emotional and mental pain, reducing fear and helping new beginnings. It re-energises the aura.

Physically, diamonds treat allergies and glaucoma, aid the brain and sight and can also be used to rebalance the metabolism.

Magickal uses: Spells for protection; strength; to increase personal power; good fortune; prosperity; peace; love; fidelity and trust.

Herkimer Diamond

Colour: Clear usually with double terminations. Can have tiny rainbows inside.

Cleaning method: All.

These clear electromagnetic pollution and radioactivity and can block geopathic stress. They energise, enliven and promote creativity. Clearing and opening the chakras so that we can connect to our higher selves.

Physically, they protect against radioactivity and treat all disease caused by it. They correct DNA; cellular disorders and balance the metabolism, clearing tension and stress from the body.

Magickal uses: Can be used as a substitute for diamond.

Emerald

Colour: Green, can be bright or cloudy.

Cleaning method: All.

This is a stone of inspiration and infinite patience. Often referred to as the stone of 'successful love', bringing domestic bliss and loyalty. It enhances unconditional love and keeps a partnership in balance. If it changes colour it is thought to signal unfaithfulness. A heart stone, opening the heart chakra to bring emotional calm. Helping one to enjoy life to the full, it overcomes any of life's setbacks and gives the energy to recover and start again. Enhances memory and mental clarity. A stone of wisdom.

Physically, Emerald treats sinuses; heart; lungs; spine; muscles and is soothing to the eyes. Detoxifies the liver; alleviates diabetes and rheumatism and improves vision.

Magickal uses: Spells to enhance memory; mental wisdom; healing, harmony; love; fidelity; loyalty; honesty; money and patience. A protective crystal good for exorcism magick.

Fluorite

Colour: Purple, clear, green, blue, yellow or brown, transparent.

Cleaning method: All.

Fluorite is a stabilising stone promoting spiritual and psychic wholeness. It produces order within the mental, emotional, physical and spiritual bodies. Brings order where there seems to be only chaos. Aiding impartiality and detached reasoning where needed and is a stone of discernment and aptitude. Protects psychically and in the physical realm. It helps one meditate and learn to go past the 'chatter' that our minds tend to generate when first learning to meditate. Helps with concentration and to develop orderly, sequential thoughts: removing mental blocks. Fluorite can help build relationship skills. A good aura-cleanser.

Physically fluorite helps general health throughout the body's main skeletal and muscular systems. It purifies, cleanses and eliminates any disorder in the body. Helps the teeth. At the start of the illness, it dissipates disorders such as tumours; colds; flu; staph and strep infections; infectious cankers; herpes, and ulcers. It treats the structure, composition and cell formation of bones and helps with DNA and RNA damage to the cells of the body.

Magickal uses: Spells to enhance mental focus and increase psychic abilities.

Fluorite comes in different colours, each one having extra properties.

Blue Fluorite

Colour: Blue, transparent.

Cleaning method: All.

Protects emotions and restores emotional balance. Enhances creativity and clears communication. It will calm or re-energise the aura and/or physical body as needed. Focuses brain activity to invoke spiritual awakening.

Physically good for the ears, eyes, nose and throat.

Magickal uses: Spells to enhance mental focus; restore emotional balance and increase psychic abilities.

Clear Fluorite

Colour: Clear, transparent.

Cleaning method: All.

Clear Fluorite energises the aura and aligns all the chakras so universal energy can enter.

Physically it stimulates the crown chakra and connects our intellect to spirit.

Magickal uses: Spells to enhance mental focus; healing and increase psychic abilities.

Green Fluorite

Colour: Green, transparent.

Cleaning method: All.

Good for absorbing negative energy from the environment, grounding excess energy and clearing emotional traumas. Connects our intuition to our subconscious mind. Green fluorite clears the aura, chakras and mental chatter, and promotes self-love.

Physically it is good for clearing infections and relieving stomach problems and intestinal cramps.

Magickal uses: Spells to enhance mental focus and increase psychic abilities.

Purple Fluorite

Colour: Purple, transparent.

Cleaning method: All.

Strengthens mystical insight, psychic awareness, and opens the third eye. A good stone for meditation.

Physically, good for treating bones and bone marrow disorders.

Magickal uses: Spells to enhance mental focus and increase psychic abilities.

Yellow Fluorite

Colour: Yellow, transparent.

Cleaning method: All.

This creative stone stabilises group energies and is good for cooperative endeavours. It also supports the intellect.

Physically Yellow Fluorite is good for treating cholesterol; liver problems and releasing toxins.

Magickal uses: Spells to enhance mental focus and increase psychic abilities.

Galena

Colour: Metallic grey-lilac.

Cleaning method: All.

A harmonising stone bringing balance to all levels of the aura and physical body. It grounds, centres and anchors the body: opening the mind and dissolving self-limiting ideas from the past, making way for new ideas.

Physically, Galena reduces inflammation in the body, stimulates the circulatory system and increases assimilation of selenium and zinc. Good for the hair and eruptive conditions in the body.

Magickal uses: Spells to help with making changes in your life.

Garnet

Colour: Red, pink, brown, black, green, yellow, orange, transparent or translucent stones.

Cleaning method: All.

Powerful cleanser and re-energiser of the chakras. Revitalises, purifies and balances energy, bringing serenity or passion as appropriate. Inspiring love and devotion, it is a stone of commitment. Fortifies, activates and strengthens survival instincts, bringing courage and hope to seemingly 'hopeless' situations. It turns crisis to challenge.

Garnet balances the sex drive and alleviates emotional disharmony. Stimulates past-life recall and sharpens perceptions of oneself and others, removing inhibitions and taboos. Opens the heart and bestows self-confidence. Activates other crystals and amplifies them. Will dissolve ingrained behaviour patterns that no longer serve. Revitalises feelings and enhances sexuality, bringing warmth, devotion, understanding, trust, sincerity and honesty to a relationship. Helps control anger, especially toward the self. Red garnet is good for the Root Chakra and the Heart Chakra.

Physically regenerates the body and stimulates the metabolism. It treats disorders of the spine and spinal fluid; bone; cellular structure and composition. Purifying to the heart, lungs and blood and regenerates DNA. Aids assimilation of minerals (iodine, calcium, magnesium) and vitamins (A, D, E). Garnet boosts the immune system and energy levels.

Magickal uses: Spells to increase sexual desire, vigour, strength and to deter thieves.

Hematite

Colour: Silver (grey) or red.

Cleaning method: All.

Hematite is a stone for the mind; it helps in sorting things out, with attunement, memory, original thinking and technical knowledge. Good for mathematical pursuits and develops mental and manual dexterity, encouraging you to reach for the stars and helping you with dissolving self-limiting concepts. Balances the yin and yang and stabilises the physical and etheric bodies. It brings balance to the mind, body and spirit and dissolves negativity. A grounding stone, bringing clarity and tranquillity into one's life and attracts kind love. Good for self-control and inner happiness. Good Base Chakra stone.

Physically it helps leg cramps, blood disorders, nervous disorders, insomnia and heals breaks and fractures. Place a piece of hematite at the top of the spine and at the base of the spine to realign the vertebrae.

Magickal uses: Spells for healing; grounding; strengthening; success in lawsuits and for protection.

Howlite

Colour: Green, white or blue (often artificially coloured).

Cleaning method: All.

Extremely calming stone, linking to the higher spiritual dimensions, opening attunement and preparing the mind to receive insights and wisdom. It assists with out-of-body journeying and helps one to access past lives. Place on Third Eye to access other lives. Helps to formulate our ambitions and helps us to achieve them. A good stone to teach oneself patience. Howlite helps to eliminate anger and uncontrolled rage. Keep a piece in your pocket and it will absorb your own anger and any that is being directed at you. Helps one to overcome criticalness and selfishness; strengthening positive character traits. It stills the mind.

Physically howlite balances calcium levels within the body and aids teeth, bones and soft tissue. It eliminates pain, stress and rage.

Magickal uses: Spells to clear rage and selfishness. Use to bring calmness into your life.

Iolite

Colour: Blue, grey, yellow or violet. Translucent and colour may change with angle of view.

Cleaning method: All.

This stone of vision activates the Third Eye Chakra. It stimulates our intuition and inner knowing. It will re-energise and align the aura and subtle bodies when it comes into contact with the aura. Helpful in cases of addiction, as iolite shows us why we are addicted and helps us release the cause/s of our addiction. A stone to show us to express our true authentic self, free from the expectations of others around us. Co-dependency issues are helped by iolite as it encourages us to take responsibility for our own pathway in life. Good for discord in relationships and for releasing unwanted thought forms.

Physically it will support and detox the liver; reduce fatty deposits in the body; clear the effects of alcohol and generally help build a strong constitution. Treats malaria and fevers; sinus problems; respiratory problems; aids the pituitary; alleviates migraines and kills bacteria.

Magickal uses: Spells to draw strength and confidence.

Iron Pyrite (Fools Gold)

Colour: Gold or brown.

Cleaning method: All.

Iron Pyrite will block negative energy and pollutants, including infectious diseases. It makes a great energy shield and will help one overcome inertia. Taps into our potential and stimulates the flow of ideas. Good to place at your workspace as it energises the area around it. Promotes diplomacy and helps us to see behind the facade to what really is. Boosts self-worth and confidence, relieving anxiety. Good to help men who feel inferior but should not be used by men who are more macho as it may trigger aggression. In women it helps overcome feelings of inferiority. Iron pyrite increases blood flow to the brain helping memory and recall. It balances our mental capabilities with our intuitive thoughts and our analytical side with our creative side. Blocks energy leaks from the body and aura and can overcome deep despair and melancholy.

Physically this stone holds the perfect ideal of health. It increases the oxygen supply to the blood and strengthens the circulatory system. This fast-acting stone will show you the root cause of the dis-ease, especially with karmic and psychosomatic dis-ease. Strengthening to the digestive tract, it neutralises toxins that have been ingested. Iron pyrite treats asthma; bronchitis; bones; stimulates cellular formation and repairs DNA damage.

Magickal uses: Spells to draw luck and money to you.

Jade

Colour: Green, brown, blue, blue-green, cream, orange, lavender, red or white.

Cleaning method: All.

Jade has an affinity with the heart chakra and increases love and nurturing. This protective stone keeps the wearer from harm and will bring harmony; luck and friendship. Promotes self-sufficiency integrating the mind and body. It releases negative thoughts; soothes the mind and helps us see our way through complex tasks. Jade helps us see we are a spiritual soul on a human journey and helps awaken hidden knowledge. Placed on the forehead it aids lucid dreaming. This serene stone can clear irritability.

Physically jade is a cleansing stone aiding the body's elimination system to remove toxins. It treats the kidneys; adrenal glands; skeletal system; balances the fluids in the body and the water-salt/acid-alkaline ratios.

Magickal uses: Spells to draw luck; health; healing; long life; love and prosperity.

In addition to all the preceding properties, specific colours have others, as listed below.

Blue/Blue-Green Jade

Colour: Blue, blue-green.

Cleaning method: All.

A stone of patience bringing slow but steady progress to your endeavours.

Magickal uses: Spells to draw luck, health, long life, love and prosperity.

Brown Jade

Colour: Brown.

Cleaning method: All.

A very grounding stone that connects to the earth and aids in adjusting to a new environment.

Magickal uses: Spells to draw luck; health; long life; love and prosperity.

Green Jade

Colour: Green.

Cleaning method: All.

Helps to harmonise dysfunctional relationships. Calming on the nervous system.

Magickal uses: Spells to draw luck; health; long life; love and prosperity.

Lavender Jade

Colour: Lavender.

Cleaning method: All.

Good at clearing emotional pain and instilling inner peace. It teaches us restraint in emotional matters and helps us set clear boundaries.

Magickal uses: Spells to draw luck; health; long life; love and prosperity.

Orange Jade

Colour: Orange.

Cleaning method: All.

This energetic stone brings joy to its users, showing us we are one with everything on Mother Earth.

Magickal uses: Spells to draw luck; health; long life; love and prosperity.

Red Jade

Colour: Red.

Cleaning method: All.

Red Jade is the most stimulating jade and helps us release anger and tension in constructive ways.

Magickal uses: Spells to draw luck; health; long life; love and prosperity.

White Jade

Colour: White.

Cleaning method: All.

A stone to direct energy to assist decision making and help filter out distractions.

Magickal uses: Spells to draw luck; health; long life; love and prosperity.

Yellow Jade

Colour: Yellow.

Cleaning method: All.

Yellow Jade is gently stimulating, bringing joy and happiness. It connects us to all that is and shows us the interconnectedness of all beings.

Physically aids the digestive and elimination systems of the body.

Magickal uses: Spells to draw luck; health; long life; love and prosperity.

Jasper

Colour: Brown, blue, green, purple, red or yellow, opaque and sometimes patterned.

Cleaning method: All.

The nurturer stone supports during times of stress and brings tranquillity. Shows us we are here to assist others not just ourselves. A stone of protection and grounding to the physical body. Aligning the aura and chakras, cleansing them and absorbing any negative energy. Balances yin and yang, and aligns the mental, emotional and physical bodies with the etheric bodies. It clears environmental and electromagnetic pollution. Jasper imparts determination and gives one the courage to pursue problems assertively. Stimulating the imagination, it transforms ideas into action.

Physically jasper is a supportive stone after prolonged illness and helps to re-energise the body.

Magickal uses: Spells to draw in healing; grounding; protection and to show us our hidden thoughts, fears and hopes.

Jasper comes in a variety of colours and types. Each contains the same basic properties plus extras as listed.

Blue Jasper

Colour: Blue.

Cleaning method: All.

A good Throat Chakra stone it connects you to the spiritual dimensions. Stabilises the aura and balances the yin and yang energies.

Physically it is good for healing degenerative dis-eases; balancing mineral deficiencies and helps energy levels to be sustained during a fast.

Magickal uses: Spells to draw in healing; grounding and to show us our hidden thoughts, fears and hopes.

Brown Jasper and Picture Jasper

Colour: Brown with mottled patterns.

Cleaning method: All.

These are connected to the earth energies and are therefore very stabilising and balancing. Good at taking you to deeper levels, helping one to connect to past lives and revealing karmic causes affecting one's life now.

Physically they boost the immune system and detoxify the body. Brown jasper strengthens one's resolve to give up smoking.

Magickal uses: Spells to draw in healing; centering and grounding (especially if you live with your head in the clouds).

Dalmatian Jasper

Colour: Grey and spotted like a Dalmatian.

Cleaning method: All.

A stone of fun: good when you are feeling depleted of energy. Dalmatian jasper reminds us that we are spiritual beings on a human journey and helps us to accept this joyfully. It contains tourmaline that quickly transmutes negative energy and outworn patterns that no longer serve us.

Encourages a determination to succeed and to see ideas through into action, this makes it a useful stone for those starting up their own business.

It helps over-intellectual people or excessive thinkers to get out of their head and into their body. Helps move you forward in life.

Emotionally, it encourages fidelity and harmonises one's emotions.

Helping to overcome potential revenge scenarios, Dalmatian jasper is very grounding, imparting calm and tranquillity.

Physically it is beneficial for cartilages; nerves; reflexes and sprains. It guards against nightmares, night terrors and assists safe sleep.

Magickal uses: Spells to draw in healing; grounding and compassion.

Flamingo Jasper

Colour: Pink and white mottled appearance.

Cleaning method: All.

A motivational stone with an 'Adrenalin kick'. Very energising, especially after illness. It rectifies unjust situations by showing us the bigger picture. Its energies repel stalkers and ex's who won't let go. Good for aiding dream recall.

Physically it calms an excessive libido. Balances the mineral content in the body and regulates the supply of iron, sulphur, zinc and manganese within the body. Supportive to the circulatory system; digestive and sexual organs; ameliorating allergies and clearing the liver and bile ducts.

Magickal uses: Spells to draw in energy after illness, and for motivation.

Green Jasper

Colour: Green.

Cleaning method: All.

Balances out the parts of your life that have become all-important to the detriment of others. It heals obsessions and is a good Heart Chakra stone.

Physically helps skin disorders; ailments of the upper torso; digestive tract and dispels bloating. Also reduces toxicity and inflammations.

Magickal uses: Spells to draw in healing; grounding and balance.

Red Jasper and Brecciated Jasper

Colour: Red.

Cleaning method: All.

Gently stimulating, these are excellent worry beads to calm the emotions. Bringing problems to light before they get too big and providing the insights into how to solve them. Good Base Chakra stones.

Physically they strengthen and detoxify the circulatory system, the blood and the liver.

Magickal uses: Spells for protection against poison and negativity; healing and to help bring down a fever.

Mookaite (Jasper)

Colour: Mottled reds, browns and white.

Cleaning method: All.

A stabilising stone to bring balance to one's inner and outer experiences.

Encourages one to follow new experiences and instils a deep calm to face them.

Mookaite encourages one to be more flexible in life. Showing us all the possibilities and helping us to choose the correct one.

Physically helps the immune system; heals wounds and purifies the blood.

Magickal uses: Spells to draw in healing; grounding; stability and when faced with difficult situations.

Yellow Jasper

Colour: Yellow.

Cleaning method: All.

A good stone to take when travelling because of its protective qualities. It channels positives energies making you feel better physically; and it energises the endocrine system. Good to stimulate the solar plexus.

Physically it heals the digestive system, stomach and releases toxins from the body.

Magickal uses: Spells to draw in healing, grounding, protection from negativity and can be used as a shield against negativity when travelling.

Jet

Colour: Black.

Cleaning method: All.

Jet is a form of fossilised wood. It is highly protective, drawing out negative energy and fears and can guard against violence and illness. Old souls who have reincarnated many times are usually attracted to jet. It aids spiritual enlightenment. Jet balances our moods and alleviates depression, bringing stability and inner balance. Helps finances when placed in a cash box and protects businesses when placed in the wealth corner of your business (or home). Jet needs to be cleansed thoroughly when bought and when used in healing because of its ability to absorb negative energies.

Physically treats colds; epilepsy; migraines; menstrual cramps and stomach pain. Use to reduce lymphatic and glandular swellings.

Magickal uses: Spells for protection; luck; prosperity; psychic awareness and healing.

Kunzite

Colour: Pink, clear, green, yellow or lilac. Translucent or transparent, and striated.

Cleaning method: All.

A high vibration stone that awakens the heart to unconditional love. Activates the heart and aligns it to the Throat and Third Eye Chakras. It encourages humility, radiating unconditional love and communication.

A good stone to use in meditation as it produces a deep state of relaxation so you can connect to the universal energies more easily. Can dispel negativity and strengthen the aura by producing a protective shield around it to clear unwanted entities and mental influences.

Kunzite facilitates introspection and combines the intellect, intuition and inspiration together. It helps us accept and act on constructive criticism and encourages self-expression. Emotional baggage is cleared with the help of kunzite (even from past lives). Can be used to block geopathic stress.

Physically, Kunzite alleviates panic attacks and strengthens the circulatory system, immune system and the heart muscle. Calms neuralgia; epilepsy and soothes joint pain.

Kunzite's lithium content is helpful for psychiatric disorders and depression when taken as an elixir. Good when recovering from the effects of emotional stress.

Magickal uses: Spells to remove emotional blocks, fears, stress and for grounding.

In addition, specific colours have other properties as follows.

Clear Kunzite

Colour: Clear.

Cleaning method: All.

Clear Kunzite helps with soul retrieval work. Trauma, shock or abuse can cause part of the soul to leave the body: kunzite can be used as a receptacle to bring the soul back to the physical body again. This kind of healing should be done by a qualified therapist in soul retrieval.

Magickal uses: Spells to remove emotional blocks, fears and stress.

Green Kunzite (Hiddenite)

Colour: Emerald green or yellow.

Cleaning method: All.

Green Kunzite connects to the higher realms to bring knowledge through and grounds spiritual love. For those who put a brave face on difficult times, kunzite will allow you to accept help from others and the universe and gently release any feelings of failure. A stone of new beginnings. Place on Third Eye to open spiritual sight.

Physically it can be used by healers to comb the aura to find areas of dis-ease or blocks. Supports the thymus and the chest area of the body.

Magickal uses: Spells to remove emotional blocks, fears and stress and spells for new beginnings.

Lilac Kunzite

Colour: Lilac.

Cleaning method: All.

This crystal provides the doorway into the higher spiritual levels. A stone of transition, useful for people who are dying, as it shows their souls what is ahead so they can embrace it without fear.

Magickal uses: Spells to remove emotional blocks, fears and stress.

Yellow Kunzite

Colour: Yellow.

Cleaning method: All.

Clears environmental smog and deflects radiation and microwaves from the aura. Can be used to align the chakras.

Physically, Yellow Kunzite can restructure DNA, balance the calcium-magnesium levels in the body and stabilise the cellular structure.

Magickal uses: Spells to remove emotional blocks, fears and stress.

Kyanite

Colour: Blue-white, black, green, grey, pink or yellow. It can be transparent or opaque and have a pearly appearance. Usually striated and bladed.

Cleaning method: Self-cleaning.

This self-cleaning crystal encourages one to speak the truth and cuts through fears and blockages. It opens the throat chakra to encourage self-expression and communication. Kyanite cuts through confusion; illusion; anger, and stress and stimulates the higher mind. It draws energy into the organs and aura.

Physically it can be used to treat the adrenal glands; brain; fevers; muscular disorders; urogenital system; thyroid and parathyroid glands. Good for pain relief; lowering blood pressure and healing infections.

Magickal uses: Spells to remove blocks and fears.

Kyanite has all the above properties as well as specific colours having others as listed here.

Black Kyanite

Colour: Black.

Cleaning method: Self-cleaning.

Good for meditation as it grounds and aligns the chakras.

Magickal uses: Spells to remove blocks and fears.

Blue Kyanite

Colour: Blue.

Cleaning method: Self-cleaning.

A good Throat Chakra stone, especially useful for performers and public speakers. Strengthens the voice and heals the throat and larynx.

Magickal uses: Spells to remove blocks and fears.

Labradorite

Colour: Greyish to black with blue, yellow. Resembles a butterfly wing in the light as the shimmery colours show through.

Cleaning method: All.

Labradorite is a magical transformational stone: it is an esoteric stone of knowledge. One of the best grounding stones to accompany astral travel and higher chakra work. Helps to maintain one's connection to Earth, whilst its light-reflectivity helps to explore higher vibrations. It ensures that you are able to bring down and integrate into physical life whatever you learn working in the higher realms. In meditation, focusing on labradorite can help you enter and maintain the meditative state. Deflects unwanted energies from the aura and prevents energy leakage. It forms a barrier to negative energies shed during therapy sessions. Stimulates the intuition and psychic gifts. Strengthening one's faith and trust in the universe; gets to the root of problems and calms an overactive mind. Energises the imagination, bringing up new ideas and clears mental confusion and indecision: allowing one to have self-understanding on a deeper level.

Physically helps the immune system. Treats disorders of the eyes and brain. It relieves stress and regulates metabolism and is good for treating colds; gout and rheumatism. Balances hormones; relieves menstrual tension and lowers blood pressure.

Magickal uses: Spells to enhance psychic abilities; intuition; perception; self-esteem; self-respect and confidence. Draws in peace of mind; happiness and tranquillity.

In addition, specific colours of Labradorite have extra properties.

Yellow Labradorite

Colour: Yellow.

Cleaning method: All.

Yellow Labradorite accesses the higher realms and can be used to enhance clairvoyance and channelling. Good for visualisation and to expand the mental body.

Physically, it heals the adrenal glands; gallbladder; liver; stomach and spleen.

Magickal uses: Spells to enhance psychic abilities; intuition; perception; self-esteem; self-respect and confidence.

Tamsin German

Lapis Lazuli

Colour: Deep blue with gold flecks.

Cleaning method: All.

A powerful thought amplifier. Stimulating higher awareness, it brings clarity and objectivity. Opens the third eye and connects one with the consciousness of the Universe and connects you to your spirit guides. Lapis Lazuli is good at protecting you against psychic attack and returning it to the source. Helps you to confront the truth and to accept its learning; harmonising conflict and aiding self-expression. Useful with dream recall and psychic work. Harmonising the physical, emotional, mental and spiritual bodies, it clears depression and lack of purpose; dissolving martyrdom, cruelty and suffering. Lapis Lazuli will help towards successful relationships. This protective stone given to children will help to keep them out of danger. Very balancing for the Throat Chakra and the Third Eye Chakra

Physically helps with pain; migraines; headaches; respiratory problems; nervous system; throat; larynx and thyroid. Cleanses organs (especially the kidneys); bone marrow; thymus and the immune system. It is good for purifying the blood; reducing high blood pressure and assisting hearing. Lapis Lazuli affects female hormonal balance and can increase the menstrual cycle by two days and for those who are menopausal, a sequence of changes is induced that may result in the return of a regular menstrual cycle. Aids weight loss by reducing the fat levels in one's tissues.

Magickal uses: Spells to enhance psychic abilities; mental clarity; virility; inner calm; courage. Spells to draw love; joy; healing and protection.

Larimar (Dolphin Stone, Blue Pectolite)

Colour: Blue, blue-green, grey, or red with white.

Cleaning method: All.

Larimar naturally raises the consciousness and harmonises the body and soul to the new vibrations of Earth. It opens to the new dimensions and helps stimulate the evolution of the planet. Induces a deep meditative state radiating love and tranquillity. This empowering stone helps steer the soul onto its true pathway in life and will clear and dissolve any self-imposed constraints. A good stone where self-sabotaging behaviour is present: it will alleviate guilt and remove fear. Teaches us to go with the flow of life. An emotional balancer bringing calmness in its wake. Promoting self-healing when placed on the Third Eye, Heart, Throat or Crown Chakras. Placed on the earth it can counteract the effects of geopathic stress.

Physically it can ameliorate bi-polar disorders. Use on the Heart, Third Eye or Solar Plexus Chakras to remove entities. Dissolves energy blocks in the head, neck and chest areas and can be placed on constricted joints and blocked arteries. Removes pain when placed on the site of the pain and is particularly good for cartilage and throat problems.

Magickal uses: Spells to increase our inherent gifts.

Lepidolite

Colour: Purple, pink, and slightly shiny.

Cleaning method: All.

Lepidolite is a stone with extremely high vibrations. A stone of transition, releasing and re-organising old patterns and then helping to induce change. Good at clearing negativity. One can access the Akashic (past life) records using lepidolite and tune into past lives to clear blockages in one's present life. Lepidolite activates and opens the Throat, Heart, Third Eye and Crown Chakras, clearing blockages and bringing cosmic awareness. Good for reducing stress and depression, it is helpful in halting obsessive thoughts and despondency. Stimulates the intellect and helps focus on what is important; encouraging one to reach goals and become more independent. Speeds up decision-making. A calming and soothing stone.

Physically use to locate the site of dis-ease. It vibrates gently when placed on an area of disease and helps to clear the blocks. Relieves allergies; strengthens the immune system; restructures DNA and enhances generation of negative ions. Also relieves exhaustion; epilepsy and Alzheimer's. Lepidolite numbs sciatica and neuralgia and overcomes joint problems. A good detoxifier for the skin and connective tissue and is helpful during menopause. Treats illnesses caused by Sick-Building Syndrome and computer-stress and clears Electromagnetic Pollution.

Magickal uses: Spells to move forward in life; inner calm and psychic awareness.

Magnesite

Colour: White, grey, brown or yellow.

Cleaning method: All.

A stone for visualisation when placed on the Third Eye. Magnesite aids relaxation and induces a deep meditative state. It opens the Heart Chakra and teaches us self-love and unconditional love. Useful where relationships are strained due to behavioural or addictive problems. Helps us explore our unconscious thoughts and feelings and shows us the reason behind them. A stone for egotistical people because it teaches us to step back and listen to others. Emotionally calming this stone supports those who are nervous or fearful and helps them overcome these feelings.

Physically it contains high levels of magnesium and helps its absorption into the body. Magnesite acts as an antispasmodic and will treat muscle; menstrual; stomach; intestinal and vascular cramps. Use to relieve the pain of kidney and gall stones; headaches and migraines. It will detoxify the body and eliminate body odours. Speeds up fat metabolism and disperses cholesterol. Good to prevent arteriosclerosis and heart problems.

Magickal uses: Spells to enhance confidence and useful in relationship troubles.

Tamsin German

Malachite

Colour: Green with light and dark bands (sometimes circles).

Cleaning method: All.

A transformation stone, it assists and supports in changing situations. A powerful stone that amplifies both positive and negative energies, so use carefully. Clears and activates all the chakras, especially the Throat and Heart helping connect to higher spiritual guidance. Clarifies emotions. It easily absorbs negative energy from the body and atmosphere, so needs to be cleansed regularly on a quartz bed. It is toxic and should only be used in its polished form. Absorbs all kinds of radiation. it will show what is blocking spiritual paths It has a strong affinity with the Devic kingdom. Place on the Third Eye to activate psychic vision, on the Heart to bring balance and harmony. Opens the heart to unconditional love. Use on the Solar Plexus to give deep emotional healing. Malachite draws out deep-seated emotions and clears anything outdated that no longer serving us. Helps us to take responsibility for actions finding the root of the problem, showing the insights we need to move on. Aids absorbing and processing information better, especially difficult concepts. Helps us to 'see' the cause of dis-ease; and will alleviate shyness and aid friendships.

Physically malachite shows the cause of dis-ease. Helpful for cramps of all kinds and sexual dis-eases. It lowers blood pressure. Asthma; arthritis; epilepsy; fractures; joint problems; growths; vertigo; tumours; the pancreas and the spleen are helped by malachite. Aligns cellular structure and DNA and will boost the immune system.

Magickal uses: Spells of protection; to draw business success; love and peace.

Marcasite

Colour: Whitish-yellow.

Cleaning method: All.

Marcasite enhances our psychic abilities, providing a shield and grounding energy to help us in everyday life. A good crystal to use for clearing our auras of entity attachments. It will increase our objectivity, so we can take a detached perception when seeking insights into the self. Helps us connect to our own power rather than seeking power over others. Increases willpower and helps us step forward and learn to shine our light. Useful for scattered or confused thinking or impaired memory. Will overcome mental exhaustion; improve concentration and bring clarity. Marcasite will dispel hysteria or victim mentality and alleviate emotional burnout. Balances the energies of the physical body to bring optimum wellbeing and high energy levels.

Physically helpful for cleansing the blood and the spleen and for freckles, moles and warts.

Magickal uses: Spells for grounding; clarity; concentration; confidence; willpower; memory and to help with sleep problems.

Tamsin German

Moldavite

Colour: Dark green and glassy in appearance.

Cleaning method: All except salt as it scratches the surface.

Moldavite was formed when a meteorite struck the earth and the heat created by the impact melted the surrounding rocks and formed a strew field of moldavite. It is considered to be a combination of earth energies and extra-terrestrial energies and can enhance other crystals by raising their vibrations. Connects us with our higher self and with extra-terrestrials, as well as with the ascended masters and will help us greatly on our path to ascension.

Holding it to the light and gazing into its depths will raise our consciousness. Recommended to use with grounding stones (hematite, smoky quartz) as it can leave you feeling spaced out. Moldavite has an extremely high vibration and will open and clear the Crown Chakra of any blocks so guidance can come through from higher dimensions. Placed at the Throat Chakra it will assist communication with other planets especially with regard to helping Mother Earth heal. At the Third Eye Chakra it can be used to journey into the past or future to facilitate our spiritual progress. Star children are very comforted by the energies of Moldavite as it helps to integrate the heavy energies of this planet into our spiritual body. If they place it at their Heart Chakra it will help relieve feelings that they don't belong on this planet. Having no crystalline structure Moldavite can take us beyond our limits, connecting us with the "why we are here" and the purpose of our incarnation. Moldavite is very much a stone for working on our spiritual side. It downloads information from our Akashic record and light body and helps it to be processed and made conscious to enhance our spiritual growth.

Physically, Moldavite can be used to find the source and cause of dis-ease and lend support during the healing. People who dislike the stone may have hidden emotional traumas or have an aversion to emotion. In these cases, they need to experience unconditional love. Working with rose quartz can help with this.

Magickal uses: Spells to enhance our psychic abilities, especially extra-terrestrial connections.

Moonstone

Colour: White, cream, blue, green or yellow with a milky or translucent appearance.

Cleaning method: All – but energise in the rays of the moon.

Strongly connected to the moon's energies and, like the moon, it shows us that everything in life is part of a cycle. A stone of new beginnings. A good emotional calmer and healer; enhancing psychic abilities and clairvoyance. It will make conscious the unconscious and help to promote empathy. Its gentle female energies will calm an overly aggressive female or an excessively macho man. Emotionally, moonstone will soothe stress and stabilise emotions.

When placed on the solar plexus it will draw out and dissolve any outworn patterns that no longer serve us, bringing with it an understanding and emotional intelligence. Clears deep, emotional stress and will heal disorders of the upper digestive tract that are caused by this stress. Moonstone helps us to be more spontaneous and allows the forces of serendipity and synchronicity to flow.

Physically, it helps the female reproductive organs; PMS; menstruation and balances the hormones. Aids the digestive system; assimilation of nutrients; elimination of toxins; clearing fluid retention; alleviating degenerative conditions of the skin, hair, eyes and helps fleshy organs (liver, pancreas). An excellent stone for conception, childbirth, and pregnancy.

Magickal uses: Spells to protect women and babies, enhance psychic abilities, soothe emotions, relieve stress, love and the green coloured moonstone is gently healing.

Muscovite (Mica)

Colour: White, pink, brown, grey, green, red, yellow or violet. Pearly layers.

Cleaning method: All.

This form of mica has angelic connections and helps stimulate our higher awareness. Opens intuition and psychic vision and can be used for astral travel. This reflective stone mirrors back what we project at the world, which we are not aware of and don't accept in others. It helps us to see and accept these traits and helps integration and transformation of these qualities.

Muscovite is good for releasing tension in the body, aligning the subtle bodies and meridians and bringing balance to the physical body. Disperses insecurities and self-doubt and is good to counter clumsiness. Aids problem solving; clears left-right confusion and is useful for those who suffer from dyspraxia.

The stone can be used to improve appearance, both internal acceptance of our self and physically by improving hair sheen, adding a sparkle to the eyes and stabilising correct body weight.

Physically muscovite balances blood sugar levels; aids the pancreas; alleviates dehydration and relieves allergies and insomnia. It can be used to heal conditions caused by distress.

Magickal uses: Spells to enhance our appearance; psychic abilities and for astral travel.

Obsidian

Colour: Brown, black, red-black, blue, green, silver, gold-sheen or rainbow.

Cleaning method: All.

This stone is without boundaries or limitations getting straight to the truth of things fast! Exposing flaws, weaknesses and blockages, it shows us how to clear any that are destructive and don't empower for our highest good, pushing us forward in life and lending us support as we go. Black Obsidian can be ruthless, so take care if you wish to use it. A gentler form is mahogany obsidian, snowflake obsidian or apache tear, but if you wish to work with black obsidian then use in conjunction with rose quartz, which will surround you with the love needed to deal with any unpleasant issues that arise. Obsidian can take you back to past lives to remove any festering emotions or trauma that need to be cleared. A very protective stone that absorbs negativity from the environment. It will block psychic attack and remove any negative spiritual influences. A large piece of obsidian can clear geopathic stress and absorb environmental pollution. Don't place in an area where people may be affected by its truth enhancing properties. Obsidian brings clarity, removing any confusions or constricting beliefs. It brings you face to face with your shadow-side to help you to integrate it and accept yourself.

Physically, obsidian shows us the root cause of dis-ease. It helps us to 'digest' anything that is hard to take and helps with the digestive tract. A good detoxifier, it helps with reducing arthritic pain, joint problems, cramps and injuries.

Magickal uses: Spells to enhance determination and clear any blocks.

Different types of obsidian also contain the properties below.

Apache Tear

Colour: Black.

Cleaning method: All.

This form of black obsidian is gentler in its effect. It brings up negativity, slowly, so it can be transmuted gently. Apache Tear is excellent for absorbing negative energy and protecting the aura. A good stone for grief, showing the source of the distress. It helps forgiveness, removing self-limiting beliefs, increasing spontaneity.

Physically, it enhances assimilation of vitamin C and D. Calms muscular spasms and is a good detoxifier.

Magickal uses: Spells to enhance determination; clear any blocks; protection and luck.

Black Obsidian

Colour: Black.

Cleaning method: All.

One of the stronger obsidians. Goes straight to the root of problems and shows faults. It helps to release that which no longer serves us so we may move into the future confidently. Black Obsidian repels negativity and disperses unloving thoughts. Clears old loves and provides support during changes. Use briefly on the Third Eye to break through mental barriers and dissolve conditioning. It compiles scattered information and promotes emotional release. Always use with rose quartz to soften the blow of what's being brought up!

Magickal uses: Spells to enhance determination; clear blocks; grounding and protection.

Mahogany Obsidian

Colour: Brown and black.

Cleaning method: All.

Gentler than black obsidian and is connected to the earth energies, making it a good grounding and protective stone. Gives one strength in times of need, and eliminates energy blockages, vitalises purpose and stimulates growth on all levels. Provides deep soul healing. Its stabilising energy strengthens a weak aura and will align the Sacral and Solar Plexus Chakras. Place by the bed to clear mental stress and tension.

Physically it relieves pain and improves circulation.

Magickal uses: Spells for strength, determination and grounding.

Rainbow Obsidian

Colour: Black with rainbow bands.

Cleaning method: All.

A gentle obsidian with very protective qualities. It will cut the cords of old love, releasing any attachments others have left and replenish the heart energy. Will absorb negative energy from the aura and draw stress from the body. It teaches us about our spiritual nature.

Magickal uses: Spells for psychic work; mediation; reflection and where there are problems in a relationship.

Snowflake Obsidian

Colour: Black with white mottled appearance.

Cleaning method: All.

When used on the Sacral Chakra it will calm and soothe, while gently showing ingrained patterns of behaviour that no longer serve us. Balances the mind, body and spirit helping us to learn from our mistakes and to accept our successes.

Physically it is good for the skeleton and it improves the blood circulation and veins.

Magickal uses: Spells to enhance determination.

Onyx

Colour: Black, blue, brown, grey, white, yellow or red.

Cleaning method: All.

A stone of change, imparting confidence for us to make changes and feel at ease in our surroundings. It connects us to a higher guidance and can take us forward to view our future. Onyx is supportive in confusing or difficult times and/or during times of enormous mental or physical stress. Providing us with the vigour, stamina and steadfastness that we need in such times. Helps you keep your own counsel. Useful in past-life work for healing old injuries or physical traumas that are affecting one now. It will take you to the source of the injury. Onyx heals old grief and sorrows. A mental tonic that alleviates overwhelming fears and worries, balances our yin and yang and will integrate any dualities within the self.

Physically treats teeth problems, bones, bone marrow, blood disorders and the feet. Best used on the left side of body.

Magickal uses: Spells to draw stability; comfort; faith; protection and grounding and for when you need to absorb intense feelings.

Opal

Colour: White, pink, beige, black, blue, brown, green, orange, red, yellow or purple. Appearance can be clear or milky with iridescence.

Cleaning method: All.

The opal's fine vibration can be used to enhance visions by helping us connect to our psychic side. Helps us to see and express our true self. It amplifies our characteristic traits and brings them to the surface so they can be transformed. Opal absorbs and reflects back what it picks up, so should only be worn as jewellery when you are in a good place mentally and emotionally. A karmic stone, showing us what we give out we get back.

Mentally opal brings spontaneity and enhances self-worth. A stone of passion that will intensify emotional states and release any inhibitions. When programmed properly opal is a good protective stone, making you unnoticeable or invisible. Can be used for earth energy healing, to repair depletions, reenergise and stabilise the earth grids.

Physically can be used to strengthen the will to live and memory. It purifies the Blood; kidneys; regulates insulin eases childbirth and alleviates PMS (use dark coloured opals). The elixir is beneficial for the eyes.

Magickal uses: Spells to draw joy; creativity; fidelity and to enhance intuition.

Peridot (Chrysolite, Olivine)

Colour: Olive green, yellowy green, honey, red, or brownish, opaque crystal.

Cleaning method: All.

This protective stone is a powerful aura cleanser releasing toxins on all levels. Purifying to the subtle and physical bodies and the mind. Peridot helps us to detach from external influences that are affecting us and shows us how to look to our own higher guidance. It releases old baggage such as guilt, burdens or obsessions from the Solar Plexus and Heart Chakra. Alleviates anger, jealousy and resentment and will help to reduce stress. Encourages us to make necessary changes in our life and gives us the motivation needed. Peridot releases negative patterns, so that new can come in and it helps one attain spiritual truth. Sharpens the mind and opens it to a new level of awareness, banishing lethargy. It shows us the things we have neglected either consciously or subconsciously and helps us accept our mistakes, showing us how to move on from them. Helps us take responsibility on our life path and to stop blaming others when it appears to go wrong.

Physically, Peridot is a tonic for the body, healing and regenerating tissues and is particularly good for skin complaints. Strengthens the metabolism and eyes; and helps the heart; thymus; lungs; spleen; intestinal tract and the gallbladder. Assists childbirth when placed on the abdomen by strengthening muscular contractions and lessening the pain. Balancing for bipolar conditions and hypochondria.

Magickal uses: Spells to draw prosperity; wealth; luck and for personal growth.

Petrified Wood

Colour: Brown.

Cleaning method: All.

This is an excellent grounding stone. It will provide one with strength in all areas of one's life. Can be used effectively to access past lives in meditation. During illness it will provide the support and insight needed to heal. During the crisis period of an illness it shows you why you are suffering and the lesson/s that you need to learn from it, so the illness doesn't have to be repeated. This 'stone of transformation', helps you to reach higher levels of consciousness. A stone of patience, of slow, steady growth towards ascension, helping you overcome limiting emotional patterns.

Physically it treats atrophied portions of the body and helps with paralysis. It will strengthen the back and align the skeleton. Good for treating hearing loss and incontinence and for balancing the liver and gallbladder. It is a good blood and liver cleanser and aids proper blood-cell manufacture in the bone marrow.

Magickal uses: Spells to draw healing and protection.

Tamsin German

Pietersite (Tempest Stone)

Colour: Golden brown to grey-blue, mottled or iridescent.

Cleaning method: All.

Pietersite otherwise known as tempest stone is connected to the storm element and is a recent discovery, and reminds us we are a spiritual being on a human journey. It is said to hold "the keys to the kingdom of heaven", connecting our everyday consciousness to our spiritual side. Use to access the Akashic records. This stone of vision can stimulate the Third Eye and pineal gland to enhance intuition, spiritual visions and precognition. Used during moving meditations it helps one reach a high level of altered awareness. Pietersite removes beliefs and patterns imposed by other people and helps us recognise the truth or falsehood of other people's words. Links us to our own inner guidance, dissolving stubborn blockages and clearing confusion. Used in past live work to remove vows, promises or dis-ease caused by not following our own truth. This stone of truth shows us the path to clear anything that blocks us using that truth.

Physically balances the endocrine system; pituitary gland; metabolic hormones; growth; sex; temperature and stabilises blood pressure. Clears and energises the meridians and clears dis-ease caused by exhaustion. Helpful to the lungs; feet; legs; liver and intestines.

Magickal uses: Spells to help find your path forward in life.

Prehnite

Colour: Green, brown, white or yellow.

Cleaning method: All.

A stone of unconditional love. A stone to heal the healer. This has a strong affinity with the elemental realm and when meditated upon, can connect you to the universal energy grid, Archangel Raphael and your spirit guides. Aids precognition and develops trust in our inner knowing. Shows you your path forward in life. Has the ability to seal the auric field in a protective shield and can aid dream recall. Use in gridding for peace and protection in the house and in the garden to create a haven of healing. Prehnite is a Feng Shui stone for de-cluttering, it helps you to let go of possessions that you no longer need. Helpful for those who hoard possessions or love, due to inner lack. Alleviates nightmares, phobias and deep fears, uncovering and healing the dis-ease that created them.

Physically prehnite is good for hyperactive children. It diagnoses dis-ease and clears the root cause. Useful for the bladder; kidney; thymus gland; shoulders; chest and lungs. Treats gout and blood disorders and repairs the connective tissue in the body. It stabilises malignancy.

Magickal uses: Spells for protection.

Tamsin German

Preseli Bluestone

Colour: Blue-grey, blue green.

Cleaning method: All.

This ancient stone of dreaming forms the inner ring of Stonehenge in Wiltshire England and links to all the other stone circles in the UK in a huge energy spiral, and then connects out to other power centres around the planet. It is thought to access multi-dimensions. The crystal emits a strong telluric electromagnetic charge (earth energy currents that run through and around the earth's mantle). It connects us to both the earth and the galactic energies via our Earth Chakra and Soul Star Chakra, allowing waves of energy to pass through and stabilises us through any earth changes. It assists shamanic journeying between the lower and upper worlds. This crystal will enhance willpower, courage and strength, aiding us through setbacks in life and helping us understand the lessons to be learnt from them. Offers protection to all levels and will boost our energy. Helps us to speak our truth. Carrying this crystal will help us be in the moment and to sense energy lines and the vibrations of crystals. Size matters with Bluestone- a small piece is very intense and larger pieces may need to be moved out of a bedroom to avoid over stimulation. These crystals are specifically directional – if you feel a headache coming when using turn the stone the other way around. It can reset your internal spiritual compass. It is a visionary stone for past life exploration, specifically Celtic heritage or Egyptian knowledge. Can be used for soul retrieval if placed on the Soma (situated at the hairline above the Third Eye Chakra) or Past Life (Alta-Major) Chakra (just behind the ears).

Physically when placed under a pillow will assist dreaming. Will bring the body's energy back into balance.

Crystal Magick

Magickal uses: Spells to connect to nature; healing and to boost your confidence.

Quartz

Colour: Clear.

Cleaning method: All.

Quartz is one of the most powerful healing and energy amplifiers. Absorbing, storing, releasing and regulating energy, also excellent for unblocking it. Quartz will work to the frequency of person being healed. Taking the energy back to before the illness set in. It will cleanse and enhance the organs and subtle bodies so the body can heal itself. A deep soul cleanser, working on all levels and enhancing psychic abilities. Use in meditation to filter out distractions. Helps concentration and will unlock memory. It can be "male" usually clear (may have inclusions) or "female" usually opaque or white.

Physically it treats the spleen; endocrine system; blood and stabilises the metabolic processes. Quartz is a 'Master' healer. Protecting against radiation and dispelling static electricity.

Magickal uses: Spells to enhance spirituality; psychic abilities; healing and power. Good for protection spells and will enhance the power of other crystals and herbs used in spell work.

There are different types of quartz as well as the clear quartz covered above. Other quartz will have the above properties plus qualities as listed in the next few pages.

Aqua Aura Quartz

Colour: Blue (Siberian), yellow (sunshine aura), red (rose or ruby aura), or rainbow, artificially bonded with gold. Usually small points or clusters.

Cleaning method: All.

The gold bonding process creates a powerful crystal to show us the alchemical process; it frees us from limitations and opens us to the new. Good crystal to heal, calm and cleanse the aura; repairing any holes as it goes.

Aqua Aura helps us express our soul energy so we can fulfil our highest potential.

Encourages communication by activating the Throat Chakra. Releases negativity from the subtle bodies, and aids channelling.

This protective stone guards against psychic or psychological attack. Good for meditation; bestowing deep peace. It will enhance other crystals when used as part of a healing spread.

Physically it heals the immune system and thymus gland.

Magickal uses: Spells to enhance spirituality; psychic abilities; healing and power. Good for protection spells and will enhance the power of other crystals and herbs used in spell work.

Blue Quartz (Dumortierite)

Colour: Blue.

Cleaning method: All.

A stone of order that can enhance organizational abilities, self-discipline, and orderliness. This is due to the effect it can have of balancing the Throat Chakra and enhancing communication between lower chakras (physical) and higher chakras (mental/spiritual). Blue Quartz brings order to all things, releasing fears and bringing courage to one's life. It boosts creativity and expression.

Emotionally it reduces problems of a scattered mind and disorganization and brings mental clarity. It helps one to see and accept reality. Assists us when building new relationships. It can lift depression and replace it with peace and happiness.

Clears stubbornness, particularly where it is ultimately bad for you. Blue Quartz reduces emotional tension; enhances spiritual development and aids contact with spirit guides and angels. It can help to express your spiritual thoughts and dreams and is excellent for meditation. It generates electromagnetism, dispels static electricity and protects against radiation.

Physically blue quartz helps with cooling the body where overstimulation is present. Treats the throat, thyroid and parathyroid; detoxification; hyperactivity and blood.

A master healer which helps stabilise the metabolic processes. Darker shades of blue that are nearer to indigo, in colour, can also be used for the Third Eye Chakra.

Magickal uses: Spells to enhance organisational skills; healing; peace and power.

Green Quartz

Colour: Green.

Cleaning method: All.

Opens the Heart Chakra. Clears negative energy and aids creativity.

Physically it helps balance the endocrine system.

Magickal uses: Spells to enhance spirituality; psychic abilities; healing and power. Good for protection spells and will enhance the power of other crystals and herbs used in spell work. Use in money spells.

Harlequin Quartz

Colour: Clear with strings of red dots inside.

Cleaning method: All.

This stone links the physical with the spiritual world; connecting the base and heart chakras to the crown chakra and helps to draw in universal energy. It balances the meridians and polarities in the body and anchors them to the etheric.

Physically it strengthens the memory and thyroid. Relieves despondency and gives us the will to recover when dis-ease is present.

Magickal uses: Spells to enhance spirituality and healing.

Natural Rainbow

Colour: Any quartz may have one or more rainbows within the crystal.

Cleaning method: All.

When held to the light the rainbow will be seen. These rainbows stimulate universal love, draw off negative energy and send healing into the body.

Magickal uses: Spells to enhance spirituality; psychic abilities; healing and power. Good for protection spells and will enhance the power of other crystals and herbs used in spell work.

Phantom Quartz

Colour: Quartz with a ghost like crystal image within the main crystal.

Cleaning method: All.

These symbolise universal awareness and are here to activate healing abilities in individuals. Connects us to our spirit guide, helps us access the Akashic Records and enhances meditation. Stimulates healing of the planet and opens clairaudience.

Physically it helps hearing disorders.

Magickal uses: Spells to enhance spirituality, psychic abilities and healing.

Rose Quartz

Colour: Pink, usually translucent, may be transparent.

Cleaning method: All.

The stone of unconditional love and infinite peace. This is the best heart crystal. It teaches you what 'true love' is.

Great to use in times of trauma or stress because its energies are very calming and reassuring. Opens and cleanses the Heart Chakra at a deep level so that you can learn to love yourself and others. Placed by your bed, rose quartz will bring a loving relationship to you if are looking for it.

A good stone if you think yourself unworthy of love. Encourages self-forgiveness and acceptance; and helps to invoke self-trust and self-worth.

Physically it strengthens the heart and circulatory system. Helps lung and chest problems, heals the kidneys and helps alleviate vertigo.

It soothes burns and is good for the complexion.

Helpful in cases of Alzheimer's, Parkinson's and senile dementia.

Magickal uses: Spells to draw love; happiness and peace.

Rutilated Quartz (Angel Hair Quartz)

Colour: Colourless or smoky with strands running through it. The strands may be golden, brown, black or reddish.

Cleaning method: All.

This is fantastic at filtering negative energy away from the body; and protects against psychic attack. This crystal gets to the root of problems and helps the transition to a new direction in life. Soothes dark moods and acts as an antidepressant. Relieves fears; phobias and anxiety; releasing constrictions and counteracting self-hatred.

Physically, it absorbs mercury poisoning from the blood, intestinal tract, muscles and nerves.

Its vitality is excellent for energy depletion and exhaustion, and it is excellent for chronic illnesses. Treats bronchitis and the respiratory tract. Stimulating and balancing on the thyroid.

Good for repelling parasites.

Magickal uses: Protection spells or those that are for bringing more security and uplifting energies into your life.

Smoky Quartz

Colour: Ranges from dark brown to yellowish, translucent.

Cleaning method: All.

A powerful Base Chakra stone, grounding us. Good anti-stress stone, which fortifies one's resolve while experiencing difficult situations.

Absorbs negative energies and replaces them with positive ones. Smoky quartz lifts depression and clears fears, even when they border on suicidal tendencies, bring an emotional calmness and helps us to leave behind anything that no longer serves us.

Clears the mind, aiding concentration and communication skills. It is good against geopathic stress and electromagnetic smog.

Physically use as a pain reliever against headaches and cramps. Treats problems of the abdomen; hips and legs; reproductive system; muscles; nerve tissue and the heart. It aids the assimilation of minerals and regulates fluids in the body.

Magickal uses: Spells to enhance healing, especially depression. Good for grounding and protection spells and will enhance the power of other crystals and herbs used in spell work.

Snow Quartz

Colour: White.

Cleaning method: All.

A stone for overcoming victimhood and martyrdom. It supports us while we learn difficult lessons, where we feel totally overwhelmed by them.

Physically it has the same healing properties as clear quartz, but has a slower more gentle energy.

Magickal uses: Spells to enhance spirituality; psychic abilities; healing and power. Good for protection spells and will enhance the power of other crystals and herbs used in spell work.

Tangerine Quartz

Colour: Naturally coated transparent orange.

Excellent to use after a shock or trauma, as it works at a soul level. Can be used for soul retrieval and will help heal after psychic attack.

Especially good in past life healing, where the soul feels it has made a mistake for which it must pay. It shows the soul the gift in the experience so it can release the trauma. Will activate the Sacral Chakra to release creative energy.

A stone to show us how like attracts like.

Magickal uses: Spells to assist us in moving forward; find our creativity and for calm.

Tourmalinated Quartz

Colour: Clear with thick dark strands running through it.

Cleaning method: All.

This stone combines the properties of quartz and tourmaline. A good grounding stone that also repels external energy influences. Dissolves tension on all levels; helping us integrate and accept our shadow side and clear self-sabotage. This harmonising stone turns negative thoughts into the positive ones.

Physically it harmonises the meridians, chakras and subtle bodies.

Magickal uses: Spells to enhance healing. Good for protection spells.

Rhodochrosite

Colour: Pink to orange and banded.

Cleaning method: All.

A stone of selfless love and balance on all levels, imparting a dynamic and positive attitude. Rhodochrosite is an excellent relationship stone, especially for people who feel unloved or who have suffered sexual abuse.

Teaches the heart to assimilate painful feelings without shutting down and removes denial. A stone to clear the Solar Plexus and Base Chakra of suppressed emotions and feelings. Shows you the truth about yourself and others, and helps identify any underlying patterns. These can then be faced and cleared without excuses but with a loving awareness. Improves self-worth and is an emotional calmer.

An aversion to the stone means that you could be suppressing something that you don't want to face. Mentally enlivening, this stone encourages a positive attitude, enhances the dream state and helps creativity. Rhodochrosite is a stone of passion, encouraging the spontaneous expression of feelings.

Physically rhodochrosite is an irritant filter relieving asthma and respiratory problems. Good for the circulatory system and purifies the blood and kidneys. It restores poor eyesight; normalises blood pressure; stabilises the heartbeat and invigorates the sexual organs.

Magickal uses: Spells to balance and calm overwrought emotions; inner conflict; love and for healing.

Rhodonite

Colour: Pink or red, mottled with black flecks.

Cleaning method: All.

An emotional balancer, this stone encourages nurturing love. It makes an excellent first-aid stone for emotional shock and panic. Rhodonite reveals both sides of an issue. Will stimulate, clear and activate both the heart and Heart Chakra. Grounding stone that balances the yin and yang helping you to achieve your highest potential.

Good for abuse, emotional self-destruction and co-dependency, clears emotional wounds and scars from the past, bringing up the emotions to be transmuted.

Good in past-life clearing, in cases of abandonment and betrayal, and in cases where we throw the blame at others for things we are unhappy about in ourselves, because rhodonite promotes unselfish self-love and forgiveness. It shows you that revenge is self-destructive. Rhodonite builds confidence and clears confusion.

Physically it is a wound healer; soothes insect bites and reduces scarring. Beneficially affects bone growth; hearing organs (fine-tuning auditory vibrations) and stimulates fertility.

Treats emphysema; inflammation of joints; arthritis; autoimmune disease; stomach ulcers and multiple sclerosis.

Magickal uses: Spells to calm emotions, bring balance and promote forgiveness.

Rhyolite

Colour: White, green light grey or red, spotted or banded in appearance.

Cleaning method: All.

Rhyolite can access karmic knowledge and help us to explore the self. Facilitates change without enforcing it; it works from our soul level.

When used in meditation can induce deep states where inner and outer journeying can occur, even past lives can be accessed to help integrate into the here and now.

It keeps us anchored in the present, so we can move forward in life. Rhyolite enhances self-esteem, self-worth, self-respect and acceptance of our true self. Balances the emotions when needed and shows us our inner strength in challenging times.

Physically treats veins; skin dis-orders; rashes; infections; dissolves kidney stones and helps the assimilation of B vitamins.

Taken as an elixir will strengthen the body and improve muscle tone. Use on solar plexus for emotional release and on the forehead for past life journeying.

Magickal uses: Spells to enhance self-esteem, self-worth and self-respect.

Ruby

Colour: Red. Transparent when polished, opaque when not.

Cleaning method: All.

A heart stone that encourages you to follow your bliss! Stimulates the pineal gland and promotes positive dreams.

Mentally, ruby enhances awareness and concentration and brings up anything negative for transmutation. A very protective stone, great where psychic attack or energy vampirism is a problem. A stone of potency and vigour, easily overcoming exhaustion and lethargy.

Physically a good detoxifier for the blood and lymph. Treats fevers; infectious disease; impaired blood flow and assists the circulatory system and heart. Stimulating on the adrenals, kidneys; spleen and the reproductive organs.

Magickal uses: Spells to draw a very deep and pure love affair; wealth; power and protection.

Ruby in Zoisite (Anyolite)

Colour: Red and green, mottled.

Cleaning method: All.

This combination stone will have the above properties of ruby as well those of zoisite. A good crystal for past life work and soul healing, it teaches us to be individual, while remembering we are all part of the whole. Activating the Crown Chakra, it creates altered states of consciousness, facilitating spiritual learning. A powerful amplifier of the aura.

Magickal uses: Spells to help troubled relationships; it will soothe, calm and harmonise.

Sapphire

Colour: Blue, black, green, purple or yellow. Transparent and bright when polished, otherwise dull and cloudy.

Cleaning method: All.

Stone of wisdom, it focuses the mind and releases unwanted thoughts. Sapphire will align the physical, mental and spiritual levels and restore balance to the body. A bringer of peace and serenity; clearing spiritual confusion and aiding concentration. Placed at the throat it will aid self-expression. Sapphires bring prosperity and abundance in all areas.

Physically will calm over activity in body systems and help regulate glands. Treats the eyes, blood dis-orders, excessive bleeding, strengthens veins and removes impurities.

Magickal uses: Spells to draw the truth; love; friendship; fidelity; protection; luck; peace of mind and healing. Also for stimulating third eye.

All sapphires have the above properties but some colours have extra properties.

Blue Sapphire

Colour: Blue.

Cleaning method: All.

Associated with love and purity, they are seekers of spiritual truth, and help keep us on our spiritual path. Good throat stone to aid communication, self-expression, and speaking our truth.

Physically they heal the thyroid.

Magickal uses: Spells to draw the truth.

Green Sapphire

Colour: Green.

Cleaning method: All.

Stimulates the Heart Chakra bringing integrity, loyalty and fidelity. Teaches us to honour others belief systems. Green Sapphire can be used to improve dream recall.

Physically it improves vision.

Magickal uses: Spells to draw the truth; love; friendship; fidelity; protection; luck; peace of mind and healing.

Pink Sapphire

Colour: Pink.

Cleaning method: All.

Teaches us to master our emotions and to integrate them positively into our being. These crystals are like magnets bringing to us that which we need to evolve on our pathway.

Magickal uses: Spells to draw the truth; love; friendship; fidelity; protection; luck; peace of mind and healing.

Purple Sapphire

Colour: Purple.

Cleaning method: All.

This awakening stone activates the kundalini energy rising up the Crown Chakra to open, enhancing our spiritual gifts. Activates the pineal gland which activates our inner vision.

Magickal uses: Spells to draw the truth; love; friendship; fidelity; protection; luck; peace of mind and healing.

Yellow Sapphire

Colour: Yellow.

Cleaning method: All.

Yellow Sapphires attract financial abundance, especially when placed in a cash box. Stimulating to the intellect, they help us see the bigger picture.

Physically when taken as an elixir it removes toxins from the body.

Magickal uses: Spells to draw prosperity.

Sardonyx

Colour: Black, brown, clear or red, banded and opaque in appearance.

Cleaning method: All.

A stone to attract friendship and good fortune; bringing lasting happiness and stability to partnerships and marriage. Use for strength and protection. Sardonyx helps willpower and will increase stamina and self-control. Grid around the house and garden to prevent crime, place at windows and doors and in each corner.

Physically alleviates depression and strengthens the immune system. Heals bones, lungs and regulates fluids and cell metabolism. Useful to help absorb nutrients and eliminate waste products.

Magickal uses: Spells to promote healthy relationships and to balance heaven and earth.

Selenite (Satin Spa, Desert Rose)

Colour: Pure white, blue, brown, green or orange. Translucent with fine striations, or larger striations in the Fishtail Selenite; or petal-like in the Desert Rose Selenite.

Cleaning method: Do not use with water as it will slowly dissolve the crystal. Selenite is self-cleaning.

Selenite links our light body to the physical, it is a stone of high vibration. Opening the Crown and Higher Crown Chakras, bringing clarity and accessing the angelic and higher levels of consciousness. Good for meditation and any spiritual work; it is a crystal for the new vibrations on this planet. It carries the imprint of all that has happened to the world and can be used to check one's progress in this life. Selenite will pinpoint lessons that need to be resolved and show us how. Assists judgement and insight, clearing confusion and showing us the bigger picture. A powerful stabiliser for erratic emotions. Use as a protective grid around the house. Place in each corner of the house, and a large piece in the centre. This will create a peaceful atmosphere that will block any external influences.

Physically aligns the spine and promotes flexibility. Neutralises mercury lost from amalgam fillings in the teeth and reverses any free radical damage. Guards against
epileptic fits and is a nurturing crystal for children.

Magickal uses: Spells to assist spiritual growth and to lend energy to the body.

Other colours of Selenite have these properties as well as those that follow.

Orange Brown Selenite

Colour: Orange-brown.

Cleaning method: Do not use with water as it will slowly dissolve the crystal. Selenite is self-cleaning.

This has a strong connection to angelic energies and heals the earth.

Magickal uses: Spells to assist spiritual growth and to lend energy to the body.

Blue Selenite

Colour: White with bluish hue.

Cleaning method: Do not use with water as it will slowly dissolve the crystal. Selenite is self-cleaning.

Use on the Third Eye to quiet intellect and mental chatter during meditation. Can help get to the core of a problem.

Magickal uses: Spells to assist spiritual growth and to lend energy to the body.

Desert Rose Selenite

Colour: Off white, creamy colour, with petal like appearance.

Cleaning method: Do not use with water as it will slowly dissolve the crystal. Selenite is self-cleaning. Use a small brush to remove any dust build up.

Dissolves self-imposed patterns that have become outdated and assists in finding new more appropriate ones.

Magickal uses: Spells to assist spiritual growth and to lend energy to the body.

Fishtail Selenite

Colour: White with a herring bone pattern to the striations.

Cleaning method: Do not use with water as it will slowly dissolve the crystal. Selenite is self-cleaning.

Extremely calming and stabilising to the emotions. Fishtail Selenite is often called Angel's Wing Selenite because it helps angelic connection.

Magickal uses: Spells to assist spiritual growth and clear emotions.

Green Selenite

Colour: Green.

Cleaning method: Do not use with water as it will slowly dissolve the crystal. Selenite is self-cleaning.

Green Selenite helps us feel good about our self, especially during the aging process. It works towards the highest good.

Magickal uses: Spells to assist spiritual growth and to lend energy to the body.

Seraphinite (Serafina)

Colour: Green.

Cleaning method: All.

Opens the Crown and Higher Crown Chakras and assists angelic connection. Used on the third eye or during meditation, it allows self-healing and enhances spiritual enlightenment. It protects the physical body during out of body journeying. Helps you connect with your heart, opening it to love. It shows our progress in life and the changes needed to continue on our path.

Physically it works at a subtle level linking to the etheric body. Use to release tension in the muscles in the neck, overcome chills and help with weight loss.

Magickal uses: Spells to remove blocks holding us back on our journey in life and for inner healing.

Serpentine

Colour: Green, brown-red, brown-yellow, black-green, red or white. It has a mottled appearance.

Cleaning method: All.

This grounding stone clears the chakras and opens the Crown Chakra to aid psychic abilities. Assists the rise of the kundalini energy and helps access past life memory and wisdom. Helps us feel more in control of our life and is said to ensure longevity. Clears emotional and mental imbalances.

Physically detoxifies the body and clears parasites. Treats diabetes and hypoglycaemia and aids the absorption of calcium and magnesium.

Magickal uses: Spells to enhance psychic abilities and repel poisonous animals.

Smithsonite

Colour: Blue-green, green, blue, brown, pink, lavender, yellow or white-grey. It has a lustrous, pearly appearance with layers of small bubbles.

Cleaning method: All.

The stone of favourable outcomes. Its gentle energies form a protective layer against life's problems. When experiencing breaking point or mental breakdown smithsonite comes to the rescue with its gentle calm and tranquil energies. It heals our inner child and clears emotional traumas from abuse.

A supportive stone that makes us feel better for its presence. Supports where leadership and tact are required. A stone of diplomacy especially in difficult relationships. Aligns the chakras and strengthens psychic abilities.

Hold during psychic communication to help discern the validity of the words. Or use at the crown to make angelic contact.

Physically can be gridded around the bed (one at each corner) and a piece placed under the pillow to boost a dysfunctional immune system. Or combine with green tourmaline or bloodstone and place over the thymus. Treats alcoholism; sinus problems; digestive problems and osteoporosis. Restores elasticity in veins and muscles.

Magickal uses: Spells to help overcome strong hurdles in life.

Sodalite

Colour: Blue with mottled dark or white areas.

Cleaning method: All.

Unites our logical with our intuitive side. Opens our spiritual side and assists the import of information from the higher mind to the physical level. Good for meditation because of its ability to stimulate the pineal gland and the Third Eye. Being a stone of truth, it helps you stand up for your beliefs. Sodalite will bring harmony and solidarity to groups. Stimulating trust and companionship and will eliminate mental confusion, encouraging rational thought, objectivity, truth and intuition. Calms the mind and clears old mind-sets and rigid thinking, allowing space for new to enter.

An emotional balancer that helps self-esteem, self-acceptance and self-trust; and brings up our shadow qualities to be faced without judgement, so they can be accepted. Clears electromagnetic pollution and when placed by a computer it clears any harmful emanations. Helps sick-

Physically balances the metabolism, overcomes calcium deficiencies, and cleanses the lymphatic system and organs. Boosts the immune system; helps radiation damage; insomnia; throat; larynx; digestion; cools fever and lowers blood pressure.

Magickal uses: Spells to assist personal growth; emotional healing and clear fear.

Spinel

Colour: Colourless, blue, black, brown, green, orange, red, white, yellow, violet.

Cleaning method: All.

A stone of rejuvenation and energy renewal; offering encouragement in difficult times. Facilitates the movement of kundalini energy and opens the chakras. Helps us see the positive traits in our self.

Magickal uses: Spells to increase your energy; assist your appearance and beauty, attract wealth and draw strength.

Different colours display additional attributes.

Black Spinel

Colour: Black.

Cleaning method: All.

Assists in material problems, giving the insights needed and the stamina to resolve them. A protective crystal connecting to the earth energies to balance the rise of the kundalini energy.

Magickal uses: Spells to increase your energy; assist your appearance and beauty.

Brown Spinel

Colour: Brown.

Cleaning method: All.

Opens the Earth Chakra and grounds you. Cleanses the aura.

Magickal uses: Spells to increase your energy; assist your appearance and beauty.

Colourless Spinel

Colour: Colourless.

Cleaning method: All.

Stimulates higher communication, linking the lower chakras with the Crown Chakra and etheric body. Good for spiritual enlightenment.

Magickal uses: Spells to increase your energy; assist your appearance and beauty.

Green Spinel

Colour: Green.

Cleaning method: All.

Opens the hearth chakra and stimulates love, compassion and kindness.

Magickal uses: Spells to increase your energy and draw wealth.

Orange Spinel

Colour: Orange.

Cleaning method: All.

Opens the Navel Chakra and stimulates creativity, intuition and balances the emotions.

Physically treats infertility.

Magickal uses: Spells to increase your energy; assist your appearance and beauty.

Red Spinel

Colour: Red.

Cleaning method: All.

Opens the base chakra and stimulates the rise of the kundalini energy. Stimulates vitality and strength.

Magickal uses: Spells to increase your energy; assist your appearance and beauty.

Violet Spinel

Colour: Violet.

Cleaning method: All.

Opens the Crown Chakra and stimulates spiritual development and astral travel.

Magickal uses: Spells to increase your energy; assist your appearance and beauty.

Yellow Spinel

Colour: Yellow.

Cleaning method: All.

Opens the Solar Plexus Chakra and stimulates personal power and intellect.

Magickal uses: Spells to increase your energy; assist your appearance and beauty.

Stillbite

Colour: White, pink, yellow, brown, orange or red. Appearance is either crystalline plates or pyramids.

Cleaning method: All.

Stillbite helps spiritual journeying and offers protection during our travels. Takes us to the higher spiritual levels and helps us remember our experiences there. Grounds spiritual energy and helps manifest intuitive thoughts into the physical dimensions.

Physically use to counteract poisoning but can also treat laryngitis; loss of taste; brain disorders and to strengthen the ligaments.

Magickal uses: Spells of protection while travelling.

Sugilite

Colour: Purple or violet-pink, opaque and lightly banded in appearance.

Cleaning methods: All.

This is a loving stone, good for dissolving hostility, especially in groups of people. It encourages loving communications. Sugilite helps us to face up to unpleasant matters and gives us the loving support to see them through. It alleviates fear, grief, sorrow, and promotes self-forgiveness. Encourages positive thoughts and reorganises our thought patterns in a more organised manner. It shows any underlying learning difficulties, such as in dyslexia, and helps us to accept and overcome them. Releases emotional turmoil and can dispel despair, drawing off negative energy and replacing it with loving, healing energy.

Physically it is an excellent pain reliever good for headaches and discomfort on all levels. Treats epilepsy; insomnia; nightmares and nerves.

Magickal uses: Spells to help deal with grief; enhance psychic awareness and healing.

Sunstone

Colour: Orange, red-brown or yellow. Can be transparent or opaque with iridescent inclusions.

Cleaning methods: All.

This stone of joy will restore the sweetness to life. Clears and draws light into all chakras and heightens intuition. This alchemical stone is connected to the sun energies and when used during meditation or in everyday life, will draw these energies in for the benefit of the user. From both the chakras and aura, Sunstone removes energy-draining hooks connected to us from other people, lovingly returning them to the sender. Good for cord-cutting after relationships have run their course. Sunstone removes co-dependency, helps self-empowerment, independence and restores one's vitality.

A natural antidepressant it will lift a dark mood. Good against feelings of discrimination and abandonment, Sunstone removes feelings of failure, inhibitions and hang-ups. Encourages optimism and enthusiasm for life. Place on the Solar Plexus to lift out heavy or repressed emotions.

Physically it is good for people who are pessimistic about life and helps SAD (Seasonal Affective Disorder). Stimulates self-healing powers, regulates the autonomic nervous system and harmonises organs. Chronic sore throat; stomach ulcers and depression can also be helped with sunstone. Gird around body to help cartilage problems, rheumatism, and general aches and pains.

Magickal uses: Spells to energise physically, mentally and emotionally, and protection.

Tanzanite

Colour: Lilac- blue. Slightly opaque.

Cleaning methods: All.

Tanzanite has extremely high vibrations and is a stone of transmutation. It links us to the angelic realms, Ascended Masters, spirit guides and Christ consciousness. Tanzanite can be used for inner and outer journeying, enhancing metaphysical abilities and for profoundly deep meditations. It links us to the soul star to assist us to evolve to higher levels. Can be used to connect to the Akashic Records for karmic and cellular healing down the timeline, assisting the soul on the ascension process.

Helps us find our true vocation in life and assists the overworked by harmonising their energy fluctuations. This stone overcomes depression and anxiety. Tanzanite should be worn with care, as it may be too strong for sensitive people. If it induces uncontrolled psychic experiences or telepathy overload, then remove and use a grounding stone such as hematite or smoky quartz. Try using for a short time and gradually increase as your body becomes accustomed to its energies.

Physically good for the skin; hair; head; throat; chest; kidneys and nerves. Calming to the mind. Reprogramming cellular memory and for past life healing.

Magickal uses: Spells to increase intuition; calm and balance.

Tektite

Colour: Black or dark brown.

Cleaning method: All.

Tektite was formed from a meteorite. These extra-terrestrial origins help us communicate with other worlds. Encourages spiritual growth by accessing higher knowledge. It will take us into the heart of a problem and show us necessary insights into the true cause, so we can take the necessary action. Helps us to release undesirable experiences and see the lesson behind them. Placed on the chakras it will bring them into balance; on the Third Eye it will enhance clairvoyance and telepathy, and aid communication with other dimensions. It strengthens the aura and balances the masculine and feminine energies.

Physically, Tektite reduces fevers, aids circulation and prevents the spread of diseases.

Magickal uses: Spells to enhance spiritual and psychic energies.

Tiger's Eye

Colour: Brown-yellow, pink, blue or red. Banded and shiny in appearance.

Cleaning methods: All.

This stone works with both the earth and sun energies. A grounding stone when you are feeling spaced out or uncommitted. Good for psychic development and attunement of the Third Eye in 'earthy' people. A stone of practicality and insight and it anchors necessary change in the body. Good for resolving internal conflict of pride or wilfulness. It will balance the left and right spheres of the brain and is good when dealing with scattered information, because it will help bring it into a coherent whole. Eliminates the 'blues' bringing brightness and optimism into one's life. Tiger's Eye will bring an awareness of both personal needs and those of others. Stimulating to the kundalini energy, it is thought to attract wealth.

Physically helpful for the eyes; night vision; throat; reproductive organs; broken bones and asthma.

Magickal uses: Spells to enhance courage; energy; strength and independence. Spells to draw luck; money and prosperity.

The variations of Tiger's Eye have the same properties as well as the following.

Blue Tiger's Eye (Hawk's Eye)

Colour: Blue and banded.

Cleaning method: All.

Also known as Hawk's Eye, it helps to enhance psychic abilities and brings to light awareness of personal needs and those of others. Enhances integrity of communication and practical communication. It helps you find the courage to recognise thoughts and ideas and the willpower to carry them into the physical realm. When stressed it is good, as it has a calming energy and aids overanxious, quick-tempered and phobic people. Blue Tiger's Eye can be used to protect the upper chakras. Said to bring good luck and wealth to one who wears or carries it. Blue Tiger's Eye is associated primarily with the Throat Chakra.

Physically it helps with the eyes; night vision; throat; reproductive organs; broken bones and asthma. Slows down the metabolism; cools an over-active sex drive and dissolves sexual frustrations.

Magickal uses: Spells to enhance courage; energy; strength; independence. Spells to draw luck; money and prosperity.

Gold Tiger's Eye

Colour: Golden brown, banded.

Cleaning method: All.

Golden Tigers Eye helps us pay attention to detail and reminds us to take action from a place of reason rather than emotion. It makes a great stone to have at meetings etc.

Magickal uses: Spells to enhance courage; energy; strength; independence. Spells to draw luck; money and prosperity.

Red Tiger's Eye

Colour: Red-brown and banded.

Cleaning method: All.

This motivating stone helps overcome lethargy, with its stimulating energies.

Physically it speeds up a slow metabolism and helps increase sex drive.

Magickal uses: Spells to enhance courage; energy; strength; independence. Spells to draw luck, money and prosperity.

Tiger's Iron

Colour: Brown with bands of black hematite and red jasper.

Cleaning method: All.

This promotes vitality throughout the whole body. A stone of change that takes you to a place of refuge when danger threatens. Good for emotional and or mental burnout or family stress, giving us the strength to carry on. Very good when you are completely exhausted, it will help you find the space for contemplation and provide you with the energy to see things through. Stimulates creativity and will bring out inherent talents.

Physically it helps the blood; balancing the white/red cell count and eliminating toxins. Heals hips; lower limbs and feet; strengthening the muscles. Aids the assimilation of vitamin B and produces natural steroids. Keep in contact with the skin for the best results.

Magickal uses: Spells to enhance courage; energy; strength; independence. Spells to draw luck; money and prosperity.

Topaz

Colour: Golden-yellow, blue, clear, brown, green or red-pink. Transparent in appearance.

Cleaning method: All.

Its vibrant energy brings abundance, joy and health. Brings our goals in life to fruition. This joyful stone imparts confidence, promotes openness and honesty and helps us to develop our inner wisdom. Stabilises the emotions and makes one receptive to love from every source. Mentally, Topaz helps problem-solving.

Physically this stone of health can help combat anorexia; aid our digestion; fortify the nerves; stimulate the metabolism and restore our sense of taste.

Magickal uses: Spells to draw money; love and affection; drive away sadness; strengthen the intellect; grant courage and protect against hatred and revenge.

It comes in different colours but they all have the above properties as well as extra ones listed below.

Blue Topaz

Colour: Blue and transparent in appearance.

Cleaning method: All.

Particularly useful for the Throat and Third Eye Chakras and aiding in verbalisation.

Magickal uses: Spells to draw love and affection; drive away sadness; strengthen the Intellect; grant courage and protect against hatred and revenge.

Clear Topaz

Colour: Clear and transparent in appearance.

Cleaning method: All.

Purifying on the emotions and good at clearing trapped energy.

Magickal uses: Spells to draw love and affection; drive away sadness; strengthen the Intellect; grant courage and protect against hatred and revenge.

Golden Topaz

Colour: Golden-yellow and transparent in appearance.

Cleaning method: All.

Like a battery charger, this energises the body, strengthening our faith and optimism.

Physically it strengthens the Solar Plexus and regenerates cellular structure. Good for nervous exhaustion; it can be used to treat the liver; gallbladder and endocrine glands.

Magickal uses: Spells to draw love and affection; drive away sadness; strengthen the Intellect; grant courage and protect against hatred and revenge. Draws money.

Pink Topaz

Colour: Pink and transparent in appearance.

Cleaning method: All.

A stone of hope. Eases out old patterns of dis-ease, dissolves any resistance and opens the way to vibrant health.

Magickal uses: Spells to draw love and affection; drive away sadness; strengthen the intellect; grant courage and protect against hatred and revenge.

Tourmaline

Colour: Brown, black, blue, green, blue-green, pink, yellow, red or watermelon. Can be transparent, shiny or opaque.

Cleaning method: All.

Magickal uses: Spells to balance the energy polarities, draw peace and harmony.

Tourmaline comes in a variety of colours, each type having distinct healing properties as shown below.

Black Tourmaline (Schorl)

Colour: Black with / without striations. Can be shiny / opaque.

Cleaning method: All.

Black Tourmaline is associated with the Root or Base Chakra. It is excellent for grounding excess energy. A purifying stone that deflects and transforms negative energy, from an individual or environment. Often used as an aura cleanser and can help with attaining higher levels of awareness. It is also used for repelling and protecting one from black magic and is believed to reflect negative spells back to their sender. Diminishes fear by promoting understanding of the self and self-confidence. It can deflect radiation energy from TV's and computer monitors. It helps maintain spirits even after messages of doom and gloom. Emotionally, it dispels fears, obsessions and neuroses, bringing emotional stability.

Physically strengthens the immune system, helps with heart disease; arthritis; dyslexia and gout. It balances and stimulates the adrenal glands.

Magickal uses: Spells to balance the energy polarities; draw peace and harmony and offer protection. Especially good at returning negative energy to the sender.

Blue Tourmaline (Indicolite)

Colour: Blue.

Cleaning method: All.

This stone carries the ray of peace and will activate the Third Eye and Throat Chakra; enabling spiritual freedom and self-expression. Aids psychic awareness, visions and is a good stone for therapists because it prevents negativity from sticking. Opens the way for service to others, encouraging tolerance, ethics, and compassion. Blocked feelings are gently brought to the surface to be cleared and an inner strength is gained, so we may take and accept responsibility of our self. Blue Tourmaline is a stone of harmony which enhances the environment around it.

Physically it can be used to find the source of dis-ease. Heals burns and prevents Scarring; heals the brain; immune and pulmonary systems; kidneys; bladder; thymus; thyroid; sore throats; speech impediments and balances the fluid levels in the body. Traditionally used for the throat; larynx; oesophagus; lungs and eyes; it can also help combat Insomnia; bacterial infections; sinusitis and night sweats. Dark Blue Tourmaline can be made into an elixir to treat the eyes and brain.

Magickal uses: Spells to balance the energy polarities; draw peace and harmony.

Brown Tourmaline (Dravide)

Colour: Brown.

Cleaning method: All.

This powerful grounding stone can be used to clear and open the Earth Chakra and the grounding cord which connects the physical body to the earth in this incarnation. It will clear, protect and align the aura and etheric body. This social and empathic stone helps us feel comfortable in large groups encouraging community spirit. Dysfunctional family relationships can be healed with this stone.

Physically used to heal intestinal disorders and skin dis-eases.

Magickal uses: Spells to balance the energy polarities; draw peace and harmony and is excellent for grounding.

Green Tourmaline (Verdelite)

Colour: Green.

Cleaning method: All.

This nurturing stone is a good healer. Promotes visualisation, opening the Heart Chakra to promote compassion, patience, tenderness and balance. Transforms negative thoughts to positive, dispels fear and offers solutions to our problems. Thought to bring prosperity to the wearer. Green Tourmaline helps us to overcome problematic father figures. It inspires creativity and has a strong affinity with plants bringing healing to them. Assists when studying plant-based healing methods such as herbalism.

Physically treats the eyes; brain; heart; thymus and immune system. Facilitates weight loss; relieves CFS and exhaustion; quiets the mind; fortifies the nervous system and aids sleep. Detoxifies the body and heals diarrhoea and constipation.

Realigns the spine and helps strained muscles. Beneficial for hyperactive children it can also reduce panic attacks and claustrophobia.

Magickal uses: Spells to balance the energy polarities and bring healing; peace and harmony. Also draws money.

Pink Tourmaline

Colour: Pink.

Cleaning method: All.

Pink Tourmaline attracts love and provides assurance that it's safe to love. Shows us how to love our self, first, so that others may love us. Clears emotional pain from the Heart Chakra and promotes peace and relaxation. Connects us to our inner wisdom and compassion and opens us to healing.

Physically it can heal a dysfunctional endocrine system and will treat the skin; heart and lungs.

Magickal uses: Draws peace; harmony; friendships and love.

Purple-Violet Tourmaline

Colour: Purple.

Cleaning method: All.

Connects the Base to the Heart Chakra and heals as it goes. Stimulates creativity. It unblocks the Third Eye, allowing our intuition to open. When used in past life healing it will show you the heart of the problem and assist with clearing it.

Physically heals depression, releases obsessive thoughts. Can treat Alzheimer's; CFS; epilepsy and pollutant sensitivity.

Magickal uses: Spells to balance the energy polarities; draw peace and harmony.

Red Tourmaline (Rubellite)

Colour: Red.

Cleaning method: All.

Heals and energises the Sacral Chakra. Helps us understand love and promotes tactfulness, sociability and extroversion. It enhances creativity on all levels.

Physically it detoxifies and energises the body. Treats the heart; reproductive system; spleen; liver; blood vessels; repairs veins and stimulates the circulation. A useful stone for muscular spasms and chills.

Magickal uses: Spells to balance the energy polarities; draw peace and harmony.

Watermelon Tourmaline

Colour: Pink enfolded in green.

Cleaning method: All.

A strong activator of the Heart Chakra, and links us to our higher self. This stone of patience teaches us diplomacy and tact. Helps us understand situations and assists us to express our self clearly. Good for releasing old emotions, it aids relationships and shows us the joy in situations around us.

Physically it encourages nerve regeneration and is good in cases of paralysis; multiple sclerosis and stress.

Magickal uses: Spells to balance the energy polarities; draw peace and harmony.

Yellow Tourmaline

Colour: Yellow.

Cleaning method: All.

A good Solar Plexus stone to strengthen personal power. Good for intellectual pursuits and business.

Physically it heals the stomach; spleen; kidneys; liver and gallbladder.

Magickal uses: Spells to balance the energy polarities; draw peace and harmony.

Turquoise

Colour: Turquoise, blue or green.

Cleaning method: All.

A stone of purification, it dispels negative energy, clears electromagnetic smog and protects against pollutants in the environment. Balances the chakras, and when placed on the Third Eye it enhances intuition and, on the throat, it releases old vows and allows the soul to express itself freely. An effective healing stone providing feelings of wellbeing to the body. Enhances spiritual growth and communication with the spiritual world, especially when used in meditation. A creative problem solver that promotes self-realisation. Dissolves self-sabotage and stabilises mood swings. Good for public speaking because it calms the nerves. It stimulates romantic love and brings inner calm.

Physically it is excellent for exhaustion; depression and panic attacks and strengthens the meridians of the body and the subtle energy bodies. Reduces excess acidity and can treat gout; rheumatism and stomach problems. Helps assimilation of nutrients and the regeneration of tissues. Its anti-inflammatory properties treat pain and cramps. Detoxifying on the body and can be used to treat viral infections. It will heal the whole body, especially the eyes and cataracts.

Magickal uses: Spells to bring good fortune; physical well-being and protection against danger when travelling.

Unakite

Colour: Green-pink, mottled in appearance.

Cleaning method: All.

A stone of vision that balances the emotions with the spiritual. Use on the third eye to aid psychic vision. Good grounding stone to use in meditation. Several tumbled stones will bring calm energy to the environment, negating electromagnetic pollution from TV's if placed near. Good for re-birthing, bringing light to blockages so they can be integrated and released. Also good for past-life work, to find the source of a problem and be able to reframe it. Place on the Third Eye to do this. Unakite draws dis-ease from past and present to the surface, to be transformed.

Physically a stone of convalescence, it is helpful for the reproductive system; stimulating weight-gain where required and aiding a healthy pregnancy. Encourages the growth of skin tissue and hair. Balances the acid/alkali balance in body, stabilises the temperature in the body and helps with impotence.

Magickal uses: Spells to draw healing.

Variscite

Colour: Grey, green or white.

Cleaning method: All.

This stone of encouragement brings hope and courage, especially during illness. Offers support and encouragement to those that are invalided. Opens the Heart Chakra and brings unconditional love into the situation at hand. It moves one out of despair and into a place of hope and acceptance. Place under your pillow at night to bring peaceful sleep. Aids clear thinking, perception and self-expression. This lively stone energises the body and supports sobriety. Used on the Third Eye for past life exploration it can show us visual images of past lives and stimulate insights into the cause of dis-ease and patterns that have been carried over to this life.

Physically treats bloating; nervous system; constricted blood flow and will regenerate the elasticity of veins and skin. Neutralises over acidity and treats gout; Rheumatism; gastritis and ulcers. Helpful for male impotence.

Magickal uses: Spells to clear anxiety and nervousness.

Zircon

Colour: Brown, green, orange, red or yellow.

Cleaning method: All.

Zircon comes in many colours, each resonating with a different chakra to bring harmony to both the physical and spiritual bodies. Helps us understand we are a spiritual being on a human journey. Promotes unconditional love for our self and others and highlights the oneness from which all souls originate. Zircon instils tenacity of purpose, clear thinking and the stamina to see things through. It shows us we are all one and overcomes racism and prejudice, clearing any imprints of discrimination, victimisation, homophobia and misogyny in this life or past lives from the emotional body. Promotes the letting go of old love and opens us to new love into our life. Helps overcome jealousy and possessiveness.

Physically benefits synergy; sciatica; depression; bones; muscles; cramp; insomnia; vertigo; menstrual irregularity and the liver. Care needs to be used by those who have a pacemaker or are epileptic, as zircon may cause dizziness. In these cases, cubic zircon can be tried as it has diluted powers.

Magickal uses: Spells to bring calm and balance.

The following is a list of properties for the specific colours of zircon, extra to the ones listed above.

Brown Zircon

Colour: Brown.

Cleaning method: All.

Good for grounding and connecting to the Earth Chakra.

Magickal uses: Spells to bring calm and balance.

Green Zircon

Colour: Green.

Cleaning method: All.

Activates the Heart Chakra. Attracts abundance.

Magickal uses: Spells to bring calm and balance and to attract abundance and money.

Orange Zircon

Colour: Orange.

Cleaning method: All.

Activates the Sacral Chakra. Boosts creativity, beauty and guards against jealousy. Good as a talisman to protect against injury when travelling.

Magickal uses: Spells to bring calm and balance, and for protection against injury when travelling.

Red Zircon

Colour: Red.

Cleaning method: All.

Adds power to rituals for drawing wealth. Activates the Base Chakra. Increases vitality, especially in times of stress and boosts libido.

Magickal uses: Spells for protection; to bring energy; calm; balance and draw wealth.

Yellow Zircon

Colour: Yellow.

Cleaning method: All.

Activates and cleanses the Solar Plexus Chakra. Lifts depression; attracts love and heightens sexual energy. Assists in attracting success in business.

Magickal uses: Spells to bring calm and balance; draw business success and love.

Zoisite

Colour: Colourless, brown, blue, green, pink (Thulite), lavender-blue, red, white or yellow.

Cleaning method: All.

Transforms negative energy into positive energy, and destructive urges into constructive ones. Encourages us to be our self, rather than who we think we should be to fit in with the norm. Draws suppressed feelings to the surface to be processed and cleared. Dispels lethargy and encourages recovery after a severe illness or stress. Zoisite is a creative stone and keeps us focused on our objections after being interrupted.

Physically a natural detoxifier it strengthens the immune system, regenerates cells, stimulates fertility and neutralises over acidification. Treats the lungs; heart; spleen; pancreas; ovaries; testicles and will reduce inflammation.

Magickal uses: Spells to clear negative energy and to give us a more optimistic view to life.

A quick reference guide for common ailments:

The following list gives helpful crystals for common ailments and uses. Crystal names which are in **bold** are specific stones for that aliment. Many crystals have multiple uses. As always, use your intuition to guide you to the most helpful ones for the aliment you wish to help clear. These are not intended as a replacement to any medication prescribed by your doctor.

Crystals can be used alongside to help support the healing process. Please NEVER self-diagnose a 'medical' condition. If you have an ailment that is causing you discomfort or pain, then consult a medical professional first.

I am including a list of contra-indications and cautions for certain crystals which is listed below. Crystals are powerful healing tools that can in some cases exasperate pre-existing characteristics in some. Please read through after making your crystal choice to check whether it is suitable for you or not.

- AGGRESSIVE TENDENCIES: avoid Iron Pyrite.
- DELICATE DISPOSITION: avoid Ruby as it may over stimulate.
- DEPRESSION: avoid Onyx and Obsidian as they will bring up your shadow side, which you may not be able to handle when depressed.
- GOITRE: avoid Fluorite.
- HYSTERIA: use Moonstone with caution.

- INFLAMMATION: avoid Hematite when present.

- INSOMNIA: avoid using Herkimer Diamond for prolonged periods.

- IRRITABILITY: avoid Ruby as it may over stimulate.

- NIGHT TERRORS: avoid Onyx.

- OBSIDIAN: use for short periods (10 mins) daily and back up with Rose Quartz Or use Mahogany Obsidian or Apache Tear as they are gentler at uncovering our shadow self.

- OPAL: avoid wearing when you are feeling negative or unhappy as Opal will enhance what we are feeling at the time.

- PSYCHIATRIC CONDITIONS, PARANOIA OR SCHIZOPHRENIA: avoid Amethyst as it may aggravate these conditions.

- SCATTERED ENERGY: avoid Opal.

- SLEEP WALKING: avoid wearing Diamond or Sapphire for prolonged periods.

ABANDONMENT: Pink Stones, Sunstone

ABSORPTION: Dendritic Chalcedony (copper), Galena (selenium and zinc)

ABUNDANCE (TO ATTRACT): Abundance Quartz, Aventurine, Carnelian, Citrine, Dendritic Agate, Diamond, Hawk's Eye, Moss Agate, Ruby, Topaz, Tourmaline, Yellow Sapphire

ABUSE: Carnelian, Red Calcite, **Rhodonite**, Rhodochrosite (sexual)

ACCEPTANCE: Agate (of love and of self), Ametrine (of others), Angelite, Aragonite, Carnelian, Charoite (of others), Chrysoprase (of others and of self), Chrysocolla (of change), Hematite (of mistakes), Moldavite (of physical body), Moonstone (of psychic gifts), Obsidian, Pink Calcite (of self), Rose Quartz (of change and of love), Rhyolite (of self), Smoky Quartz, Sodalite, Iron Pyrite (of self)

ACIDIFICATION OF TISSUE (TO CORRECT): Bloodstone, Chiastolite, Diamond, Jade (acid / alkaline imbalance), Green Jasper, Malachite, Turquoise, Variscite, Zoisite

ACIDITY: Peridot

ACHES: Hematite, Rose Quartz

ACNE: Amethyst

ADDICTIONS: **Amber**, **Amethyst**, Kunzite, Lavender-Pink Smithsonite, Lepidolite, Onyx, Peridot, Tiger's Eye (to overcome addictive behaviour)

ADRENALS: Aventurine, Black Tourmaline, Green Calcite (calm), Kyanite, Peridot, Rose Quartz (balance), Yellow Labradorite (balance)

AGGRESSION (AMELIORATE): Amethyst, **Bloodstone**, Carnelian, Garnet, Lepidolite, Rose Quartz, Ruby

ALCOHOLISM: **Amethyst,** Black Onyx, Smithsonite

ALLERGIES: Aquamarine, Carnelian (pollen), Chrysoprase, Iolite, Lepidolite, Moss Agate, Muscovite, Picture Jasper, Red Jasper, Zircon

ALZHEIMERS: Blue Obsidian, Kunzite, Lepidolite, Purple Tourmaline, Rose Quartz, Rutilated Quartz

ANEMIA: Black Tourmaline, **Bloodstone**, Carnelian, Citrine, Garnet, Hematite, Kunzite, **Ruby,** Tiger's Eye, Tourmaline

ANGER (AMELIORATE): Amethyst, Blue Lace Agate, Carnelian, Garnet, Lepidolite, Peridot, Rose Quartz

ANGINA: Amethyst, Emerald, **Rhodonite**, Rhodochrosite, Rose Quartz

ANIMAL DISORDERS: Dalmatian Jasper (calm), Lithium Quartz, Turquoise

ANOREXIA NERVOSA: Ametrine, Carnelian, Lepidolite, Moss Agate, Rhodochrosite, Rose Quartz, Topaz, Turquoise

ANTIBACTERIAL: Amber, Iolite

ANTI-INFLAMMATORY: Blue Chalcedony, **Moss Agate**, Turquoise

ANTISEPTIC: Amber, Amethyst, Calcite

ANTISPASMODIC: Aragonite, Azurite, Magnesite

ANTIVIRAL: Fluorite

ANXIETY / STRESS: Amber, Apatite, Aventurine, Beryl, Black Tourmaline, Calcite, Chrysoprase, Emerald, Fluorite, Hematite, Herkimer Diamond, Iron Pyrite, **Kunzite**, Labradorite, Malachite, Moonstone, Peridot, Rose Quartz, Rutilated Quartz, Sapphire, Smithsonite, Tiger's Eye, Turquoise

APHRODISIAC: Amethyst, Carnelian, Pink Tourmaline, Red Jasper, Rose Quartz

APPENDICITIS: Citrine, Peridot, Yellow Sapphire

APPETITE (SUPPRESSANT): Apatite

ARTERIES: Bloodstone (strengthens), Larimar (blocked), Obsidian (blocked)

ARTERIOSCLEROSIS: Amethyst, Aventurine, Beryl, Magnesite, Obsidian, Petrified Wood

ARTHRITIS: Amethyst, Apatite, Azurite, Black Tourmaline, Blue Lace Agate, Carnelian, Green Calcite, Chrysocolla, **Fluorite**, Garnet, Hematite, Malachite, Obsidian, Petrified Wood, Rhodonite

ASSIMILATION OF: Blue Opal (iron), Chrysocolla (iron and vitamin C), Chrysoprase (vitamin C), Fluorite (oxygen), Honey Calcite (calcium), Howlite (calcium), Magnesite (magnesium), Opal (protein), Serpentine (calcium & magnesium), Turquoise (nutrients)

ASTHMA: **Amber,** Amethyst, Ametrine, Beryl, Blue Sapphire, Iron Pyrite, Malachite, Rhodochrosite, Rose Quartz, Tiger's Eye, Topaz

ATMOSPHERE POLLUTANT CLEANERS: Black Tourmaline, Smoky Quartz, Turquoise

AURA: Amber (aligns aura with physical body when held over crown or solar plexus, removes negativity), Amethyst (to repair holes, hold over site, cleanse and protect), **Apache Tear** (removes negativity, protects aura), Aqua Aura (to repair holes, hold over site), Diamond (protects aura), Green Tourmaline (to repair holes, hold over site), Iolite (to energise), Kunzite (to remove entities, comb through aura), Labradorite (protects aura), **Quartz** (to energise, hold over solar plexus, to cleanse, comb through aura, to repair holes, hold over site and protects aura), Selenite (cleanses), **Smoky Quartz** (to cleanse or to remove entities comb through aura), Zircon (strengthens aura)

AUTISM: Apatite, Charoite, Malachite, Moldavite, Opal, **Sugilite**

AUTOIMMUNE DISORDERS: Aquamarine, Rhodonite

BACK PROBLEMS: **Amber,** Aragonite (disc elasticity), Blue Agate (backache), Cathedral Quartz (aches/pain), Hematite (backache), **Iolite** (backache), Lapis Lazuli (pain), Malachite (pain), Sapphire (pain)

BACTERIAL INFECTIONS: Apache Tear, Blue Tourmaline, Green Calcite, Iolite

BAD BREATH: Sunstone

BAD TEMPER (AMELIORATE): Bloodstone, Emerald

BEDSORES: Amethyst, Blue Lace Agate, Ruby

BELCHING: Beryl

BI-POLAR: Charoite, Kunzite, Larimar, Peridot

BITES (VENOMOUS): Emerald

BLACKOUTS: Lapis Lazuli

BLADDER: Amber, Black Tourmaline, Bloodstone, Jade, Picture Jasper, Orange Calcite, Prehnite, Topaz, Yellow Sapphire

BLEEDING: **Bloodstone** (to stop excessive bleeding), Carnelian (to stop excessive bleeding including menstrual), Chiastolite (to stop excessive bleeding), Jasper (to stop excessive menstrual bleeding) **Ruby** (to stop excessive bleeding), Sapphire (to stop bleeding), Topaz (nose)

BLOOD POISONING: Black Tourmaline, Carnelian, Smoky Quartz (mercury poisoning)

BLOOD (CELLS): Tiger's Iron

BLOOD CLEANSER: Amethyst, Ametrine, Aquamarine, Black Tourmaline, Blue Quartz, **Bloodstone,** Citrine, Garnet, **Hematite**, Lapis Lazuli, Mookaite, Moss Agate, Opal, Ruby, Serpentine, Sugilite

BLOOD CLOTS (DISSOLVE): Amethyst, Bloodstone, Hematite

BLOOD CLOTTING (IMPROVE): Calcite, Red Chalcedony, Sapphire

BLOOD DISORDERS: Amethyst, Bloodstone, Blue Quartz, Chrysocolla, Cherry opal, Lapis Lazuli, Mookaite, Onyx, Prehnite, Sapphire

BLOOD PRESSURE: Amethyst (high), Aventurine (equalise), Bloodstone (high), Blue Chalcedony (high), Carnelian (low),Charoite (equalise and high), Chrysocolla (high), Chrysoprase (high), Emerald (high), Jade (high), Kyanite (high), Labradorite (high), Lapis Lazuli (high), Malachite (high), Red Calcite (low), Rhodochrosite (high/ low), Sodalite (high/ low), Tourmaline (equalise/ low)

BLOOD SUGAR IMBALANCE: Muscovite, Peridot

BLOOD VESSELS: Agate (strengthens), Angelite (repairs), Bloodstone (capillaries), Carnelian (capillaries), Malachite (capillaries), Red Tourmaline (repairs veins), Rhodochrosite (dilates), Rose Quartz (strengthens)

BOILS: Amber, Lapis Lazuli, Sapphire

BONES: Amber (marrow), Apatite (broken/ healing), Aragonite (healing), Blue Lace Agate (disorders), Calcite (growth/ structure/ calcium uptake/ strengthening), Carnelian (healing), Cathedral Quartz (aching), Chalcedony (marrow/ healing), Chrysocolla (disease/ disorders/ strengthening), Desert Rose Selenite (strengthening), Fluorite (strengthening), Green Calcite (adjustments), Hematite (broken), Howlite (structure/ calcium levels), Iron Pyrite (healing), Lapis Lazuli (marrow), Magnesite (broken/ disorders), Malachite (broken), Onyx (healing/ marrow), Purple Fluorite (marrow/ disorders), Rhodonite (growth), Rose Quartz (aching), Rutilated Quartz (healing), Selenite (strengthening), Spinel (aching), Tiger's Eye (disease/ broken), Topaz (disorders/ strengthening), Tourmaline (disorders/ strengthening), Zircon

BONE MARROW DISORDERS: Lapis Lazuli, Onyx, Purple Fluorite

BOWEL: Hawk's Eye, Jasper (especially yellow), Malachite, Tourmaline

BRAIN: Amber, Amethyst (neural pathways), Beryl, Blue Lace Agate (as elixir brain fluid imbalance), Carnelian, Emerald (tumour), Green Tourmaline, Iron Pyrite (improve blood flow), Kyanite, Labradorite (disorders), Lapis Lazuli (damage/ stimulate activity), Larimar (stimulate activity), Magnesite, Moss Agate (balance left/right hemispheres), Ruby (detox), Sapphire (disorders), Stillbite (disorders), Sugilite (balance left/right hemispheres/ neural pathways), Turquoise (fatigue), Zircon (damage)

BREASTFEEDING: Chalcedony, Chiastolite, **Moonstone,** Pink Chalcedony, Selenite

BREATHLESSNESS: **Amber**, Amethyst, Black Onyx, Jet, Moss Agate

BREATHING DISORDERS: Moss Agate

BRONCHITIS: **Amber,** Black Onyx, Iron Pyrite, Jet, Rutilated Quartz

BRUISES: Amethyst, Blue Lace Agate, Hematite, Rose Quartz

BULIMIA: Carnelian, Rose Quartz

BURNS: Amethyst, Blue Tourmaline (soothes), Carnelian, Chrysocolla (soothes), Chrysoprase, Emerald, Green Calcite (cools), Hematite, Moonstone, **Quartz, Rose Quartz** (soothes)

BURSITIS: Amber

CALCIFICATION: Calcite, Malachite

CALCIUM: Apatite (absorption), Amazonite (deficiency/deposits), Aragonite (absorption), Calcite (absorption), Howlite (imbalance), Peridot (excess), Serpentine (calcium/magnesium balance), Sodalite (deficiency), Yellow Kunzite (calcium/magnesium balance)

CANEROUS GROWTHS: Amethyst

CANCER-PRECANCER: Amethyst (skin-growths), Beryl, Blue Quartz, Carnelian, Emerald (skin cancer), Fluorite, Garnet, Herkimer Diamond, Malachite, Moonstone, Red Jasper, Smoky Quartz (treats radiation related illness and chemotherapy), Sugilite (offers emotional support during cancer)

CANDIDA ALBICANS: Carnelian, Dendritic Chalcedony

CAPILLARIES: Blue Lace Agate (aids), Dendritic Agate (reverses degeneration), Tektite (aids)

CARDIOVASCULAR SYSTEM: Beryl, Kunzite, Peridot

CATARACTS: Turquoise

CATARRH: Amber, Blue Agate, Sapphire, Topaz

CARTILAGE PROBLEMS: Apatite, Aragonite, Dalmatian Jasper, Larimar, Sunstone

CELLULAR PROBLEMS: Celestite (disorders), Chiastolite (chromosome damage), Garnet (regenerates DNA), Herkimer Diamond (corrects DNA), Iron Pyrite (disorders), Jasper (regeneration), Rhodonite protection (tape to phone)" (regeneration), Sardonyx (cell metabolism), Selenite (structure), Sodalite (regeneration), Tanzanite (cellular memory) Yellow Kunzite (disorders)

CELL PHONE RADIATION PROTECTION (TAPE TO PHONE): Amazonite, **Black Tourmaline**, Diamond, **Shungite**, Smoky Quartz

CELLULITE: Apatite, Citrine

CENTRAL NERVOUS SYSTEM (DEPLETED OR DISTURBED): Amethyst, Aventurine, Celestite, Rhodonite, Rose Quartz

CERVIX: Carnelian

CHAKRAS:

ALIGN Amber, Citrine, Kyanite, Quartz

BALANCE: Sunstone

BLOWN CHAKRA: Fire Agate

CLEANSE: Amethyst, Bloodstone, Calcite, Citrine, Quartz

CLEAR BLOCKAGES CHAKRAS: Azurite, Bloodstone, Lapis Lazuli, Quartz

ENERGY LEAKS (SEAL): Green Aventurine, Labradorite, Quartz

ENTITIES (CLEAR) CHAKRAS: Smoky Amethyst

HOLES (TO REPAIR): Amethyst, Green Tourmaline Quartz

INFLUENCES FROM OTHERS: Kunzite, Selenite

TECT CHAKRAS: Apache Tear, Jet, Labradorite, Quartz

STRENGTHEN CHAKRAS: Quartz

EARTH CHAKRA: Brown Stones, Brown Jasper, Fire Agate, Hematite, Mahogany Obsidian, Rhodonite, Smoky Quartz, Tourmaline

BASE CHAKRA: Red Stones, Azurite, Black Tourmaline, Bloodstone, Carnelian, Chrysocolla, Citrine, Fire Agate, Garnet, Golden Topaz, Obsidian, Red Calcite, Red Jasper, Smoky Quartz, Pink Tourmaline

SACRAL/ NAVEL CHAKRA: Orange Stones, Blue Jasper, Citrine, Orange Calcite, Orange Carnelian, Red Jasper, Topaz

SOLAR PLEXUS CHAKRA: Yellow Stones, Citrine, Golden Beryl, Jasper, Malachite, Rhodochrosite, Tiger's Eye, Yellow Tourmaline

SPLEEN CHAKRA: Aventurine, Rhodonite, Ruby, Zircon

HEART CHAKRA: Pink or Green Stones, Aventurine, Chrysocolla, Green Jasper, Green Quartz, Green Sapphire, Green Tourmaline, Jade, Kunzite, Lepidolite, Pink Danburite, Pink Tourmaline, Red Calcite, Rhodonite, Rhodochrosite, Rose Quartz, Ruby, Watermelon Tourmaline, Variscite

HIGHER HEART/ THYMUS CHAKRA: Pink or Green Stones, Amethyst, Angelite, Aqua Aura, Bloodstone, Blue Tourmaline, Citrine, Green Tourmaline, Kunzite, Rose Quartz

THROAT CHAKRA: Blue Stones, Amber, Amethyst, Aqua Aura (underactive), Aventurine, Azurite, Blue Lace Agate, Blue Obsidian, Blue Topaz, Blue Tourmaline, Citrine, Kunzite, Lapis Lazuli (underactive), Lepidolite, Peridot (underactive), Quartz, Rose Quartz, Smithsonite (underactive), Turquoise

THIRD EYE (BROW) CHAKRA: Indigo Stones, Aquamarine, Azurite, Electric-Blue Obsidian, Garnet, Herkimer Diamond, Iolite, Kunzite, Labradorite, Lapis Lazuli, Lepidolite, Malachite with Azurite, Moldavite, Purple Fluorite, Sodalite, Yellow Labradorite

CROWN CHAKRA: Purple or White Stones, Angelite, Citrine, Clear Tourmaline, Golden Beryl, Larimar, Lepidolite, Moldavite, Purple Jasper, Purple Sapphire, Quartz, Red Serpentine, Selenite

HIGHER CROWN CHAKRA: White Stones, Celestite, Kunzite, Selenite

CHANGE: Aqua Aura (adapting to), Bloodstone (adapting to), Brown Jade (adapting to), Chalcedony (adapting to), Chiastolite (facilitating), Chrysanthemum Stone (accepting), Chrysocolla (accepting), Clear Calcite (new beginnings), Danburite (facilitating), Diamond (new beginnings), Fire Opal (facilitating), Green Kunzite (new beginnings), Labradorite (support during), Larimar (accepting), Malachite (encouraging), Mookaite (encouraging), Moonstone (new beginnings), Peridot (encouraging), Rose Quartz (accepting), Rutilated Quartz (facilitating), Seraphinite (facilitating), Tiger's Iron (support during)

CHEMOTHERAPY: Smoky Quartz

CHEST PROBLEMS: Amber (pains), Emerald (pains), Green Kunzite (Hiddenite), Larimar, Malachite (pains), Prehnite, Rhodonite, Rhodochrosite, Rose Quartz, Zoisite

CHICKEN POX: Azurite, Malachite, Topaz

CHILDBIRTH: Amber (ease pain), Carnelian, Cathedral Quartz (ease pain), Chalcedony (fosters maternal instincts), Emerald (ease pain), Jade, Lapis Lazuli (ease pain), Malachite, Moonstone (ease pain), Moss Agate (ease pain), Opal (ease pain), Peridot (ease pain)

CHILLS: Aragonite, Kunzite, Magnesite, Red Black Obsidian, Red Tourmaline, Seraphinite

CHOLERA: Malachite

CHOLESTEROL: Aventurine (lowers), Beryl (balances), Magnesite (lowers), Yellow Fluorite

CHRONIC FATIGUE SYNDROME: Ametrine, Citrine, Green Tourmaline, Purple Violet Tourmaline, Yellow Apatite

CIRCULATION: Amethyst, Azurite with Malachite, Beryl (strengthening), Black Tourmaline, Bloodstone (purifies and regulates blood), Blue Tiger's Eye, Candle Quartz, Carnelian, Chalcedony (balances), Citrine (stimulating), Diamond (defective), Electric Blue-Obsidian (disorders), Emerald, Fire Agate (disorders), Galena (stimulates), Hawk's Eye (disorders), Hematite (disorders), Howlite, Iron Pyrite (strengthening), Kunzite (strengthening), Malachite, Mookaite (cleanses), Moss Agate (cleansing), Obsidian (hardened arteries), Red Chalcedony (stimulating), Red Jasper, Red Tourmaline (stimulating), Rhodochrosite (purifies), Rose Quartz (strengthening), Ruby (poor/ disorders), Tektite, Turquoise, Yellow Topaz

CLAIRAUDIENCE (ENHANCE): Phantom Quartz

CLAIRSENTIENCE (ENHANCE): Cherry Opal

CLAIRVOYANCE: Amethyst (enhance), Aquamarine (open), Celestite (stimulate), Cherry Opal (open), Emerald (enhance), Hawk's Eye (stimulate), Herkimer Diamond (stimulate), Moonstone (stimulate), Tektite (enhance), Yellow Labradorite (enhance)

CLARITY (MENTAL): Amethyst, Aventurine, Beryl, Bloodstone, Calcite, Citrine, Chrysoprase, Jade, Opal, Peridot, Sapphire

CLAUSTROPHOBIA: Aventurine, Chrysoprase, Emerald, Green Tourmaline

CLEANSERS OF PHYSICAL BODY: Amber, Chalcedony Charoite, Clear Quartz (physical body and soul), Fluorite

CODEPENDENCY: Chrysoprase, Iolite, Rhodonite, Sunstone

COLD EXTREMITIES: Obsidian

COLDS: Ametrine, Carnelian, Emerald, Fluorite, Green Opal, Jet, Labradorite, Larimar, Moss Agate

COLIC: Jade, Malachite

COLON PROBLEMS: Bloodstone, Brown Tourmaline, Carnelian, Citrine, Garnet, Obsidian, Smoky Quartz, Yellow Jasper

COMMITMENT: Garnet, Tiger's Eye

COMMUNICATION : Apatite (enhance), Aqua Aura (enhance), Aquamarine (unblocks), Azurite (unblocks), Blue Calcite (encourage), Blue Chalcedony (calming and enhance), Blue Fluorite (enhance), Blue Obsidian (enhance), Blue Opal (encourage), Celestite (enhance), Chrysocolla (enhance and teaches when to keep silent), Green Calcite (enhance), Howlite (calming), Kunzite (enhance), Kyanite (encourage), Lapis Lazuli (encourage), Larimar (angelic communication), Moldavite (higher self and extra-terrestrial communication), Moss Agate (enhance), Smoky Quartz (encourage), Tektite (communication with other worlds)

COMPASSION: Angelite, Aventurine, Beryl, Chrysoprase, Green Spinel, Kyanite, Lapis Lazuli, Moldavite, Obsidian, Rhodochrosite, Tourmaline

COMPLACENCY: Gold Tiger's Eye

COMPULSIONS: Charoite, Chrysoprase, Hematite

COMPUTER STRESS: Amazonite, Lepidolite, Purple Sugilite, Smoky Quartz

COMPUTERS (PROTECTION FROM ELECTROMAGNETIC EMISSIONS ETC): Amazonite, Fluorite, Sodalite, Yellow Kunzite

CONCENTRATION (IMPROVE): Agate, Ametrine, Aragonite, Carnelian, Citrine, Fluorite, Hematite, Lepidolite, Quartz, Ruby, Sapphire, Smoky Quartz, Yellow Apatite

CONCUSSION: Beryl

CONFIDENCE: Agate, Beryl, Black Tourmaline, Carnelian, Chrysanthemum Stone, Chrysocolla, Citrine, Fluorite, Garnet, Hematite, Iron Pyrite, Lapis Lazuli, Peridot, Red Chalcedony, Rhodonite, Rose Quartz, Ruby, Tourmaline, Variscite

CONFUSION: Apatite, Aquamarine, Bloodstone, Kyanite, Obsidian, Onyx, Rhodonite, Selenite, Sodalite

CONJUNCTIVITIS: Agate, Blue Sapphire

CONNECTIVE TISSUE: Lepidolite (detoxifies)

CONSTIPATION: Amber, Citrine, Emerald, Green Tourmaline, Red Calcite, Red Jasper, Ruby, Serpentine

CONVALESCENCE: Blue Calcite, Emerald, Flamingo Jasper, Moss Agate, Petrified Wood, Ruby, Unakite, Zoisite

CONVULSIONS: Chrysoprase, Jasper

COORDINATION: Fluorite, Sugilite, Tourmaline

COUGHS: Amber, Ametrine, Aquamarine, Blue Agate, Topaz

COURAGE: Aquamarine, Beryl, Bloodstone, Carnelian, Diamond, Garnet, Jasper, Ruby, Topaz, Variscite

CRAMPS: Amethyst, Apache Tear (Obsidian), Bloodstone, Charoite, Chrysocolla (muscle, menstrual), Green Fluorite, (intestinal), Hematite (legs), Jet (menstrual), Lepidolite (legs), Magnesite (intestinal, stomach, menstrual and vascular), Malachite, Obsidian, Serpentine, Smoky Quartz, Turquoise, Zircon

CRAVINGS: Fire Agate

DEAFNESS: Amber, Black Tourmaline, Onyx, Rhodonite, Sapphire

DEATH (ASSISTING THE TRANSITION): Amethyst, Carnelian (fear), Chiastolite (understanding immortality), Danburite, Isis (Goddess) Quartz, Kyanite, Lilac Kunzite

DEBILITY: Black Tourmaline, Fire Agate

DECISION MAKING: Amethyst (facilitate), Bloodstone (enhancing), Charoite (enhancing), Green Agate (enhancing), Onyx (wise decisions), White Jade (facilitate)

DEGENERATIVE PROBLEMS: Citrine (disease), Picture Jasper (disease), Moonstone (skin, hair, eyes, organs)

DEHYDRATION: Moss Agate, Muscovite

DELIRIUM: Peridot

DEMENTIA: Chalcedony, Rose Quartz

DENIAL: Rhodochrosite, Watermelon Tourmaline

DENTAL PROBLEMS: Fluorite

DEPRESSION: Amber, **Ametrine**, Apatite, Black Calcite, Carnelian (elderly), Charoite (Bi-polar), Citrine, Garnet, Hematite, Iron Pyrite, Jade, Jet, **Kunzite**, Lapis Lazuli, Larimar (Bi-polar), **Lepidolite** (Bi-polar and depression), Moss Agate, Orange Calcite, Peridot (Bi-polar), Purple Tourmaline, Rutilated Quartz, Smoky Quartz, Sapphire, Sardonyx, Spinel, Smithsonite (mental breakdown), **Sunstone** (S.A.D), Tiger's Eye, Turquoise

DESIRE: Black Spinel (reducing), Hematite (unfulfilled), Opal, Blue-Green Smithsonite, Zircon

DESPAIR: Carnelian, Iron Pyrite, Rhodonite, Serpentine, Sugilite, Variscite

DESPONDENCY: Lepidolite

DETERMINATION: Jasper

DETOXIFIERS: Brown or Black stones, Amethyst (body and mind), Azurite, Bloodstone, Blue Quartz, Calcite, Chrysanthemum Stone, Citrine, Chrysoprase (heavy metals), Danburite, Green Tourmaline, Herkimer Diamond, Iolite (liver), Jade, Lapis Lazuli (etheric body), Magnesite (body odour), Malachite (liver), Moonstone, Moss Agate, Obsidian, Orbicular Jasper (body odour), Peridot, Red Tourmaline, Ruby, Rose Quartz (emotions), Sapphire, Serpentine, **Smoky Quartz** (body and emotions), Stillbite, Topaz, Turquoise, Yellow Apatite, Yellow Fluorite, Yellow Sapphire

DIABETES: Amethyst, Chrysocolla (regulates insulin), Citrine, Diamond, Emerald, Jade, Malachite, Moss Agate, Opal (regulates insulin), Red Jasper, Serpentine

DIARRHOEA: Beryl, Green Tourmaline, Lapis Lazuli, Malachite, Quartz, Serpentine

DIGESTION: Agate (stimulate), Amber, Amethyst (disorders), Beryl, Bloodstone (cleanse), Calcite (disorders), Carnelian, Chrysocolla (calm), Chrysoprase (calm), Citrine (stimulate), Emerald, Fire Opal, Green Jasper (calm), Iron Pyrite (calming and strengthening), Jasper (strengthening), Labradorite, Malachite, Moonstone (stress related), Moss Agate (stimulate and cleanse), Obsidian, Peridot, Pink Tourmaline, Red Jade, (stimulate), Red Tourmaline, Rhodonite, Sapphire, Sardonyx, Smithsonite (disorders), Snowflake Obsidian, Sodalite (disorders), Tiger's Eye, Topaz (strengthening), Yellow Apatite, Yellow Jade, Yellow Jasper

DISCS (LOSS OF ELASTICITY): Aragonite

DIZZINESS: Aragonite, Candle Quartz, Clear Quartz, Lapis Lazuli, Malachite, White Sapphire

DNA PROBLEMS: Ametrine (stabilising), Fluorite (repair), Garnet (repair), Herkimer Diamond (repair and reverse degeneration of) , Iron Pyrite (repair), Lepidolite (repair), Malachite (aligning), Selenite (repair), Yellow Kunzite (repair and reverse degeneration of)

DREAMS: Amethyst (stimulating and understanding), Bloodstone (stimulating and understanding), Chalcedony (bad), Celestite (recall), Danburite (promote lucid), Green Sapphire (recall), Herkimer Diamond (recall), Kyanite (recall), Lapis Lazuli (understanding) Malachite (stimulating), Moonstone (promote lucid), Red Jasper (recall), Rhodochrosite (enhancing),

DROPSY-EDEMA: Amber, Bloodstone, Jet, Moonstone

DYSENTERY: Emerald

DYSPEPSIA: Emerald

DYSLEXIA: Amethyst, Malachite, Opal, Picture Jasper, Royal Sapphire, **Sugilite**, Tourmaline, Tourmalined Quartz

EAR PROBLEMS: Amber, Amazonite, Amethyst, Black Tourmaline, Blue Agate, Blue Chalcedony, Celestite, Fluorite, Orange Calcite, Red Obsidian, Rhodonite, Snowflake Obsidian, Sapphire, Tourmaline

ECZEMA: Amethyst, Green Aventurine, Sapphire

ELECTROMAGNETIC POLLUTION: Amazonite (protection against), Aventurine (absorb), Black Tourmaline (protection against), Diamond (protection against), Fluorite (protection against), Herkimer Diamond (clearing), Jasper (clearing), Kunzite (protection against), **Lepidolite** (clearing), Malachite (clearing), Sodalite (clearing), **Smoky Quartz** (absorb), Turquoise (clearing)

EMOTIONAL ABUSE: Rose Quartz, Pink Agate, Pink Carnelian, Smithsonite

EMOTIONAL BALANCE: Amethyst, Apatite, Aventurine, Chiastolite, Chrysocolla, Citrine, Emerald, Jet, Lepidolite, Moonstone, Moss Agate, Opal, Peridot, Petrified Wood, Rhodonite, Rhyolite, Rose Quartz, Serpentine, Sodalite, Stillbite

EMOTIONAL BLOCKAGES: Yellow Stones, Blue Tourmaline, Kunzite, Kyanite, Lepidolite (past life), Malachite, Rose Quartz

EMOTIONAL CALMING: Amethyst, Calcite, Carnelian, Citrine, Emerald, Howlite, Opal, Magnesite, Moonstone, Rose Quartz, Smoky Quartz, Variscite

EMOTIONAL CLEANSER: Blue Lace Agate, Green Opal, Peridot, Rhodochrosite

EMOTIONAL DEPENDENCY: Lepidolite

EMOTIONAL EXHAUSTION: Apatite, Amethyst, Aragonite, Azurite, Kunzite, Lepidolite, Magnesite, Orange Carnelian

EMOTIONAL PATTERNS: Moonstone

EMOTIONAL RECOVERY: Chrysocolla, Green Opal, Lapis Lazuli

EMOTIONAL RELEASE: Ametrine, Azurite, Beryl, Chiastolite, Chrysocolla, Fluorite, Green Calcite, Green Opal, Lapis Lazuli, Lepidolite, Malachite, Moldavite, Peridot, Rhodochrosite, Fishtail Selenite, Serpentine, Turquoise, Yellow Smithsonite

EMOTIONAL TRAUMA: Amazonite, Amethyst, Aqua Aura, Charoite, Rose Quartz, Smoky Quartz

EMOTIONAL WOUNDS: Charoite, Blue-Green Smithsonite, Rhodochrosite

EMPATHY (PROMOTE): Aventurine, Green Tourmaline, Malachite, Moldavite, Moonstone, Pink Chalcedony, Rose Quartz, Turquoise

EMPHYSEMIA: Amber, Amethyst, Aqua Aura, Emerald, Malachite, Pink Beryl, Rhodonite, Rose Quartz, Tiger's Eye

EMPOWERMENT: Beryl, Chrysocolla, Royal Plume Jasper, Lapis Lazuli, Larimar, Fire Opal, Obsidian, Sunstone, Yellow Spinel, Yellow Tourmaline

ENDOCRINE SYSTEM: Amber, Amethyst, Apatite, Aquamarine (balance), Chrysoprase(balance), Citrine (balance), Fire Agate, Golden Topaz, Green Quartz, Howlite, Labradorite (balance), Moonstone (balance), Peridot, Pietersite (balance), Sapphire, Tourmaline, Topaz, Yellow Jasper (energises)

ENERGY: Red or Orange Stones, Amethyst (boost), Apatite (stagnant), Black Tourmaline (blockages), Calcite (stagnant), Carnelian (boost), Clear Topaz (stagnant), Diamond (boost), Fire Opal (boost), Garnet (boost and cleanse), Herkimer Diamond (boost), Kyanite (boost), Larimar (blockages), Malachite (boost), Obsidian (blockages), Quartz (boost and blockages), Variscite (boost)

ENTITIES (REMOVE): Amethyst and Smoky Quartz, Fairy Quartz, Larimar, Smoky Amethyst

ENVIRONMENTAL POLLUTANTS: Brown Stones, Amethyst, Apatite, Aventurine, Black Tourmaline, Blue Quartz, Citrine, Green Fluorite, Herkimer Diamond, Jasper, Kunzite, Malachite, Moldavite, Moss Agate, Obsidian, Petrified Wood, Prehnite, Rose Quartz, Smoky Quartz, Turquoise, Variscite

ENVY (AMELIORATE): Carnelian, Picture Jasper, Ruby

EPILEPSY: Amethyst, Black Onyx, Emerald, Jasper, Jet, Kunzite (calms), Lapis Lazuli, Lepidolite, Magnesite (prevents), Malachite, Opal, Selenite (prevents), Sugilite, Tourmaline, Yellow Sapphire

EXHAUSTION: Red or Orange Stones, Apatite (emotional), Bloodstone, **Carnelian**, Charoite, Fire Opal, Green Tourmaline, Lepidolite, Pietersite, Ruby, Rutilated Quartz, Tiger's Eye, Tiger's Iron, Turquoise

EYE: Agate, Aqua Aura (watering), Aquamarine (itchy and watering), Aventurine (soothe), Beryl, Blue Fluorite, Blue Lace Agate (infection), Blue Chalcedony (glaucoma), Blue Obsidian, Carnelian, Celestite, Chalcedony, Charoite, Citrine, Chrysanthemum Stone, Chrysoprase, Dark-blue Tourmaline, Dendritic Agate, Diamond (glaucoma), **Emerald** (blood shot, tired and to soothe), Fire Agate (improve night vision), Green Sapphire (improve vision), Hematite, Jade (disease), Labradorite, Lepidolite, Malachite, Moonstone, Moss Agate, Opal (strengthens), Optical Calcite, Orange Calcite, Peridot (strengthens), Quartz (infection), Rhodochrosite (restore vision), Ruby (irritated and infection), Sapphire (infection/ulcerated), Snowflake Obsidian (clear), Tiger's Eye, Turquoise (cataracts)

FAINT: Amethyst, Lapis Lazuli, Malachite

FALLOPIAN TUBES: Carnelian, Chrysoprase

FAT DEPOSITS: Amethyst (boost metabolism), Iolite (reduce fat deposits)

FATIGUE: Amethyst, Ametrine, Bloodstone, Blue Opal, **Carnelian**, Citrine (menopause), Dendritic Agate, Hematite, Herkimer Diamond, Iron Pyrite, Rose Quartz, Sunstone, Yellow Apatite

FEAR: Amazonite (alleviate), Azurite (finding root cause), Black Tourmaline, Blue-Green Smithsonite, Blue Quartz (alleviate), Charoite (alleviate), Chiastolite (alleviate fear of going mad), Citrine (of responsibility), Diamond (alleviate), Emerald, Green Tourmaline (alleviate), Hematite (of failure), Jet (unreasonable), Labradorite (remove), Larimar (remove), Lepidolite, Magnesite (support during), Moss Agate (alleviate), Onyx (alleviate), Orange Calcite (alleviate), Pink Calcite (remove), Rhodochrosite (irrational), Rose Quartz, Rutilated Quartz, Serpentine, Smoky Quartz (alleviate and fear of failure), Sugilite (alleviate)

FEET: Aquamarine (swollen), Blue Lace Agate (burning), Jet, Larimar, Onyx, Pietersite, Smoky Quartz, Tiger's Iron

FEMALE PROBLEMS: Moonstone, Malachite

FEMALE REPRODUCTIVE PROBLEMS: Orange Stones, Amber, Carnelian, Chrysoprase, Dendritic Chalcedony (inflammation), Malachite, Moldavite, Moonstone, Moss Agate, Unakite

FERTILITY (INCREASE): Carnelian, Chrysoprase, Jade (enhance), Moonstone (conception), Orange Sapphire, Rhodonite (stimulate), Rose Quartz (enhance), Ruby in Zoisite, Thulite (enhance)

FEVER (LOWER): Agate, **Blue Chalcedony**, Blue Lace Agate (reduces), Carnelian, Chiastolite (reduces), Chrysoprase, Green Calcite (cools), Hematite, Iolite, Iron Pyrite, Kyanite, Larimar, Magnesite (balances temperature), Moldavite, Moss Agate (reduces), Opal, Peridot, Red Jasper, Red-Black Obsidian, Ruby, Sapphire, Sodalite (cools), Tektite (reduces)

FLATULENCE: Diamond, Emerald, Green Garnet

FLU: Fluorite, Green Opal, Labradorite, Moss Agate

FLUID RETENTION: Amber, Aqua Aura, Aquamarine, Jade, Moonstone

FOOD POISONING: Emerald

FORGETFULNESS: Emerald, Moss Agate, Rhodonite, Tourmaline

FORGIVENESS: Apache Tear, Beryl, Chrysoprase, Peridot (of self), Pink Calcite, Rhodonite, Rose Quartz (of self), Rutilated Quartz, Serpentine (of self), Sugilite (of self), Topaz

FRACTURES: Blue Lace Agate, Calcite, Hematite, Malachite, Onyx, Tiger's Eye

FRIGIDITY: Carnelian, Rose Quartz

FRUSTRATION: Apatite, Charoite, Iron Pyrite, Kyanite, Obsidian, Sapphire

FUNGAL INFECTION: **Moss Agate,** Chrysoprase with Smoky Quartz

GALLBLADDER: Amber, Azurite with Malachite, Carnelian, Chalcedony, Citrine, Danburite, Golden Topaz. Green Obsidian, Magnesite (pain), Orange Calcite, Peridot, Red Jasper, Tiger's Eye, Topaz, Yellow Apatite, Yellow Labradorite, Yellow Tourmaline

GALLSTONES: Carnelian, Red Jasper, Rhyolite

GANGRENE: Citrine

GASTRIC ULCER: Agate, Emerald, Sapphire

GASTRIC UPSET: Agate (gastritis), Carnelian, Jasper, Variscite (gastritis)

GEOPATHIC STRESS: Amazonite (block), Amethyst (block), Aragonite (transforms), Aventurine (for gridding), Black Tourmaline, Brown Jasper (alleviate), Dendritic Agate (stabilises), Diamond (block), Fluorite (block), Herkimer Diamond (block), Kunzite, Larimar (block), Obsidian (block), Selenite, Smoky Quartz (block)

GIDDINESS: Emerald, Quartz

GINGIVITIS: Blue Lace Agate

GLANDS: Amber (glandular swellings), Aquamarine (swollen), Blue Lace Agate (swollen), Golden Topaz, Jet (swollen), Mookaite, Ruby (regulate), Topaz (swollen)

GLANDULAR FEVER: Blue Lace Agate

GLAUCOMA: Blue Chalcedony, Diamond

GOITRE: **Amber**, Chrysoprase

GOUT: Chiastolite, Chrysoprase, Labradorite, Prehnite, Topaz, Tourmaline, Turquoise, Variscite

GRIEF: Amethyst (alleviate), Apache Tear (comfort), Azurite (alleviate), Clear Obsidian, Fire Agate (release), Lapis Lazuli, Onyx (old), Pink Calcite (release), Red Jasper, Rhodochrosite, Sugilite (alleviate)

GROUNDING: Brown Stones, Agate, Amber (energy), Aragonite (energy), Beryl, Black Kyanite (in chakra work), Black Obsidian (in chakra work), Black Tourmaline (energy), Bloodstone (energy), Brown Sardonyx (energy), Brown Spinel, Brown Tourmaline, Citrine (energy), Fire Agate, Green Fluorite (energy), Hawk's Eye (energy), Hematite, Herkimer Diamond, Jasper (energy), Mahogany Obsidian, Moldavite (star children), Petrified Wood, Pietersite (etheric body), Rhodonite (energy), Selenite (light body), Smoky Quartz, Sugilite (autism), Tourmalined Quartz, Unakite

GROWTH: Agate (spiritual), Aventurine (physical 0-7yrs), Calcite (physical, in small children), Moldavite (spiritual), Pietersite (physical), Rutilated Quartz (spiritual), Tektite (spiritual), Topaz (spiritual), Unakite (spiritual)

GUILT: Chiastolite (alleviate), Chrysocolla (alleviate), Jasper, Larimar (alleviate), Peridot (alleviate), Picture Jasper (hidden), Rose Quartz, Sodalite (alleviate)

HAEMORRHOIDS: Ametrine, Bloodstone, Clear Obsidian, Chrysocolla, Golden Topaz, Ruby, Sapphire, Topaz

HAIR: Agate, Aquamarine, Aragonite (loss), Black Tourmaline (improve condition), Blue Opal (loss), Chrysocolla (improve condition), Galena, Larimar, Moonstone (alopecia), Opal (improve condition), Petrified Wood (stimulate), Quartz (improve condition), Rutilated Quartz, Tanzanite, Smithsonite (improve condition), Unakite (baldness and improve condition)

HALLUCINATIONS: Lapis Lazuli

HANDS: Aquamarine (swollen), Moldavite, Moonstone (swollen), Smoky Quartz

HAPPINESS: Sunstone

HARA: Sapphire

HARDENING DISEASES: Beryl, Petrified Wood

HAY FEVER: Amber, Aquamarine, Blue Lace Agate, Jet, Tiger's Eye

HEADACHES: Amber, Amethyst, Ametrine, Bloodstone, Blue Sapphire, **Cathedral Quartz**, Cherry Opal, Hematite, Jet, Lapis Lazuli, Larimar, Magnesite, Rose Quartz, Smoky Quartz (electromagnetic stress), **Sugilite**, Turquoise

HEARING: Amethyst, Blue Agate, Lapis Lazuli, Petrified Wood, Phantom Quartz, Rhodonite

HEART: Pink or Green Stones, Blue Aventurine (attacks and regeneration), Bloodstone, Blue Quartz, Calcite (strengthen), Carnelian (disease), Charoite (disorders), Chrysoprase (disorders), Citrine, Emerald, Green Aventurine (attacks and regeneration), Green Garnet, Green Obsidian, Green Tourmaline, Hematite (inflammation), Jade (irregular beat),

Kunzite (strengthen), Larimar (trauma and disorders), Magnesite (disorders and good preventative), Malachite, Peridot, Petrified Wood, Pink Chalcedony (strengthen), Pink Tourmaline, **Rhodochrosite** (disease and irregular beat), Rhodonite (disease), Red Jasper (disease), Rose Quartz (unblock and strengthen), Ruby (disease), Sapphire, Serpentine (disturbed rhythm), Smoky Quartz, Tourmalined Quartz (disease), Watermelon Tourmaline

HEARTACHE: Chrysocolla, Kunzite, Lapis Lazuli, Lepidolite, Rhodonite, Rose Quartz, Topaz

HEARTBURN: Carnelian, Emerald, Garnet, Peridot, Quartz

HEAT STROKE (MOBILISE): Blue Lace Agate, Hematite

HEAVY METALS: Chrysoprase

HEMORRHAGING: Carnelian, Hematite, Malachite, Moss Agate, Topaz

HEPATITIS: Calcite, Emerald

HERNIA: Mookaite

HERPES: Fluorite, Lapis Lazuli

HICCUPS: Beryl, Peridot

HIPS: Azurite (pain), Jade, Red Calcite, Smoky Quartz, Tiger's Eye, Tiger's Iron

HOARSENESS: Sodalite

HORMONES: Amethyst (boosting), Aquamarine (balance), Chrysoprase (balance), Citrine (balance), Garnet, Green Quartz (balance), Labradorite (balance), Moonstone (balance), Pietersite (boosting, balance and growth), Watermelon Tourmaline (balance)

HOT FLUSHES: Fire Agate, Citrine

HYDROCEPHALUS: Blue Lace Agate

HYPERACIDITY: Emerald

HYPERACTIVITY: Apatite, Garnet, Green Tourmaline, Moonstone, Ruby

HYPOCHONDRIA: Blue Agate, Peridot, Tiger's Eye

HYPOGLYCEMIA: Moss Agate, Pink Opal, Serpentine

HYSTERIA: Amber, Amethyst, Lapis Lazuli, Moonstone, Rose Quartz, Topaz, Turquoise

IMMUNE SYSTEM: Amethyst, Ametrine (strengthen), Aquamarine (calm), Aragonite (strengthen), Black Tourmaline (strengthen), **Bloodstone** (stimulate), Blue Agate, Blue Chalcedony (enhance and strengthen), Blue Quartz (strengthen), Brown Jasper (boost), Calcite (strengthen), Chiastolite (balance), Citrine, Carnelian, Emerald, Green Calcite (stimulate), Green Opal (strengthen), Green Tourmaline, Lepidolite (strengthen), Kunzite (stimulate), Lapis Lazuli (boost), Malachite, Mookaite (fortify), Moss Agate (boost), Picture Jasper (stimulate), Quartz (stimulate), Rhyolite (strengthen), Ruby in Zoisite, Sardonyx (strengthen), Sodalite (boost), **Smithsonite**, Turquoise (enhance)

IMPOTENCE: Carnelian, Garnet, Pink Beryl, Rhodonite, Rutilated Quartz, Sodalite, Variscite

INCONTINENCE: Petrified Wood

INDIGESTION: Candle Quartz, Citrine, Jasper, Peridot, Tourmaline

INERTIA: Red Stones, Iron Pyrite

INFECTION: Amethyst, Apache Tear, Bloodstone (acute), Blue Lace Agate (lymph and throat), Blue Tourmaline (bacterial), Chrysocolla (acute), Chrysoprase (bacterial), Citrine (kidney and bladder), Emerald (infectious), Fluorite (infectious and viral), Green Calcite (bacterial), Iron Pyrite (protects against), Kunzite, Kyanite, Malachite, Moss Agate (fungal), Opal, Petrified Wood, Rhodochrosite (acute), Rhyolite, Ruby, Smoky Quartz, Turquoise (viral)

INFERTILITY: Chrysoprase (arising from infection), Garnet, Moonstone

INFLAMMATION IN BODY: Agate (bladder and intestinal), Amber, Apache Tear (Obsidian), Aventurine, Blue Lace Agate, Blue Chalcedony, Dendritic Chalcedony, Fluorite, Galena (reduces), Garnet, Green Calcite, Green Jasper, Hematite, Iron Pyrite, Jade (kidneys), Larimar, Lavender-Violet Smithsonite, Malachite (joints), Moss Agate, Rhodonite (joints), Spinel, Topaz, Turquoise

INHIBITIONS: Garnet, Malachite, Opal, Sunstone

INJURIES: Amethyst, Obsidian

INNER CHILD: Amethyst, Chrysoprase, Smithsonite

INSECT BITES: Rhodonite

INSOMNIA: Amethyst (overactive mind and stress), **Black Tourmaline** (nightmares and geopathic/electromagnetic stress), Blue Selenite (overactive mind), Blue Tourmaline, Candle Quartz, Celestite, Charoite, Chrysoprase (stress), Hematite, **Herkimer Diamond** (geopathic/electromagnetic stress), Howlite (overactive mind), Iron Pyrite (overeating), Lapis Lazuli, Lepidolite, Malachite, Moonstone (over eating), Muscovite, Rose Quartz (stress), Smoky Quartz (nightmares and geopathic/electromagnetic stress), Sodalite, Topaz, Yellow Labradorite (overactive mind), Zircon

INTESTINAL TRACT: Amber, Amethyst, Beryl, Brown Tourmaline (disorders), Bloodstone, Calcite, Carnelian, Celestite, Emerald, Fire Opal, Green Fluorite (cramps and disorders), Magnesite (cramps), Orange Calcite (disorders), Peridot, Pietersite, Sapphire, Sardonyx, Snowflake Obsidian, Yellow Jasper

INTUITION: Amazonite (open), Amethyst (enhance and open), Aquamarine (enhance), Electric-Blue Obsidian (enhance), Citrine (open), Fluorite (enhance), Kyanite (stimulate), Labradorite (stimulate), Malachite (enhance and facilitate), Moonstone (enhance), Pietersite accessing), Royal Sapphire (open), Sapphire (trusting), Selenite, Sodalite (facilitate), Stillbite (facilitate and open), Sunstone (enhance), Turquoise (enhance), Violet Spinel (stimulate)

IRON ABSORPTION: Garnet, Hematite

IRRITABILITY: Apatite, Bloodstone, Green Aventurine, Jade, Magnesite, Rhodonite

IRRITABLE BOWEL SYNDROME: Calcite

IRRITANT FILTER: Rhodochrosite

IRRITATION: Peridot

ITCHING: Azurite, Green Aventurine, Hematite, Malachite

JAW: Aquamarine

JEALOUSY: Amethyst, Peridot, Rhodochrosite, Chrysanthemum Stone

JET LAG: Black Tourmaline

JOINTS: Amber (problems), Apatite (problems), Aragonite (strengthen), Azurite, Calcite (calcified and strengthen),

Fluorite (mobilise and problems), Hematite (inflammation), Kunzite (pain), Larimar (pain), Lepidolite (problems), Malachite (inflammation and swollen), Obsidian (problems), Red Calcite (mobilise), Rhodonite (inflammation)

JOY: Chalcedony, Chrysocolla, Citrine, Emerald, Green Tourmaline, Orange Jade, Sunstone, Topaz

JUDGEMENTALISM (OVERCOME): Aquamarine, Chrysoprase

JUSTICE: Red Jasper, Fire Opal

KARMA: Brown Jasper (cause), Charoite (redress), Clear Topaz (aware), Danburite (cleanser), Opal, Quartz (dissolve karmic seeds)

KIDNEYS: Amber, Aquamarine, Azurite, Beryl, Bloodstone (cleanse), Blue Tourmaline, Carnelian (regulate), Chrysocolla (detoxify), Citrine (infections), Emerald, Fire Opal (underactive), Garnet, Hematite (cleanse), Honey Calcite (degeneration), **Jade** (cleanse), Jasper (stones), Magnesite (stones), Malachite, Moss Agate, Muscovite, Opal (cleanse), Orange Calcite, Prehnite (underactive), Red Jasper (degeneration), Rhodochrosite (cleanse, stimulate and underactive), Rhyolite (stones), Rose Quartz (cleanse), Ruby (stimulate and underactive), Serpentine, Smoky Quartz (detoxify), Tanzanite, Topaz, Yellow Jasper (degeneration), Yellow Tourmaline

KNEES: Azurite, Blue Lace Agate

KUNDALINI: Apatite (raises), Garnet (raises), Jet (direct and stimulate), Purple Sapphire (stimulates), Red-Black Obsidian (raises), Red Spinel (balance), Serpentine (open new pathways), Spinel (raises), Tiger's Eye (stimulates)

LABOUR PAINS: Lapis Lazuli, Moss Agate

LACK OF PURPOSE: Lapis Lazuli

LACTATION: Chalcedony (impaired), Jade (increase), Moonstone (impaired)

LARYNX: Blue Kyanite, Blue Tourmaline, Lapis Lazuli, Sodalite, Stillbite

LARYNGITIS: Amber, Blue Lace Agate, Rhodonite, Sodalite, Stillbite, Tourmaline

LAXATIVE: Brown Jasper, Picture Jasper

LEFT-RIGHT BRAIN: Amethyst, Moss Agate, Malachite, Opal

LEGAL SITUATIONS: Malachite

LEGS: **Aquamarine**, Bloodstone, Blue Tiger's Eye, Garnet, Hawk's Eye, Hematite (cramps), Jade (hips), Jasper, Pietersite, Red Calcite (legs and hips), Ruby, Smoky Quartz (legs and hips), Tiger's Iron (legs and hips)

LEPROSY: Ruby

LETHARGY: Ametrine, Calcite, Carnelian, Peridot, Red Tiger's Eye, Ruby, Tourmaline

LEUCORRHAEA: Turquoise

LEUKEMIA: Bloodstone, Cherry Opal, Garnet, Malachite

LIBIDO (LOSS OF): Tourmaline

LIFE FORCE (ENHANCE): Amazonite, Amber, Apache Tear, Aquamarine, Fluorite, Petrified Wood, Poppy Jasper

LIGAMENTS: Green Calcite (constriction), Carnelian (healing), Stillbite (torn)

LIGHT BODY: Herkimer Diamond (activate), Kyanite, Moldavite, Selenite (anchor)

LIGHTHEADEDNESS: Amethyst

LIVER: Amber, Amethyst, Aquamarine, Azurite (stimulate), Azurite with Malachite, Beryl, Bloodstone, Carnelian, Charoite (alcohol damage), Citrine, Chrysoprase (stimulate), Danburite, Dendritic Chalcedony (detox), Emerald (stimulate and detox), Fluorite, Garnet, Gold Calcite, Golden Topaz, Hematite, Iolite (detox and regenerate), Labradorite, Malachite (detox), Moonstone, Moss Agate, Peridot (alcohol damage), Picture Jasper (stimulate), Pietersite, Rhodonite, Red Jasper (blockages), Red Tourmaline (blockages and stimulate), Rose Quartz, Ruby (cleanse), Seraphinite (spots), Sapphire, Tiger's Eye, Yellow Apatite, Yellow Fluorite, **Yellow Jasper,** Yellow Labradorite, Yellow Tourmaline

LOGIC: Kyanite, Sodalite

LONELINESS: Snowflake Obsidian

LONGEVITY: Agate, Beryl, Chrysoprase, Diamond, Jade, Peridot, Rhodonite, Serpentine, Sodalite

LOVE: Pink Stones, Agate (accept and foster), Beryl (reawaken), Celestite (attract), Charoite (unconditional), Chrysanthemum Stone (attract), Chrysocolla (increase capacity), Diamond (fidelity and promote), Emerald (unconditional), **Garnet** (fidelity and attract)**, Green Aventurine** (mature), Green Spinel (attract), Kunzite (unconditional), Lapis Lazuli**,** Larimar (attract), Magnesite (unconditional, for self and attract), Pink Agate (parent to child), Pink Calcite (accept and unconditional), Pink Sapphire (promote)**,** Pink Topaz (attract), Pink Tourmaline (attract), Rainbow Obsidian (letting go), **Rhodochrosite** (promote)**,** Rhodonite (attract and promote), **Rose Quartz** (self-love, accept and attract), **Sugilite** (self-love and attract), Topaz (attract), Turquoise (attract), Variscite (attract)

LOWER EXTREMITIES: Black Tourmaline

LUMBAGO: Candle Quartz, Carnelian, Sapphire

LUNGS: Amber (fluid in), Amethyst (disorders), Angelite, Aventurine, Beryl, Blue Chalcedony, Blue Quartz, Blue Tourmaline, Carnelian, **Charoite**, Chrysocolla (difficulty breathing and disorders), Diamond (fluid in), Emerald, Fluorite, Garnet (regenerate), Hematite, Iron Pyrite, Kunzite, Lapis Lazuli, Moss Agate (congested), Peridot, Picture Jasper, Pietersite, Pink Beryl (disorders), Pink Tourmaline, Prehnite, Rhodochrosite, Rose Quartz (disorders), Sardonyx, Serpentine, Sodalite, Turquoise, Watermelon Tourmaline, Yellow Sapphire (fluid in)

LYMPHATIC SYSTEM: Agate (cleansing), Amethyst (swellings), Aquamarine (strengthen), Bloodstone (stimulate), Blue Chalcedony (stimulate), Blue Lace Agate (infections), Emerald, Jet (swellings), Moss Agate (swellings), Rose Quartz (cleansing), Ruby (cleansing), Sodalite (cleansing), Sugilite (cleansing), Tourmaline, Yellow Apatite (cleansing)

M.E: Ametrine, Ruby, Tourmaline

MALARIA: Turquoise

MALIGNANT CONDITIONS: Amethyst, Azurite, Carnelian, Emerald, Garnet, Green Aventurine, Malachite, Prehnite, Smoky Quartz

MANIFESTATION STONES: Apatite, Citrine, Diamond, Golden Beryl, Kyanite, Prehnite, Red Chalcedony, Stillbite, Tiger's Eye, Topaz

MASTECTOMY: Chrysocolla

MEASLES: Leopard-skin Jasper, Topaz, Turquoise

MEDITATION: Amethyst (aids), Ametrine (enhance), Apatite (deepen), Aqua Aura (aids), Aquamarine (higher dimensions), Aragonite (prepares), Azurite (prepares), Black Kyanite (ground), Blue Topaz (enhance), Brown Jasper (deepen), Carnelian (aid), Celestite (angelic realms), Chrysocolla (aids), Chrysoprase (deepen), Fire Agate (enhance), Gold Calcite (higher dimensions), Howlite (aids), Kyanite (enhance), Larimar (aids), Lavender-Violet Smithsonite (higher dimensions), Magnesite (aids), Phantom Quartz, Pink Calcite (angelic realms), Prehnite (deepen), Quartz (aid), Selenite (aids), Serpentine (enhance), Silver-Sheen Obsidian (enhance), Smoky Quartz (aids), Snowflake Obsidian (enhance), Tibetan Quartz (ancient wisdom), Turquoise (enhance), Unakite (ground), Violet Purple Fluorite (enhance), Yellow Labradorite (aids)

MELANCHOLY: Chalcedony, Iron Pyrite, Lapis Lazuli, Sapphire, Sardonyx, Tourmaline

MEMORY: Agate (enhance), Amber (improve), Amethyst (improve), Azurite (enhance), Blue Chalcedony (enhance), Calcite (enhance), Emerald (improve), Hematite (enhance), Iron Pyrite (enhance), Moss Agate (improve), Opal (improve), Rhodonite (improve), Unakite (improve)

MENOPAUSE: Cherry Opal, Citrine, Diamond, Garnet, Lapis Lazuli, Lepidolite, Moonstone, Rose Quartz, Ruby

MENSTRUATION: Beryl, Carnelian (excessive bleeding and regulate), Chrysocolla (tension and cramps), Citrine (cramps), Jasper (excessive bleeding), Jet (cramps and disorders),

Labradorite (tension and cramps), Lapis Lazuli (cramps), Magnesite (cramps), Malachite (cramps), Moonstone (regulate and tension), Opal (tension), Red Jasper (bring on and irregular), Rose Quartz (cramps), Serpentine (cramps), Topaz (cramps and disorders), Zircon (balances)

MENTAL CHATTER: Blue Selenite, Rhomboid Calcite

MENTAL IMBALANCE: Amethyst (lighten burdens), Celestite (dysfunction), Emerald, Fluorite (remove influences), Lepidolite (dependency), Malachite, Moonstone, Sapphire, Smithsonite (breakdown), Sunstone (remove influences), Tiger's Eye (burn out and dis-ease)

MERCURY POISONING: Rutilated Quartz, Selenite, Smoky Quartz

METABOLISM: Amazonite (balances), Amber, Amethyst (balances and stimulates), Apatite (speeds up and stimulates), Aventurine (stimulates), Bloodstone (stimulates), Blue Opal (balances), Blue Tiger's Eye (slows down), Carnelian (stimulates), Chrysocolla (balances), Citrine, Diamond (balances), Garnet (stimulates), Herkimer Diamond (balances), Labradorite (regulate), Magnesite (speeds up), Multicoloured Gem Tourmaline (stimulates), Peridot (strengthens), Petrified Wood, Pietersite (balances), Red Tiger's Eye (speeds up), Sapphire, Sodalite (balances), Topaz (stimulates), Watermelon Tourmaline (balances)

MIASMS: Azurite with Malachite, Chrysocolla, Danburite, Jet, Lapis Lazuli, Magnesite, Rhodochrosite, Sugilite

MID-LIFE CRISIS: Rose Quartz

MIGRAINES: Aventurine, Iolite, Jet, Lapis Lazuli, Magnesite, Pink Calcite, Rhodochrosite, Rose Quartz, Sugilite, Topaz

MIND: Agate (enhance powers), Amethyst (calming and focusing), Aquamarine (calm), Azurite (cleanses), Beryl (calm), Black Obsidian (clear patterns/programmes), Bloodstone (enhance powers), Blue Selenite (calm), Brecciated Jasper (enhance powers), Carnelian (calm), Celestite (breakdown and enhance powers), Chrysoprase (disorders and enhance powers), Citrine (enhance powers), Emerald (enhance powers), Fluorite (stop undue influences, focusing and disorders), Green Calcite (enhance powers), Green Fluorite (enhance powers), Green Tourmaline (calm), Howlite (calm), Iron Pyrite (enhance powers), Jade (calming), Kunzite (stop undue influences), Labradorite (calm), Onyx (tonic), Peridot (enhance powers), Pietersite (stop undue influences and clear patterns/ programmes), Rhomboid Calcite (calm), Selenite (stop undue influences), Smithsonite (breakdown), Snowflake Obsidian (clear patterns/ programmes), Sodalite (clear patterns/ programmes and calms), Sunstone (stop undue influences), Tiger's Eye (disorders), Tourmaline (disorders), Yellow Labradorite (enhance powers)

MINERALS: Carnelian (improve absorption), Chalcedony (build up and improve absorption), Garnet (improve absorption), Jasper (balance), Smoky Quartz (improve absorption)

MISTAKES: Peridot (admitting), Snowflake Obsidian (valuing)

MOODSWINGS: Jet, Lepidolite, Turquoise

MOTHER IMAGE PROBLEMS: Moonstone

MOTIVATION: Amethyst, Apatite, Calcite, Carnelian, Citrine, Ruby, Red Tiger's Eye, Topaz

MOUTH: Apatite, Beryl (problems), Clear Quartz (ulcer), Lapis Lazuli (ulcer), Rose Quartz (ulcer), Ruby (ulcer), Sodalite, Tiger's Eye, Tourmaline (ulcer), Yellow Sapphire

MUCUS MEMBRANES: Amber (strengthen), Blue Chalcedony (regeneration), Emerald, Fluorite, Turquoise

MULTIPLE PERSONALITY: Blue Obsidian

MULTIPLE SCLEROSIS: Carnelian, Lapis Lazuli, Red Jasper, Rhodonite, Rose Quartz, Watermelon Tourmaline

MUMPS: Aquamarine, Topaz

MUSCLE SYSTEM: Apache Tear (cramp/ spasm), Amazonite (spasm), Apatite (strengthen and motor responses), Apache Tear (cramps), Aragonite (spasms), Aventurine, Azurite with Malachite (spasm), Black Tourmaline (strengthen and tone), Celestite (relax), Cherry Opal (tension), Chrysocolla (spasm), Citrine, Danburite (strengthen), Electric-Blue Obsidian (spasm), Emerald, Fluorite (strengthen and tone), Green Tourmaline (strained), Hematite, Herkimer Diamond, Kyanite (motor responses), Larimar (relax), Light Green Serpentine (pain), Malachite (torn), Magnesite (relax and spasm), Obsidian, Peridot (strengthen and tone), Red Tourmaline (spasm), Rhodonite, Rhyolite (strengthen), Sapphire, Seraphinite (tension), Smithsonite (relax and flexibility), Sugilite (motor responses), Tiger's Iron (strengthen), Tourmaline (strengthen and tone), Turquoise, Zircon

MUSCULAR DISORDERS: Kyanite, Peridot

NAILS: Blue Lace Agate, Calcite (strengthen), Fluorite (strengthen), Rhodochrosite (strengthen)

NARROW MINDEDNESS: Chrysanthemum Stone, Fluorite

NASAL PASSAGES: Larimar, Turquoise

NAUSEA: Blue Sapphire, Brown Agate, Emerald, Jasper, Red Aventurine

NECK: Aquamarine, Blue Lace Agate, Hawk's Eye (stiff), Hematite (tension), Larimar, Quartz, Rose Quartz (tension), Seraphinite (tension), Siberian Blue Quartz (stiff)

NEGATIVITY: Amazonite (clear), Amber (clear and transmute), Amethyst (clear), Apache Tear (transmute), Apatite (clears), Aventurine (clears and protect from psychic vampirism), Black Obsidian (repel), Black Sardonyx (absorbs), Black Tourmaline (psychic attack), Blue Sapphire (transmute), Calcite (clears), Carnelian (clear), Chalcedony (absorbs), Charoite (transmute), Chiastolite (clear thoughts), Chrysocolla (clears), Citrine (absorbs, transmutes and clears), Emerald (clears), Green Calcite (absorbs), Green Fluorite (absorbs), Green Quartz (transmute), Hematite (clears), Jade (clear thoughts), Jasper (absorbs), Jet (clears), Lapis Lazuli (clear and clear thoughts), Lavender-Violet Smithsonite (clears), Lepidolite (clears), Malachite (absorbs), Natural Rainbow Quartz (draws off), Obsidian (absorbs), Rose Quartz (clears), Ruby (transmute), Rutilated Quartz (draws off), Smoky Quartz (clear and neutralise), Snowflake Obsidian (clear), Sugilite (draws off), Topaz (clear), Tourmaline (clears), Turquoise (clears)

NEPHRITIS: Jade, Tourmaline

NERVES AND NERVOUS SYSTEM: Amber, Amethyst, Amazonite (calming), Ametrine (autonomic system), Aragonite (involuntary movements), Aventurine, Black Tourmaline, Blue Calcite (calming), Blue Lace Agate, Charoite (autonomic system), Chiastolite (nerve damage and strengthen), Chrysoprase (disorders), Citrine (strengthen),

Dendritic Agate, Emerald (tension), Fire Agate, Fishtail Selenite (nerve damage), Fluorite (pain relief), Golden Topaz (nervous exhaustion), Green Jade (calms), Green Tourmaline, Jade (strengthen), Kunzite (nerve damage and disorders), Lapis Lazuli, Malachite, Opal, Pink Calcite (disorders), Pink Tourmaline, Rose Quartz, Sapphire (disorders), Smoky Quartz (strengthen), Sugilite (align), Sunstone (autonomic system), Tanzanite, Thulite (nervous exhaustion), Topaz (strengthen), Variscite, Watermelon Tourmaline (regenerate)

NERVOUSNESS: Fishtail Selenite, Lapis Lazuli, Magnesite, Rhodochrosite, Sapphire, Smoky Quartz, Topaz, Variscite

NERVOUS TIC: Green Aventurine

NEURALGIA: Amber, Amethyst, **Cathedral Quartz**, Carnelian, Dendritic Agate, Hematite, Kunzite, Lapis Lazuli, Lavender-Violet Smithsonite, Lepidolite, Rose Quartz

NEURITIS: Tourmaline

NEUROSES: Green Aventurine

NEUROTIC PATTERNS: Chrysoprase, Sapphire

NIGHT SWEATS: Blue Tourmaline

NIGHT VISION (AID): Tiger's Eye

NIGHTMARES: Amethyst, Celestite, Chrysoprase, Garnet, Hematite, Jet, Pink Calcite (prevents), Prehnite, Ruby, Smoky Quartz, Turquoise

NOSE BLEEDS: **Carnelian, Ruby,** Sapphire, Topaz

NOSE PROBLEMS: Blue Fluorite, Jet (blocked nostrils)

NURTURING STONES: Blue Lace Agate, Chalcedony, Green Tourmaline, Jade, **Jasper**, Lavender-Pink Smithsonite, Rhodonite, Selenite, Sunstone

NUTRIENT ABSORPTION PROBLEMS: Carnelian, Fluorite, Golden Topaz, Hematite, Moonstone, Peridot, Petrified Wood, Pietersite, Sardonyx, Serpentine, Turquoise, Yellow Smithsonite

OBESITY: Black Onyx, Diamond, Moonstone, Tourmaline, Zircon

OBSESSION: Blue Agate, Black Onyx, Bloodstone, Charoite, Green Jasper, Peridot, Red Tourmaline

OBSESSIVE THOUGHTS: Lepidolite, Purple Tourmaline

OBSTACLES (REMOVE): Amber, Kunzite, White Sapphire

OEDEMA: Carnelian

OESOPHAGUS: Blue Tourmaline

OPTIC NERVE: Malachite

OPTIMISM: Amber, Ametrine, Beryl, Blue Chalcedony, Citrine, Golden Topaz, Moss Agate, Sunstone

OSTEOPOROSIS: Amazonite, Larimar, Smithsonite

OVARIES: Amber, Bloodstone, Carnelian, Chrysoprase, Gold Calcite, Peach Aventurine, Rose Quartz, Ruby in Zoisite, Topaz

OVERACTIVE: Amethyst, Garnet

OVEREATING: Hematite

OVERINDULGENCE: Amethyst, Hematite

OVERREACTING: Moonstone

OVERSENSITIVE: Rose Quartz, Sodalite

OVERSTIMULATION: Beryl

OVERTHINKING: Beryl, Blue Selenite, Rhomboid Calcite, Yellow Labradorite

OVERWHELM: Blue-Green Jade

OXYGENATORS: Botswana Agate, Ametrine, Iron Pyrite, Pink Beryl

PAIN RELIEF: Amber (chest), Amethyst, Aragonite, Black Tourmaline, Blue Calcite (dissolves), **Cathedral Quartz**, Celestite (dissolves), Dendritic Agate, Diamond (emotional), Fluorite, Hematite, Lapis Lazuli, Larimar, Light Green Serpentine, Mahogany Obsidian, Malachite, Obsidian, Peridot (childbirth), Quartz, Rose Quartz (chest), Sapphire, Seraphinite, Smoky Quartz, Sugilite, Turquoise

PANCREAS: Agate (cleanse), Amber, Amethyst, Apatite, Bloodstone, Blue Lace Agate, Carnelian, Charoite, Chrysocolla (regulates insulin), Citrine, Emerald, Green Calcite, Jasper, Malachite, Moonstone, Moss Agate, Peridot, Pink Tourmaline, Red Tourmaline Smoky Quartz, Topaz

PANIC ATTACKS: Blue-Green Smithsonite, Green Tourmaline, Kunzite, Sodalite (calms), Turquoise

PARALYSIS: Amethyst, Chiastolite, Emerald with Blue Sapphire, Watermelon Tourmaline

PARANOIA: Rhodochrosite, Sugilite, Tourmaline

PARASITES: Amethyst, Ruby Aura Quartz , Rutilated Quartz, Serpentine

PARATHYROID: Kyanite, Malachite

PARKINSONS DISEASE: Celestite, Opal, Rose Quartz

PAST LIVES: Amber (accessing), Apatite (accessing), Aragonite (accessing), Black Tourmaline (deflect effects of), Blue Lace Agate (rejection), Blue Opal (healing), Brown Jasper (accessing), Carnelian (accessing), Cathedral Quartz (access Akashic records), Charoite (accessing, healing, wound imprints and emotional pain), Danburite (cleansing and healing), Electric-Blue Obsidian (accessing), Fire Opal (unhealed grief), Garnet (accessing), Green Aventurine (regression), Green Obsidian (tie cutting), Hawk's Eye (sourcing problems), Herkimer Diamond (accessing, sourcing problems and injuries), Howlite (accessing and healing), Iolite (causes of addiction), Kunzite (releasing ties and entity attachment), Labradorite (healing), Larimar (entity attachment and relationships), Laser Quartz (entity attachment), Lavender-Violet Smithsonite (death trauma and healing), Lepidolite (blockages), Light Green Serpentine (healing), Lithium Quartz (healing and relationships), Malachite (sexual trauma and tie cutting), Moldavite (accessing), Obsidian (healing), Onyx (injuries), Opal (accessing), Petrified Wood, Peridot (learn from and phobias), Phantom Quartz (accessing), Picture Jasper (releasing ties), Pietersite (healing and releasing ties), Pink Tourmaline (abandonment), Prehnite (deprivation trauma and access Akashic records), Quartz (releasing ties), Rainbow Obsidian (tie cutting), Rhodochrosite (heart pain), Rhodonite (betrayal, resentment, healing, trauma, heart pain and abandonment), Rhyolite (healing), Rose Quartz (broken heart), Ruby in Zoisite (healing), Rutilated Quartz (healing), Sceptre Quartz (wound imprints), Selenite (entity attachment and wound imprints), Serpentine (accessing), Smoky Amethyst (entity attachment), Smoky Quartz (wound imprints), Spirit Quartz (family patterns and unhealed grief), Sugilite (sourcing problems), Sunstone (tie cutting), Tangerine Quartz (healing), Tanzanite (access Akashic records), Tibetan Turquoise (blockages), Turquoise (releasing vows), Tiger's Eye (break curse), Unakite (sourcing problems), Variscite (accessing and sourcing problems)

PATIENCE: Amber, Danburite, Emerald, Green Tourmaline, Howlite, Orbicular Jasper, Silver-Sheen Obsidian, Watermelon Tourmaline

PEACE (INNER): Amber, Aqua Aura, Blue/Blue-Green Jade, Danburite, Hematite, Kunzite, Lapis Lazuli, Larimar, Magnesite, Malachite with Chrysocolla, Prehnite, Rose Quartz, Sapphire, Selenite

PERCEPTION (ENHANCE): Agate, Ametrine, Angelite, Aquamarine, Aventurine, Carnelian, Charoite, Sardonyx, Sodalite, Tiger's Eye, Variscite

PERIOD PAINS: Serpentine

PERSEVERANCE: Dendritic Agate, Aventurine, Jasper, Silver-Sheen Obsidian

PERSONAL POWER: Carnelian

PESSIMISM: Hawk's Eye, Sunstone

PHOBIAS: Aquamarine, Azurite, Blue Tiger's Eye, Chrysocolla, Citrine, Obsidian, Opal, Prehnite, Rutilated Quartz, Sodalite

PINEAL GLAND: Amethyst, Malachite, Moonstone, Opal, Pietersite (stimulate), Purple Tourmaline (stimulate), Quartz, Rhodonite (activate), Ruby (stimulate), Sodalite (stimulate), Yellow Labradorite

PITUITARY GLAND: Aquamarine, Garnet, Iolite, Pietersite, Opal, Sapphire

PLUTONIUM POISONING: Malachite

PMS: Chrysocolla, Labradorite, Moonstone, Opal

PNEUMONIA: Diamond, Fluorite

POISON (ANTIDOTE): Amethyst, Bloodstone, Blue Lace Agate, Diamond, Emerald, Sapphire, Stillbite, Zircon

POLLEN ALLERGIES: Carnelian

POLLUTION: Aquamarine (protection from), Aventurine (environmental), Beryl (protection from), Jasper (environmental), Malachite (absorb), Moss Agate (sensitivity to), Obsidian (environmental), Purple-Violet Tourmaline (sensitivity to), Turquoise (environmental and protection from), Yellow Kunzite (environmental)

POLTERGEISTS: Chrysocolla

POSITIVITY: Black Tourmaline, Carnelian, Emerald, Howlite, Iron Pyrite, Magnesite, Opal, Rhodochrosite, Ruby, Smoky Quartz, Spinel, Sugilite, Sunstone, Tourmalined Quartz

POST-NATAL DEPRESION: Rose Quartz

POTENTIAL: Aqua Aura (fulfilling), Beryl (fulfilling), Herkimer Diamond (fulfilling), Iron Pyrite (tap into), Moldavite (accessing), Opal (understand), Orange Calcite (maximise), Rhodonite (fulfilling), Rhyolite (fulfilling), White Sapphire (accessing)

PREGNANCY: Azurite (support during), Hematite (fatigue), Jasper (support during), Lapis Lazuli, Moonstone, Moss Agate (birthing stone), Peridot (support during), Unakite

PROLONGED ILLNESS: Jade

PROSTATE: Chrysoprase, Obsidian

PROTECTION: Amber, Amethyst, Angelite, Beryl, Black Tourmaline, Bloodstone, Carnelian, Chiastolite, Emerald (against enchantment), Fire Agate, Fire Opal (against danger), Fluorite (psychic), Iron Pyrite, Jade, Jasper, Jet, Kunzite, Labradorite, Malachite, Obsidian, Prehnite, Sardonyx (against crime), Selenite (for the home), Smoky Quartz, Tiger's Eye, Tourmaline, Turquoise

PSYCHIC ABILITIES: Apatite (developing), Azurite (developing), Blue Tourmaline (enhance), Calcite, Emerald (enhance), Herkimer Diamond (stimulating), Hawk's Eye (enhance), Jet (opening), Kyanite (stimulating), Labradorite (stimulating), Lapis Lazuli (enhance), Moonstone (accepting and enhance), Quartz (enhance), Serpentine (opening), Smithsonite (enhance), Tiger's Eye (enhance), Violet Purple Fluorite (enhance)

PSYHIC ATTACK: Amethyst (protection), Ametrine (neutralise and protection), Apache Tear, Aqua Aura, Black Tourmaline (protection), Labradorite, Lapis Lazuli (return to source), Moss Agate, Ruby (protection), Rutilated Quartz (protection), Selenite, Tourmaline (neutralise)

PSYCHIC SURGERY: Tektite

PSYCHIC VAMPIRISM: Aventurine

PSYCHIC VISION: Chrysocolla (open), Green Sapphire, Malachite, Opal, Siberian Blue Quartz (stimulate), Unakite (open and enhance)

PSYCHOMETRY: Onyx

PSYCHO-SEXUAL PROBLEMS: Malachite

PSYCHOSOMATIC DIS-EASE: Amethyst, Aventurine, Azurite, Garnet, Hawk's Eye, Iron Pyrite, Kunzite, Malachite (understanding cause), Sugilite (understand cause of), Pink Chalcedony

PUBLIC SPEAKING: Apatite, Blue Kyanite, Turquoise

PURIFIERS: Clear Sardonyx, Clear Topaz (emotions), Garnet, Peridot (subtle and physical body), Snowflake Obsidian, Turquoise (negative energy)

PUS: Bloodstone

QI (LIFE FORCE): Aqua Aura, Kyanite

QUINSY: Amber, Topaz

RADIATION: Black Tourmaline (counteract), Emerald, Herkimer Diamond, Jasper (counteract), **Malachite** (counteract and protection), Quartz (protection), Smoky Quartz (counteract and sickness), Sodalite (counteract), Turquoise, Yellow Kyanite (counteract)

RAGE: Amethyst, Carnelian, Howlite

RASHES: Rhyolite

RATIONAL THOUGHT: Black Tourmaline, Sodalite

RE-BIRTHING: Angelite, Carnelian, Chiastolite, Malachite Red Jasper, Smithsonite, Unakite

RECOVERY (TO AID): Ruby in Zoisite

RECUPERATION: Peridot

RED BLOOD CELLS: Red Stones, Amethyst, Hematite, Tiger's Iron

REIKI: Blue-Green Obsidian

REJECTION: Rose Quartz (ease pain)

REJUVENATION: Spinel

RELATIONSHIPS: Celestite (enhance), Chrysocolla (enhance), Diamond (enhance), Emerald (balancing), Fluorite (balancing), Green Jade (difficult), Green Opal (enhance), Iolite (difficult), Lapis Lazuli (enhance), Magnesite (difficult), Peridot (difficult), Rhodochrosite (enhance), Rose Quartz (restoring trust), Smithsonite (difficult), Sunstone (possessiveness)

RELAXATION: Amethyst, Aventurine, Blue Calcite, Fire Agate, Gold Calcite, Jasper, Magnesite, Peridot, Pink Tourmaline, Rhodonite, Smoky Quartz, Topaz

RELIABILITY: Hematite

REPRESSION: Blue Lace Agate (counteracts), Botswana Agate (release), Fluorite (process), Lapis Lazuli (release), Picture Jasper (process), Pietersite (process), Rhodochrosite (process), Rose Quartz (release), Sunstone (process)

REPRODUCTIVE SYSTEM: Red and Orange Stones, Carnelian, Dendritic Chalcedony (female), Jasper, Malachite (female), Moonstone, Orange Calcite, Red Tourmaline, Rhodochrosite, Rose Quartz, Ruby (stimulate), Smoky Quartz, Tiger's Eye, Unakite, Variscite (male)

RESENTMENT: Carnelian, Chrysanthemum Stone, Peridot, Rainbow Aura Quartz, Rhodonite

RESISTANCE: Celestite (healing), Charoite (clear), Kunzite (clear), Lepidolite (change), Orange Calcite (clear), Pink Beryl (to healing), Pink Topaz (clear)

RESPIRATORY SYSTEM: Amethyst, Candle Quartz, Iolite, Iron Pyrite, Lapis Lazuli, Pietersite (problems), Rhodochrosite (problems), Rutilated Quartz

RESPONSIBILITY: Aquamarine (overwhelming), Blue Tourmaline (taking), Citrine (fear of), Iolite (of self), Malachite (of self), Orbicular Jasper (accept), Peridot (of self), Royal Sapphire (of self), Snow Quartz (overwhelming)

REYNAUDS DISEASE: Hematite

RHEUMATISM: Agate, Amber, Azurite, Carnelian, Chiastolite, Chrysocolla, Emerald, Fluorite, Hematite, Labradorite, Malachite, Petrified Wood, Sunstone, Turquoise, Variscite

RICKETS: Apatite, Calcite, Rutilated Quartz

RINGWORM: Calcite, Diamond, Zircon

RISK-TAKING: Malachite

RNA (STABILISE): Ametrine, Azurite with Malachite and Chrysocolla

SADNESS: Azurite, Red Jasper, Ruby, Sodalite

SCARRING: Blue Tourmaline, Rhodonite, Rose Quartz

SCHIZOPHRENIA: Blue Obsidian, Emerald, Lepidolite, Ruby, Sugilite, Tiger's Eye

SCIATICA: Citrine, Hematite, Kunzite, Lepidolite, Rose Quartz, Sapphire, Tourmaline, Zircon

SCROFULA: Sapphire

SEASONAL AFFECTIVE DISORDER (SAD): Yellow Stones, Sunstone, Topaz

SECURITY: Agate (emotional), Chrysoprase, Fire Agate (emotional), Moldavite (letting go of), Smithsonite (rebuilding), Watermelon Tourmaline (emotional), Yellow Tourmaline (emotional)

SELF-ACCEPTANCE: Agate, Chrysoprase, Pink Calcite, Rhyolite, Sodalite

SELF-ANALYSIS: Agate

SELF-AWARENESS: Chrysocolla, Dendritic Chalcedony, Lapis Lazuli

SEL-BELIEF: Labradorite

SELF-CONFIDENCE: Citrine, Moss Agate, Onyx, Rose Quartz

SELF-CONTAINMENT: Kunzite

SELF-CONTROL: Black Obsidian, Onyx, Sardonyx, Topaz

SELF-CRITICISM: Tiger's Eye

SELF-DECEIT: Magnesite

SELF-DESTRUCTIVENESS: Rhodonite

SELF-DOUBT: Chalcedony

SELF-ESTEEM: Amethyst, Beryl, Citrine, Garnet, Hematite, Iron Pyrite, Moss Agate, Opal, Pink Calcite, Rhodochrosite, Rhodonite, Rose Aura Quartz, **Rose Quartz,** Rhyolite, Sodalite, Sunstone, Tiger's Eye

SELF-EXPLORATION: Rhyolite

SELF-EXPRESSION: Amber, Apatite, Aqua Aura, Aquamarine, Azurite with Chrysocolla, Blue Lace Agate, Blue Tourmaline, Citrine, Emerald, Iolite, Kunzite, Kyanite, Lapis Lazuli, Malachite, Moss Agate, Opal, Sapphire, Sodalite, Watermelon Tourmaline, Variscite

SELF-HATRED (OVERCOMING): Rutilated Quartz

SELF-HEALING: Amber, Beryl, Larimar, Malachite, Peridot, Seraphinite, Sunstone, Tourmaline with Lepidolite

SELF-KNOWLEDGE: Jade, Lapis Lazuli, Obsidian, Opal

SELF-LIMITATION: Apache Tear, Hematite

SELF-LOVE: Magnesite, Rhodonite, Rose Quartz, Pink Tourmaline

SELF-REALISATION: Chlorite Phantom Quartz, Topaz, Turquoise

SELF-RIGHTEOUSNESS: Chrysanthemum Stone

SELF-SABOTAGE: Larimar, Tourmalined Quartz, Turquoise

SELF-SUFFICIENCY: Jade

SELF-TRUST: Kunzite, Rose Quartz

SELF-WORTH: Larimar, Pink Calcite

SELFISHNESS: Howlite

SELFLESSNESS: Bloodstone

SENILE DEMENTIA: Chalcedony, Rose Quartz

SENSITIVITY: Aquamarine (increase), Aragonite (reduce), Blue Lace Agate (in men), Chrysocolla (increase), Citrine (reduce), Moldavite (reduce), Rose Quartz, Selenite (to light), Sodalite (reduce), Sugilite (to Earth vibrations)

SEPTICEMIA: Quartz

SEXUAL: Bloodstone, Blue Spinel (decrease libido), Blue Tiger's Eye (decrease libido), Brown Opal (tension), Carnelian (frigidity and impotence), Chrysoprase (sexually transmitted diseases), Fire Agate (enhance), Fluorite (increase libido), Garnet (balance sex drive and impotence), Jasper (prolong pleasure), Malachite (sexually transmitted diseases), Pietersite (balance sex hormones), Pink Agate (healing abuse), Pink Carnelian (healing abuse), Pink Beryl (impotence), Red Tiger's Eye (increase libido), Rhodochrosite (healing abuse), Rose Quartz, Ruby (enhance and impotence), Ruby Aura Quartz (healing abuse), Rutilated Quartz (impotence), Smoky Quartz (impotence), Tourmaline (increase libido), Variscite (impotence)

SHADOW SIDE: Obsidian, Rutilated Quartz, Sodalite, Tourmalined Quartz

SHINGLES: Blue Lace Agate, Chrysoprase, Fluorite, Jade, Lapis Lazuli, Moonstone, Rose Quartz

SHOCK: Lapis Lazuli, Obsidian, Rose Quartz, Rhodonite, Sugilite, Tangerine Quartz

SHOULDERS: Beryl, Blue Lace Agate, Hawk's Eye, Larimar, Prehnite, Selenite

SHYNESS: Hematite, Malachite, Tiger's Eye

SICK BUILDING SYNDROME: Lepidolite, Sodalite, Smoky Quartz

SIGHING (EXCESSIVELY): Aquamarine, Emerald

SIGHT: Aquamarine, Emerald

SINUSES: Azurite, Blue Lace Agate, Black Onyx, Emerald (sinusitis), Fluorite (sinusitis), Jet (sinusitis), Sodalite, Smithsonite (sinusitis)

SKELETAL SYSTEM: Amazonite, Apatite, Azurite, Blue Lace Agate (strengthen), Calcite (strengthen), Chrysanthemum Stone, Chrysocolla, Dendritic Agate, Fluorite (strengthen), Garnet, Green Selenite (help overcome effects of aging), Iron Pyrite, Jade, Lapis Lazuli (strengthen), Petrified Wood (alignment), Purple Fluorite (strengthen), Sardonyx, Snowflake Obsidian, Topaz (support in youngsters)

SKIN: Agate (disorders), Amethyst (disorders), Angelite (repair), Aventurine (eruptions), Azurite, Brown Jasper (disorders), Brown Tourmaline (disorders), Calcite (disorders), Carnelian, Chrysanthemum Stone, Chrysoprase (disorders), Emerald (cancer), Fluorite (disorders, removes wrinkles and regenerates), Garnet, Green Aventurine (disorders), Green Jasper (disorders), Hematite, Lepidolite (detoxify), Moonstone (disorders), Moss Agate (infections), Peridot, Pink Tourmaline, Rhodochrosite (disorders), Rhyolite (disorders), Rose Quartz (disorders and smoothing), Rutilated Quartz (repair), Selenite (help overcome effects of aging), Snowflake Obsidian (disorders), Unakite, Variscite (repair), Yellow Smithsonite (disorders), Zircon (disorders)

SLEEP WALKING: Moonstone, Topaz

SLEEP SICKNESS: Amethyst

SLUGGISHNESS: Red Stones, Amethyst, Carnelian, Ruby

SMELL (RESTORE SENSE OF): Red Jasper, Sardonyx, Tiger's Eye, Tourmaline

SMOKING: Blue Chalcedony (clear lungs), Botswana Agate (quitting), Brown Jasper (quitting), Hematite (quitting), Peridot

SNAKE BITE: Emerald, Jasper

SNEEZING: Zircon

SOOTHING STONES: Agate, Amazonite, Fluorite, Jade, Snowflake Obsidian, Topaz

SORE THROAT: **Blue Lace Agate** (soothe). Aquamarine, Blue Tourmaline (chronic), Blue Jasper, Larimar (soothe), Pink Opal (soothe), Sunstone (chronic)

SORES: Amethyst, Carnelian, Chalcedony, Green Aventurine, Lapis Lazuli, Quartz, Ruby

SORROW: Apatite, Sugilite

SOUL: Aqua Aura (activates, Black Calcite (dark night of), Black Obsidian (growth), Charoite (overcome fear in), Chiastolite (soul's purpose), Clear Calcite (healing), Clear Kunzite (retrieval), Danburite (growth), Diamond (aspirations of), Herkimer Diamond (soul's purpose), Larimar (growth), Lavender Jade (healing), Lavender-Violet Smithsonite (healing and retrieval), Moss Agate (energise), Obsidian (healing), Pink Beryl (aspirations of), Quartz (cleanse), Ruby in Zoisite (growth and healing), Rutilated Quartz (growth), Selenite (retrieval), Tangerine Quartz (retrieval)

SOULMATE (ATTRACTING): Larimar, Rhodochrosite, Soulmate Quartz

SPASMS: Amethyst, Amazonite, Apache Tear, Aragonite, Azurite, Carnelian, Chrysocolla, Electric-Blue Obsidian, Magnesite, Red Tourmaline, Ruby

SPEECH: Aventurine (defects), Blue Agate, Blue Apatite (public speaking), Blue Chalcedony (fluent), Blue Kyanite (public speaking), Blue Obsidian (defects), Blue Topaz, Blue Tourmaline (defects), Chrysoprase (fluent), Dark Blue Tourmaline (impediments), Emerald (fluent), Lapis Lazuli (fluent), Rhodonite, Turquoise (public speaking)

SPINE: Aragonite (disc elasticity), Azurite (aligning), Beryl, Cherry Opal (injuries), Electric-Blue Obsidian (aligning and impacted vertebrae), Emerald (injuries), Fire Opal (blocked energy), Fluorite (injuries), Garnet (disorders and strengthen base of), Hematite (aligning), Labradorite (aligning), Orange Carnelian (strengthen base of), Red Spinel (blocked energy), Tiger's Eye (aligning), Tourmaline (aligning), Selenite (aligning, inflexible and injuries)

SPIRITUAL VISION: Azurite (unblock), Charoite, Emerald, Herkimer Diamond, Pietersite, Purple Sapphire, Topaz

SPITE: Peridot

SPLEEN: Amber, Apatite, Aquamarine, Azurite, Bloodstone (detoxify), Calcite, Chalcedony, Citrine, Fluorite, Green Aventurine (protection), Green Obsidian, Honey Calcite (poor functioning), Jade, Malachite, Mookaite (poor functioning), Moonstone, Moss Agate, Peridot, Pink Tourmaline (detoxify), Red Jasper (deterioration), Red Obsidian, Red Tourmaline (stimulate), Ruby (stimulate), Sunstone, Yellow Jasper (deterioration), Yellow Labradorite, Yellow Tourmaline, Zircon

SPONDULYTIS: Labradorite

SPONTANEITY: Apache Tear, Opal, Rhodochrosite

STABILISING: Black Obsidian, Blue Jasper (aura), Brecciated Jasper (emotions), Calcite (emotional), Charoite (emotions), Chiastolite (emotions), Chrysanthemum Stone (emotions), Chrysocolla (domestic), Fishtail Selenite (emotions), Fluorite (emotions), Jade (personality), Jet (emotions), Kyanite (bio-magnetic field), Lepidolite (emotions), Mahogany Obsidian, Onyx, Opal (emotions), Royal Plume Jasper (emotions and mental), Selenite (emotions), Topaz (emotions), Turquoise (emotions), Yellow Fluorite (group energy)

STAGNANT ENERGY: Calcite, Clear Topaz, Quartz, Smoky Quartz, Yellow Apatite

STAMINA: Agate, Amethyst, Black Spinel, Carnelian, Dalmatian Jasper, Fire Agate, Onyx, Red Tourmaline, Sardonyx

STAMMERING: Green Aventurine

STATIC ELECTRICITY: Quartz

STEADFASTNESS: Carnelian, Onyx

STEROIDS (NATURAL BOOST): Tiger's Iron

STIFF NECK: Hawk's Eye, Siberian Blue Quartz

STIMULATING: Carnelian, Jasper, Tiger's Eye

STITCHES (HEAL): Jade

STOMACH-ABDOMEN: Agate (ulcers), Amber, Amethyst, Aquamarine (upset), Beryl, Bloodstone (upset), Carnelian, Chrysocolla, Chrysoprase (stress), Emerald (swollen and upset), Fire Agate, Green Fluorite (disorders), Iron Pyrite (night time problems), Jade, Jasper (strengthen), Jet (pains), Lapis

Lazuli (pains), Magnesite (cramps), Malachite, Mookaite, Moonstone (ulcers), Opal, Peridot (acidity), Pink Beryl (upset), Quartz (ulcers), Rhodonite (ulcers), Sapphire, Serpentine, Siberian Blue Quartz (ulcers), Snowflake Obsidian, Sunstone (ulcers), Tiger's Eye (ulcers), Turquoise, Yellow Jasper, Yellow Labradorite, Yellow Tourmaline

STRENGTHENERS: Aragonite (immune system), Chrysocolla (inner), Mahogany Obsidian (weak aura), Onyx (strength), Peridot (body), Pietersite, Red Spinel (strength), Rhyolite, Ruby (strength), Sardonyx (strength), Thulite, Turquoise (meridians)

STREPTOCAL INFECTIONS: Amber, Fluorite

STRESS: Amber (relieve), Ametrine (mental and dis-ease caused), **Amethyst** (relief, emotional, physical), **Aquamarine** (reduce and mental), **Aragonite** (emotional), Azurite (releasing and emotional), Beryl (relieve), Black Tourmaline (releasing), Blue Lace Agate (mental), **Charoite** (reduce), Fluorite (reduce), **Green Aventurine,** Herkimer Diamond (physical), Jasper (supports during), Kunzite (emotional), Kyanite (releasing), Labradorite, Lapis Lazuli (releasing), Larimar (supports during), Lepidolite (emotional and reduce), Magnesite (emotional), Moonstone (reduce), Moss Agate (reduce), Obsidian (mental), Onyx (supports during, mental and physical), Peridot (reduce), Rainbow Obsidian (physical), Rhodochrosite (reduce), Rhodonite, Rose Quartz, Siberian Quartz, Smithsonite (releasing), Smoky Quartz (releasing and supports during), Watermelon Tourmaline (reduce)

SUBCONSCIOUS: Black Obsidian (revealing), Chrysocolla (blocks), Labradorite (understanding), Magnesite (recognising), Malachite (accessing and blocks), Moonstone (revealing), Selenite (understanding)

SUICIDAL THOUGHTS: Amber, Lapis Lazuli, Smoky Quartz

SUNBURN: Angelite, Larimar, Rose Quartz, Siberian Blue Quartz

SUPPORATING WOUNDS: Calcite

SUPRA-ADRENALS: Jade

SURVIVAL INSTINCTS: Hematite, Ruby Aura Quartz

SWELLING: Amethyst, Aquamarine (glands), Blue Chalcedony, Jet (feet, glands and lymphatic), Malachite (joints), Rhodonite (joints)

TACHYCARDIA: Garnet

TACT: Iron Pyrite, Red Tourmaline, Smithsonite, Snow Quartz

TALENTS (REALSING): Chrysoprase, Golden Topaz, Tiger's Eye, Tiger's Iron

TASTE (RESTORE): Stillbite, Topaz, Tourmaline

TEETH: Amazonite (decay), Amber (teething pain), Amethyst, Apatite, Aquamarine, Azurite with Malachite, Calcite (strengthen), Fluorite, Howlite (calcium levels), Jet (loose), Magnesite, Malachite, Onyx (enamel deficiency), Rutilated Quartz, Selenite (counteract mercury poisoning), Topaz, Tourmaline

TEETHING PAIN: Amber, Cathedral Quartz

TELEPATHY: Angelite (enhance and stimulate), Chalcedony (enhance), Electric-Blue Obsidian (enhance), Herkimer Diamond (enhance and stimulate), Selenite (enhance), Siberian Blue Quartz (stimulate), Tektite (enhance)

TEMPER: Blue Tiger's Eye, Rose Quartz

TEMPERATURE: Blue Chalcedony (lowers), Magnesite (regulates), Pietersite (regulates)

TENACITY: Moss Agate

TENDONITIS: Lepidolite

TENSION (RELEASE): Carnelian, Herkimer Diamond, Kunzite, Red Jade, Rose Quartz

TESTICLES: Amber, Carnelian, Chrysoprase, Citrine, Gold Calcite, Peach Aventurine, Rose Quartz, Topaz, Variscite

TESTS (TAKING): Gold Tiger's Eye

THROAT: **Amber** (infected and relaxed), Angelite (inflammation), Apatite, Aquamarine (inflammation), Azurite, Beryl (inflammation), Blue Fluorite (problems), Blue Jasper, **Blue Lace Agate**, Blue Tourmaline, Celestite, Chrysocolla (ulcerated), Hematite, Kyanite, Lapis Lazuli, Larimar, Malachite, Siberian Blue Quartz (inflammation), Tanzanite, Tiger's Eye, Turquoise

THROMBOSIS: Magnesite

THRUSH (CANDIDA): Chrysocolla, Dendritic Chalcedony

THYROID: Amber, Angelite (balance), Aqua Aura, Aquamarine (balance), Azurite, Beryl, Blue Lace Agate (deficiencies), Blue Tourmaline, Candle Quartz, Celestite, Citrine (balance), Harlequin Quartz (deficiencies and strengthens), Kyanite (deficiencies), Lapis Lazuli (regulate and deficiencies), Rhodochrosite (balances), Rhodonite (regulate and stimulate), Rutilated Quartz (balance and stimulate), Sapphire, Sodalite, Turquoise

TICS: Azurite

TIMIDITY: Hematite

TINNITUS: Celestite

TIREDNESS: Amethyst, Carnelian, Fire Agate, Rose Quartz

TISSUE: Amber (revitalise and repair), Angelite (repair), Aventurine (regenerating), Calcite (regenerating), Cherry Opal (regenerating), Hematite (regenerating), Howlite (balance calcium levels), Lepidolite (connective), Peridot (regenerating), Prehnite (connective), Rhyolite (hardened), Rutilated Quartz (repair and torn), Turquoise (regenerating)

TOENAILS: Blue Lace Agate, Moss Agate (fungal infection)

TOES: Aragonite

TOLERANCE: Aquamarine, Aragonite, Dendritic Chalcedony, Kunzite, Tourmaline

TONIC: Peridot

TONSILITIS: Amber, Blue Lace Agate, Sodalite, Tourmaline

TONSILS: Chrysocolla (inflamed)

TOOTHEACHE: **Amber**, Aquamarine, Jet, Lapis Lazuli, Malachite

TOXICITY: Green Jasper, Rutilated Quartz, Smoky Quartz, Sunshine Aura Quartz

TOXINS: Ametrine (remove), Beryl (strengthen resistance to), Celestite (remove), Chrysanthemum Stone (clear environment), Iolite (remove), Iron Pyrite (ingested), Moss Agate (remove), Serpentine (remove), Yellow Apatite (remove)

TRANCE STATES: Channelling Quartz, Electric-Blue Obsidian, Yellow Labradorite

TRANQUILLITY: Pink and Green Stones, Amethyst, Blue Sapphire, Chrysocolla, Emerald, Jade, Jasper, Kyanite, Smithsonite

TRANQUILLISER: Amethyst

TRANSFORMATIONAL STONES: Ametrine, Bloodstone, Charoite, Herkimer Diamond, Labradorite, Malachite, Opal

TRANSITIONAL STONES: Chiastolite, Danburite, Kyanite, Lepidolite, Lilac Kunzite, Moldavite, Water Opal

TRAUMA: Agate (emotional), Amazonite (emotional), Chiastolite (emotional), Lavender Jade Malachite (past life), Moldavite (emotional), Moss Agate, Obsidian (emotional and past life), Pink Calcite, Rhodonite, Rose Quartz, Sunshine Aura Quartz (emotional), Tangerine Quartz

TRAPPED NERVE: Kunzite

TRUST: Amber, Chrysanthemum Stone, Chrysoprase, Green Sapphire, Labradorite, Lavender-Pink Smithsonite, Pink Chalcedony, Prehnite, Sodalite, Variscite

TRUTH: Angelite (speaking), Apatite (promoting), Blue-Green Obsidian (speaking), Blue Lace Agate (spiritual), Celestite (revealing), Chrysocolla (promoting), Chrysoprase (promoting), Emerald (promoting), Fluorite (revealing), Kyanite (promoting and speaking), Lapis Lazuli (confronting and revealing), Peridot (spiritual), Obsidian (promoting and revealing), Pietersite (personal and recognising), Rhodochrosite (confronting), Sapphire (personal), Siberian Blue Quartz (speaking), Sodalite (personal), Topaz (personal and promoting)

TUBERCULOSIS: Amber, Blue Sapphire, Emerald, Pink Beryl, Topaz

TUMOURS: Amethyst, Bloodstone, Chrysanthemum Stone, Electric-Blue Obsidian, Fluorite, Jet, Malachite, Rose Quartz, Sapphire, Sardonyx

ULCERS: Agate (gastric), Ametrine (intestinal), Bloodstone (varicose), Blue Lace Agate (varicose, skin and stomach), Calcite (skin), Chrysocolla (throat), Emerald (skin and stomach), Fluorite, Green Aventurine, Moonstone, Peridot (stomach), Rhodonite (stomach), Ruby (varicose, mouth and skin), Sapphire (eyes and stomach), Siberian Quartz, Siberian Blue Quartz (stomach), Sunstone (stomach), Tiger's Eye, Tourmaline, Variscite

UNACCEPTABLE THOUGHTS: Picture Jasper

UNCERTAINTY: Topaz

UNCONDITIONAL LOVE: Kunzite, Magnesite, Rhodochrosite, Rose Quartz

UNDERSTANDING: Chiastolite, Emerald, Green Sapphire, Herkimer Diamond, Iolite, Malachite (complex concepts), Selenite, Tourmaline

UNGROUNDEDNESS: Hematite, Smoky Quartz

URINARY PROBLEMS: Amber, Blue Lace Agate, Citrine (urinary system), Jade (urinary system), Jasper, Red Calcite, Ruby

URO-GENITAL TRACT: Blue Aventurine, Citrine, Kyanite

UTERUS: Agate, Jasper (uterine bleeding)

VAGINA: Carnelian

VAMPIRISM: Aventurine, Ruby

VASCULAR CRAMPS: Magnesite

VEINS: Amber (varicose), Aquamarine (varicose), Blue Lace Agate (varicose), Harlequin Quartz (strengthens), Magnesite (vascular cramps), Red Tourmaline (repairs), Rhodochrosite, Rhodonite (varicose), Rhyolite, Ruby, Rutilated Quartz (strengthen walls), Sapphire (strengthen walls), Smithsonite (elasticity), Snowflake Obsidian, Opal (varicose), Topaz (varicose), Tourmaline (varicose), Variscite (elasticity)

VENEREAL DISEASE: Zircon

VENOMOUS BITES: Emerald

VERTEBRAE: Labradorite

VERTIGO: Blue Sapphire, Lapis Lazuli, Malachite, Pink Beryl, Red Jasper, Rose Quartz, Zircon

VIGOUR (INCREASE): Peridot

VIOLENCE (NEGATE): Apatite, Bloodstone, Jet, Rose Quartz, Ruby Aura Quartz

VIRAL INFECTION: Fluorite, Turquoise

VIRILITY (INCREASE): Red or Orange Stones, Lapis Lazuli, Red-Black Obsidian, Ruby in Zoisite, Smoky Quartz

VIRUSES: Fluorite, Turquoise

VISION: Bloodstone (night vision), Blue Chalcedony (glaucoma), Blue Obsidian, Clear Calcite, Clear Fluorite (poor), Diamond (glaucoma), Emerald (poor), Rhodochrosite, Tiger's Eye (night vision), Topaz

VISUALISATION (ENHANCE): Amethyst, Iolite, Green Tourmaline, Magnesite, Malachite, Prehnite, Ruby, Siberian Blue Quartz, Topaz, Unakite, Yellow Labradorite

VITALITY (INCREASE): Red Stones, Amber, Black tourmaline, Bloodstone, Carnelian, Fire Agate, Fire Opal, Jade, Red-Black Obsidian, Red Jasper, Ruby, Rutilated Quartz

VITAMIN ABSORPTION: Apache Tear (vitamins C and D), Blue-Green Obsidian (vitamins A and E), Carnelian, Chrysoprase (vitamin C), Rhyolite (vitamin B), Tiger's Iron (vitamin B)

VOCAL CORDS: Amber, Blue Lace Agate, Blue Calcite, Rhodonite, Sodalite, Tourmaline

VOICE: Blue Kyanite (strengthen)

VOMITING: Emerald, Lapis Lazuli, Moonstone

WALKING (DIFFICULTIES): Brown Aragonite

WARMING STONES: Aragonite (extremities), Citrine, Fire Opal, Obsidian (extremities), Red Carnelian

WARTS: Calcite, Emerald

WASTING DISEASES: Carnelian, Red Jasper

WATER – SALT IMBALANCES: Jade

WATER PURIFIERS: Lithium Quartz

WATER RETENTION: Mookaite, Moonstone

WEAKNESS: Amethyst (muscles and general), Hematite (muscles and general), Quartz (aura), Thulite, Turquoise

WEALTH: Abundance Quartz (abundance), Aventurine, Carnelian (abundance), Citrine, Dendritic Agate (abundance), Diamond (abundance), Hawk's Eye (abundance), Moss Agate, Ruby, Topaz (abundance), Yellow Sapphire, Yttrian Fluorite

WEATHER SENSITIVITY: Blue Chalcedony, Moss Agate

WEIGHT: Angelite (control), Apatite (control), Danburite (to gain), Green Tourmaline (to lose), Iolite (to lose), Kyanite (to lose), Lepidolite (anorexia), Magnesite (to lose), Prehnite (to lose), Red Chalcedony (reduces hunger), Seraphinite (to lose), Topaz (anorexia), Unakite (to gain), Yellow Apatite (reduces hunger)

WELLBEING (ENHANCE): Green Aventurine

WHITLOW: Fluorite, Topaz, Tourmaline

WHOOPING COUGH: Amber, Blue Lace Agate, Topaz

WILL TO BE HEALED: Garnet

WILL TO LIVE: Opal

WILLPOWER: Black Onyx, Garnet, Gold Calcite, Hematite, Orange Calcite, Rose Quartz, Ruby, Sardonyx, Tiger's Eye, Yellow Calcite

WISDOM: Amber (attuning to), Amethyst, Carnelian, Citrine (attuning to), Danburite (ancient), Emerald, Etched Quartz (ancient), Howlite, Opal Aura Quartz (attuning to), Record Keeper Quartz (attuning to), Sapphire, Scepter Quartz (ancient), Serpentine, Topaz (attuning to)

WORRY: Amazonite, Azurite, Charoite, Onyx, Red Jasper

WOUND HEALERS: Amber, Calcite, Chalcedony, Fluorite, Garnet, Mookaite, Rhodonite, Rose Quartz, Ruby, Sapphire

WRINKLES: Fluorite

X-RAY DAMAGE PREVENTION: Amazonite, Herkimer Diamond, Lepidolite, Malachite, Smoky Quartz

YIN-YANG IMBALANCE: Agate, Celestite, Hematite, Jasper, Kyanite, Onyx, Rhodonite, Tiger's Eye

A quick guide for common magickal uses:

CALM and BALANCE: Amethyst, Ametrine, Aquamarine, Citrine, Coral, Diamond, Jade, Malachite, Pink Tourmaline, Tanzanite, Zircon.

HAPPINESS: Agate, Amethyst, Calcite, Diamond, Jade.

INTUITION: Lapis Lazuli, Moonstone, Tanzanite.

LOVE: Jade, Malachite, Red Jasper, Rose Quartz.

LOVE and FRIENDSHIP: Alexandrite, Amber, Amethyst, Emerald, Moonstone, Pink Tourmaline, Sapphire, Topaz.

LUCK: Alexandrite, Amber, Aventurine, Opal, Pearl, Turquoise.

MENTAL CLARITY: Amber, Lapis Lazuli, Moonstone, Silver, Smoky Quartz, Topaz.

PRODUCTIVITY: Agate, Garnet, Opal.

PROTECTION: Garnet, Obsidian, Onyx, Quartz Crystal in a white bag.

PROSPERITY: Alexandrite, Calcite, Emerald, Gold Tiger's Eye in a green bag, Jade, Opal, Pearl, Peridot, Ruby, Sapphire, Topaz, Tourmaline.

SELF-ESTEEM: Aventurine, Carnelian, Diamond, Emerald, Garnet.

SERENITY: Amethyst, Blue Lace Agate, Jade, Quartz Crystal.

STRENGTH and CONFIDENCE: Agate, Amber, Aquamarine, Carnelian, Diamond, Garnet, Iolite, Malachite, Onyx, Ruby, Sapphire, Topaz (blue).

JOY: Orange Sunstone.

WISDOM: Coral, Jade, Pearl.

Conclusion

As you can see crystals can be used to bring many things into our life. They are gifts from the universe to help us adapt to life here on beautiful Mother Earth. Always trust your intuition as this too is a gift we are given.

Remember life is a journey so enjoy each and every experience.... the good, the bad and the just plain ugly experiences are all learning lessons to make us evolve into the best that we can be.

Love Light and Blessings on your journey.

Tamsin German

Index

Abandonment, 243

Absorption, 243

Abundance, 25

Abundance (to attract), 243

Abundance Quartz, 243, 304

Abuse, 243

Acceptance, 244

Aches, 244

Acidification of tissue (to correct), 244

Acidity, 244

Acne, 244

Adamite, 100

Addictions, 244

Adrenals, 244

Agate, 33, 34, 41, 52, 63, 89, 97, 101, 244, 248, 256, 259, 263, 264, 265, 266, 267, 270, 274, 275, 276, 278, 283, 285, 289, 290, 293, 294, 296, 301, 302, 305, 306, 307

Agatised Coral, 52

Aggression (ameliorate), 244

Aggressive tendencies), 242

Alabaster (orange), 52

Alcoholism, 244

Alexandrite, 105, 306

Align chakras, 251

Allergies, 244

Alzheimers, 244

Amazonite, 34, 52, 95, 106, 250, 251, 256, 260, 261, 263, 265, 271, 273, 277, 279, 280, 282, 293, 294, 295, 298, 301, 305

Amber, 33, 34, 35, 41, 56, 63, 91, 97, 107, 244, 245, 246, 247, 248, 249, 250, 251, 252, 253, 254, 255, 257, 258, 259, 260, 261, 262, 264, 265, 266, 267, 269, 270, 271, 272, 273, 274, 275, 276, 277, 279, 280, 281, 282, 283, 285, 286, 288, 289, 291, 295, 296, 297, 298, 299, 300, 301, 302, 303, 304, 305, 306, 307

Amethyst, 33, 34, 53, 56, 57, 58, 64, 87, 88, 97, 98, 108, 243, 244, 245, 246, 247, 248, 249, 250, 251, 252, 254, 255, 257, 258, 259, 260, 261, 262, 263, 265, 266, 267, 268, 269, 270, 271, 273, 274, 275, 276, 277, 278, 280, 281, 282, 283, 285, 286, 287, 288, 289, 291, 293, 294, 295, 296, 297, 298, 300, 301, 303, 304, 305, 306, 307

Ametrine, 34, 110, 244, 245, 246, 247, 254, 255, 256, 257, 258, 259, 261, 263, 267, 269, 273, 275, 276, 280, 282, 283, 285, 287, 290, 297, 300, 301, 302, 306

Anemia, 245

Angel Hair Quartz, 197

Angelite, 33, 111, 244, 248, 252, 253, 256, 275, 285, 286, 288, 293, 298, 299, 300, 301, 304

Anger (ameliorate), 245

Angina, 245

Animal disorders, 245

Anorexia Nervosa, 245

Anthophyllite, 53

Antibacterial, 245

Anti-inflammatory, 245

Antiseptic, 245

Antispasmodic, 245

Antiviral, 245

Anxiety/Stress, 245

Anyolite, 203

Apache Tear, 34, 179, 180, 243, 246, 247, 251, 257, 265, 266, 270, 273, 279, 280, 287, 291, 295, 296, 303

Apatite, 33, 41, 112, 245, 246, 248, 250, 251, 255, 256, 258, 260, 261, 262, 265, 269, 271, 272, 275, 276, 277, 278, 279, 280, 283, 287, 289, 291, 293, 294, 295, 298, 299, 301, 303, 304

Aphrodisiac, 245

Apophyllite, 33, 34

Appendicitis, 245

Appetite (suppressant), 245

Aqua Aura, 246, 252, 253, 255, 261, 263, 264, 276, 285, 286, 287, 291, 294, 299

Aqua Aura Quartz, 192

Aquamarine, 33, 34, 53, 113, 244, 246, 247, 253, 255, 256, 257, 262, 263, 264, 266, 267, 268, 269, 271, 272, 273, 274, 275, 276, 278, 279, 280, 285, 286, 289, 291, 292, 293, 294, 295, 296, 297, 298, 299, 300, 302, 306, 307

Aquarius, 33

Aragonite, 33, 58, 114, 244, 245, 247, 248, 250, 254, 256, 259, 261, 265, 266, 267, 269, 271, 276, 279, 280, 283, 292, 295, 297, 300, 304

Aries, 33

Arteries, 245

Arteriosclerosis, 246

Arthritis, 246

Assimilation of, 246

Asthma, 246

Astral body, 47

Atacamite, 33, 95

Atmosphere pollutant cleaners, 246

Aura, 246

Aura Quartz, 283, 298, 303, 305

Auricalcite, 95

Autism, 246

Autoimmune Disorders, 246

Aventurine, 33, 34, 53, 63, 89, 97, 98, 243, 244, 245, 246, 248, 251, 252, 254, 255, 256, 260, 261, 262, 263, 265, 266, 267, 270, 275, 277, 279, 280, 285, 286, 287, 288, 293, 295, 300, 302, 304, 306, 307

Azeztulite, 36

Azurite, 33, 34, 35, 64, 95, 117, 245, 246, 251, 252, 253, 254, 255, 258, 261, 263, 265, 266, 268, 271, 272, 274, 275, 276, 277, 278, 279, 285, 286, 287, 289, 290, 291, 293, 295, 297, 298, 299, 305

Azurite with Malachite, 118

Back problems, 247

Bacterial infections, 247

Bad breath, 247

Bad temper (ameliorate), 247

Balance chakras, 251

Barnacle Quartz, 25

Base chakra, 47, 63

Base chakra, 252

Bedsores, 247

Belching, 247

Beryl, 33, 34, 97, 119, 245, 246, 247, 249, 250, 254, 255, 256, 257, 259, 261, 263, 265, 266, 267, 268, 271, 272, 274, 275, 276, 278, 279, 282, 286, 291, 293, 295, 296, 297, 299, 300

Bi-polar, 247

Bites (venomous), 247

Black, 64

Black Amethyst, 109

Black Calcite, 122, 258, 294

Black Kyanite, 165, 266, 276

Black Obsidian, 179, 180, 266, 278, 280, 291, 294, 296, 297

Black Onyx, 244, 249, 262, 282, 305

Black Sardonyx, 280

Black Spinel, 33, 215, 258, 296

Black Tourmaline, 33, 59, 229, 244, 245, 246, 247, 251, 252, 254, 256, 257, 260, 262, 263, 265, 266, 267, 269, 270, 271, 275, 279, 280, 283, 286, 287, 288, 297

Blackouts, 247

Bladder, 247

Bleeding, 247

Blood cleanser, 247

Blood pressure, 248

Blood sugar imbalance, 248

Blood vessels, 248

Blood (cells), 247

Blood clots (dissolve), 248

Blood clotting (improve), 248

Blood disorders, 248

Blood poisoning, 247

Bloodstone, 33, 34, 53, 97, 98, 120, 244, 245, 247, 248, 251, 252, 253, 254, 255, 256, 257, 258, 259, 260, 262, 263, 266, 267, 269, 270, 271, 272, 273, 274, 275, 277, 278, 282, 283, 285, 286, 292, 295, 296, 301, 302, 303

Blown chakras, 251

Blue, 64

Blue Agate, 247, 250, 257, 260, 267, 269, 282, 295

Blue Apatite, 295

Blue Aventurine, 116, 302

Blue Banded Chalcedony., 53

Blue Calcite, 53, 122, 255, 257, 280, 283, 288, 304

Blue Celestite, 33

Blue Chalcedony, 64, 129, 245, 248, 255, 260, 263, 264, 266, 269, 270, 275, 276, 279, 282, 294, 295, 298, 299, 303, 304

Blue Fluorite, 142, 255, 263, 281, 299

Blue Jasper, 156, 252, 294, 296

Blue Kyanite, 166, 273, 287, 295, 304

Blue Lace Agate, 33, 34, 56, 64, 102, 245, 246, 247, 248, 249, 250, 252, 261, 263, 264, 265, 266, 267, 268, 269, 270, 272, 273, 275, 279, 280, 281, 283, 285, 289, 291, 292, 293, 294, 297, 299, 300, 301, 302, 304, 305, 307

Blue Obsidian, 33, 244, 252, 255, 263, 290, 295, 303

Blue Opal, 246, 255, 263, 267, 277, 283

Blue Pectolite, 170

Blue Quartz, 193, 247, 248, 250, 258, 262, 263, 267, 269, 275

Blue Sapphire, 204, 246, 256, 267, 280, 283, 300, 301, 303

Blue Selenite, 209, 270, 277, 278, 282

Blue Spinel, 33, 34, 292

Blue Tiger's Eye, 224, 254, 273, 277, 285, 292, 298

Blue Topaz, 34, 227, 252, 276, 295

Blue Tourmaline, 230, 247, 249, 252, 260, 270, 272, 273, 275, 281, 282, 287, 289, 290, 291, 294, 295, 299

Blue/Blue-Green Jade, 285

Blue-Green Jade, 152, 283

Blue-Green Obsidian, 301, 303

Blue-Green Smithsonite, 258, 263, 283

Boils, 248

Boji Stone, 33, 34

Bone marrow disorders, 249

Bones, 248

Botswana Agate, 283, 289, 294

Bowel, 249

Brain, 249

Breastfeeding, 249

Breathing disorders, 249

Breathlessness, 249

Brecciated Jasper, 54, 159, 296

Bridge Quartz, 25

Bronchantite, 95

Bronchitis, 249

Brown Agate, 280

Brown Aragonite, 304

Brown Jade, 152, 253

Brown Jasper, 156, 251, 265, 269, 272, 273, 276, 283, 293, 294

Brown Sardonyx, 266

Brown Spinel, 33, 215, 266

Brown Tourmaline, 231, 255, 266, 271, 293

Brown Zircon, 238

Bruises, 249
Bulimia, 249
Burns, 249
Bursitis, 249
Calcification, 250
Calcite, 33, 35, 41, 121, 245, 248, 250, 251, 253, 255, 258, 259, 261, 262, 265, 266, 267, 268, 269, 271, 273, 276, 278, 279, 280, 287, 289, 290, 293, 295, 296, 298, 300, 302, 303, 304, 305, 306
Calcium, 250
Calm and balance, 306
Cancer, 33
Cancerous growths, 250
Cancer-precancer, 250
Candida albicans, 250
Candle Quartz, 254, 259, 269, 270, 275, 289, 299
Capillaries, 250
Capricorn, 33
Cardiovascular system, 250
Carnelian, 33, 34, 41, 63, 87, 88, 98, 126, 243, 244, 245, 246, 247, 248, 249, 250, 252, 254, 255, 256, 257, 258, 259, 261, 262, 263, 264, 265, 267, 268, 269, 271, 272, 273, 274, 275, 276, 277, 278, 279, 280, 281, 282, 283, 284, 285, 286, 288, 289, 292, 293, 294, 295, 296, 299, 300, 302, 303, 304, 305, 307
Cartilage problems, 250
Cat's Eye, 34
Cataracts, 250

Catarrh, 250
Cathedral Quartz, 25, 247, 248, 254, 267, 281, 283, 284, 298
Celestial body, 47
Celestite, 57, 127, 250, 251, 253, 255, 259, 260, 263, 270, 271, 274, 276, 277, 278, 279, 281, 283, 288, 289, 299, 300, 301, 305
Cell phone radiation, 251
Cellular problems, 250
Cellulite, 251
Central nervous system (depleted or disturbed), 251
Cervix, 251
Chakras, 251
Chalcantite, 95
Chalcedony, 33, 34, 128, 248, 249, 253, 254, 255, 258, 259, 263, 265, 272, 273, 276, 278, 280, 281, 290, 291, 292, 294, 295, 298, 299, 301, 305
Chalcopyrite, 95
Change, 253
Channelling Quartz, 26, 300
Charoite, 34, 130, 244, 246, 247, 248, 255, 256, 257, 258, 261, 262, 263, 265, 267, 270, 272, 274, 275, 280, 282, 283, 284, 285, 289, 294, 295, 296, 297, 301, 305
Chemotherapy, 253
Cherry Opal, 248, 254, 255, 267, 273, 276, 279, 295, 300
Chest problems, 253

Chiastolite, 34, 131, 244, 247, 249, 250, 253, 257, 260, 261, 263, 264, 266, 269, 280, 283, 286, 288, 289, 294, 296, 301, 302

Chicken pox, 253

Childbirth, 254

Chills, 254

Chlorite Phantom Quartz, 291

Cholera, 254

Cholesterol, 254

Chronic Fatigue Syndrome, 254

Chrysanthemum Stone, 132, 253, 256, 258, 263, 271, 274, 279, 289, 291, 293, 296, 300, 301

Chrysocolla, 33, 34, 58, 95, 133, 244, 246, 248, 249, 252, 253, 255, 256, 257, 259, 260, 261, 266, 267, 268, 270, 272, 274, 275, 276, 277, 279, 280, 283, 285, 286, 287, 288, 289, 290, 291, 292, 293, 295, 296, 297, 299, 300, 301, 302

Chrysolite, 34, 185

Chrysoprase, 33, 58, 134, 244, 245, 246, 248, 249, 255, 256, 257, 258, 259, 262, 263, 264, 265, 266, 267, 268, 270, 272, 274, 276, 278, 280, 281, 282, 286, 290, 292, 293, 295, 296, 298, 299, 301, 303

Chrysotile, 135

Chrysotite, 135

Cinnabar, 95

Circulation, 254

Citrine, 33, 34, 36, 57, 63, 87, 98, 136, 243, 245, 247, 251, 252, 253, 254, 255, 256, 257, 258, 259, 260, 261, 262, 263, 265, 266, 267, 268, 269, 270, 271, 272, 274, 275, 276, 277, 278, 279, 280, 282, 283, 285, 289, 290, 291, 292, 295, 299, 302, 304, 305, 306

Clairaudience (enhance), 254

Clairsentience (enhance), 254

Clairvoyance (enhance), 255

Clarity (mental), 255

Claustrophobia, 255

Cleanse chakras, 251

Cleansers of physical body, 255

Clear blockages chakras, 251

Clear Calcite, 122, 294

Clear Fluorite, 142

Clear Kunzite, 163

Clear Quartz, 98, 259

Clear Topaz, 228

Codenpendency, 255

Cold extremities, 255

Colds, 255

Colic, 255

Colon problems, 255

Colourless Spinel, 216

Commitment, 255

Communication, 255

Compassion, 256

Complacency, 256

Compulsions, 256

Computer stress, 256

Computers (protection from electromagnetic emmissions ETC), 256
Concentration (improve), 256
Concussion, 256
Confidence, 256
Confusion, 256
Conicalcite, 95
Conjunctivitis, 256
Connective tissue, 256
Constipation, 257
Convalescence, 257
Convulsions, 257
Coordination, 257
Coral, 306, 307
Coughs, 257
Courage, 257
Cramps, 257
Cravings, 257
Cross Quartz, 26
Crown chakra, 48, 64, 253
Crystal balls/spheres, 19
Crystal bowls, 19
Crystal clusters/beds, 19
Crystal wands, 20
Cuprite, 95
Dalmatian Jasper, 53, 157, 245, 250, 296
Danburite, 34, 137, 253, 257, 258, 259, 265, 272, 274, 277, 279, 284, 285, 294, 301, 304, 305
Dark Blue Tourmaline, 97, 263, 295

Deafness, 257
Death (assisting the transition), 257
Debility, 257
Decision making, 257
Degenerative problems, 257
Dehydration, 258
Delicate disposition, 242
Delirium, 258
Dementia, 258
Dendritic Agate, 33, 58, 103, 243, 250, 263, 265, 281, 283, 285, 293, 304
Dendritic Chalcedony, 243, 250, 264, 270, 274, 289, 300
Denial, 258
Dental problems, 258
Depression, 242, 258
Desert Rose Selenite, 208, 209, 248
Desire, 258
Despair, 258
Despondency, 258
Determination, 258
Detoxifiers, 258
Diabetes, 259
Diamond, 33, 40, 41, 64, 138, 243, 244, 246, 251, 253, 254, 257, 259, 260, 262, 263, 264, 265, 266, 274, 275, 276, 277, 282, 283, 285, 288, 290, 294, 303, 304, 306, 307
Diamond Window Quartz, 26
Diarrhoea, 259
Digestion, 259

Dioptase, 34, 35, 95
Discs (loss of elasticity), 259
Dizziness, 259
DNA problems, 259
Dolphin Stone, 170
Double termination (point), 21
Dravide, 231
Dreams, 259
Dropsy-edema, 260
Dumortierite, 53, 193
Dysentery, 260
Dyslexia, 260
Dyspepsia, 260
Ear problems, 260
Earth chakra, 251
Eczema, 260
Egg shaped crystals, 21
Electric-Blue Obsidian, 253, 254, 271, 279, 284, 295, 298, 300, 301
Electromagnetic pollution, 260
Elestial, 21
Emerald, 33, 34, 41, 140, 245, 247, 248, 249, 250, 253, 254, 255, 257, 259, 260, 261, 262, 263, 264, 265, 267, 268, 269, 270, 271, 272, 274, 275, 276, 277, 278, 279, 280, 281, 283, 285, 286, 287, 288, 289, 290, 291, 293, 294, 295, 296, 300, 301, 302, 303, 304, 305, 306, 307
Emotional blockages, 260
Emotional dependency, 261

Emotional exhaustion, 261
Emotional abuse, 260
Emotional balance, 260
Emotional body, 47
Emotional calming, 261
Emotional cleanser, 261
Emotional patterns, 261
Emotional recovery, 261
Emotional release, 261
Emotional trauma, 261
Emotional wounds, 261
Empathy (promote), 261
Emphysemia, 261
Empowerment, 261
Endocrine system, 262
Energy, 262
Energy leaks (seal) chakras, 251
Entities (clear) chakras, 251
Entities (remove), 262
Environmental pollutants, 262
Envy (ameliorate), 262
Epilepsy, 262
Etched Quartz, 26, 305
Etheric body, 47
Etheric template, 47
Exhaustion, 262
Eye, 263
Faint, 263
Fairy Quartz, 262
Fallopian tubes, 263
Fat deposits, 263
Fatigue, 263

Fear, 263
Feet, 264
Female problems, 264
Female reproductive problems, 264
Fertility (increase), 264
Fever (lower), 264
Fire Agate, 33, 34, 251, 252, 254, 257, 262, 263, 266, 269, 276, 281, 286, 288, 290, 292, 296, 300, 303
Fire Opal, 253, 259, 261, 262, 271, 272, 284, 286, 295, 303, 304
Fishtail Selenite, 208, 210, 261, 281, 296
Flamingo Jasper, 158, 257
Flatulence, 264
Flu, 264
Fluid retention, 264
Fluorite, 33, 41, 54, 64, 141, 242, 245, 246, 248, 250, 255, 256, 257, 258, 259, 260, 261, 262, 264, 265, 268, 270, 271, 272, 273, 274, 275, 277, 278, 279, 281, 282, 283, 285, 286, 288, 289, 292, 293, 294, 295, 296, 297, 298, 301, 302, 303, 305
Food poisoning, 264
Fools Gold, 150
Forgetfulness, 264
Forgiveness, 265
Fractures, 265
Frigidity, 265
Frustration, 265
Fungal infection, 265
Galena, 33, 95, 145, 243, 254, 267, 270
Galenite, 95
Gallbladder, 265
Gallstones, 265
Gangrene, 265
Garnet, 33, 34, 41, 63, 89, 98, 146, 244, 245, 246, 247, 250, 252, 253, 255, 256, 257, 258, 259, 262, 268, 269, 270, 271, 272, 273, 274, 275, 276, 277, 278, 281, 282, 284, 285, 287, 291, 292, 293, 295, 298, 305, 306, 307
Garnierite, 95
Gastric ulcer, 265
Gastric upset, 265
Gem Silica, 95
Gemini, 33
Generator Quartz, 26
Geodes, 21
Geopathic stress, 265
Giddiness, 265
Gingivitis, 265
Girasol Quartz, 54
Glands, 266
Glandular fever, 266
Glaucoma, 266
Goitre, 242, 266
Gold, 64
Gold Calcite, 123, 274, 276, 282, 288, 299, 305

Gold Sheen Obsidian, 34
Gold Tiger's Eye, 225, 256, 299, 306
Golden Beryl, 34, 252, 253, 275
Golden Topaz, 228, 252, 262, 265, 266, 267, 274, 281, 282, 298
Green, 64
Green Agate, 257
Green Aventurine, 116, 260, 267, 271, 274, 275, 281, 284, 293, 294, 295, 296, 297, 302
Green Calcite, 123, 244, 246, 247, 248, 249, 255, 261, 264, 269, 270, 273, 278, 280, 283
Green Fluorite, 143, 257, 266, 271, 278, 280, 296
Green Garnet, 264, 267
Green Jade, 152, 281, 288
Green Jasper, 158, 244, 252, 259, 270, 282, 293, 300
Green Kunzite, 163, 253
Green Obsidian, 265, 284, 295
Green Opal, 255, 261, 264, 269, 288
Green Quartz, 194, 252, 262, 268, 280
Green Sapphire, 205, 252, 259, 263, 287
Green Sapphire, 302
Green Sapphire,, 301
Green Selenite, 210, 293
Green Smithsonite, 261
Green Spinel, 34, 216, 256, 274
Green Tourmaline, 33, 34, 58, 205, 231, 246, 249, 251, 252, 254, 255, 257, 258, 259, 261, 262, 263, 267, 269, 272, 278, 279, 281, 283, 284, 285, 303, 304
Green Zircon, 239
Grief, 266
Grounding, 266
Growth, 266
Guilt, 266
Gypsum, 41
Haemorrhoid, 267
Hair, 267
Hallucinations, 267
Hands, 267
Happiness, 267, 306
Hara, 267
Hardening diseases, 267
Harlequin Quartz, 194, 299, 302
Hawk's Eye, 224, 243, 249, 254, 255, 266, 273, 280, 284, 285, 287, 293, 296, 304
Hay fever, 267
Hearing, 267
Heart, 267
Heart chakra, 48, 63, 252
Heartache, 268
Heartburn, 268
Heat stroke (mobilize), 268
Heavy metals, 268
Hematite, 41, 54, 63, 78, 98, 147, 243, 244, 245, 246, 247, 248, 249, 251, 254, 256, 257,

258, 263, 264, 265, 266, 267, 268, 270, 271, 272, 273, 274, 275, 276, 279, 280, 281, 282, 283, 285, 286, 288, 289, 290, 291, 293, 294, 295, 298, 299, 300, 302, 304, 305

Hemorrhaging, 268

Hepatitis, 268

Herkimer Diamond, 34, 56, 64, 139, 243, 245, 250, 253, 255, 258, 259, 260, 262, 263, 265, 266, 270, 274, 277, 279, 284, 286, 287, 288, 294, 295, 297, 298, 299, 301, 302, 305

Hernia, 268

Herpes, 268

Hiccups, 268

Hiddenite, 34, 163, 253

Higher crown chakra, 253

Higher heart/thymus chakra, 252

Hips, 268

Hoarseness, 268

Holes (to repair) chakras, 251

Honey Calcite, 246, 272, 295

Hormones, 268

Hot flushes, 269

Howlite, 148, 246, 248, 250, 254, 255, 261, 262, 270, 276, 278, 284, 285, 286, 288, 292, 298, 300, 305

Hydrocephalus, 269

Hyperacidity, 269

Hyperactivity, 269

Hypochondria, 269

Hypoglycemia, 269

Hysteria, 242, 269

Immune system, 269

Impotence, 269

Incontinence, 269

Indicolite, 230

Indigestion, 269

Inertia, 269

Infection, 270

Infertility, 270

Inflammation, 243

Inflammation in body, 270

Influences from others chakras, 251

Inhibitions, 270

Injuries, 270

Inner child, 270

Insomnia, 243, 270

Intestinal tract, 271

Intuition, 271, 306

Iolite, 149, 244, 245, 246, 247, 253, 255, 258, 263, 264, 274, 277, 284, 285, 288, 289, 291, 300, 302, 303, 304, 307

Iron absorption, 271

Iron Pyrite, 98, 150, 242, 244, 245, 246, 248, 249, 250, 254, 256, 258, 259, 263, 264, 265, 269, 270, 275, 276, 278, 283, 286, 287, 289, 291, 293, 296, 298, 300

Irritability, 243, 271

Irritable bowel syndrome, 271

Irritant filter, 271

Irritation, 271

Isis (Goddess) Quartz, 27, 257

Itching, 271

Jade, 34, 41, 63, 98, 151, 244, 247, 248, 252, 254, 255, 258, 259, 263, 264, 267, 268, 270, 271, 272, 273, 274, 278, 280, 281, 286, 291, 292, 293, 294, 295, 296, 298, 300, 302, 303, 304, 306, 307

Jadeite, 33

Jasper, 33, 41, 57, 98, 155, 247, 249, 250, 252, 257, 258, 259, 260, 262, 264, 265, 266, 269, 272, 273, 276, 278, 280, 281, 283, 285, 286, 288, 289, 292, 294, 296, 297, 299, 300, 302, 305

Jaw, 271

Jealousy, 271

Jet, 33, 41, 54, 63, 90, 161, 249, 251, 255, 257, 258, 260, 262, 263, 264, 266, 267, 272, 275, 276, 277, 278, 280, 281, 286, 287, 293, 296, 298, 300, 301, 303

Jet lag, 271

Joints, 271

Joy, 272, 307

Judgementalism (overcome), 272

Justice, 272

Kabamba Jasper, 54

Karma, 272

Ketheric template, 47

Kidneys, 272

Knees, 272

Kundalini, 272

Kunzite, 33, 34, 97, 162, 244, 245, 246, 247, 250, 251, 252, 253, 254, 256, 258, 260, 261, 262, 265, 268, 269, 270, 272, 274, 275, 278, 281, 282, 283, 284, 285, 286, 287, 289, 290, 291, 292, 294, 297, 299, 300, 301, 302

Kyanite, 33, 35, 36, 92, 165, 244, 248, 249, 251, 256, 257, 259, 260, 262, 264, 265, 270, 271, 274, 275, 279, 283, 287, 291, 296, 297, 299, 300, 301, 302, 304, 305

Labour pains, 273

Labradorite, 33, 34, 41, 54, 98, 167, 245, 246, 248, 249, 251, 253, 255, 259, 262, 263, 264, 266, 268, 271, 274, 276, 277, 278, 284, 285, 286, 287, 289, 290, 295, 297, 301, 303

Lack of purpose, 273

Lactation, 273

Lapis Lazuli, 33, 34, 41, 54, 64, 89, 95, 98, 169, 247, 248, 249, 251, 252, 253, 254, 256, 258, 259, 261, 262, 263, 266, 267, 268, 269, 270, 273, 274, 275, 276, 277, 279, 280, 281, 283, 285, 286, 287, 288, 289, 290, 291, 292, 293, 294, 295, 297, 298, 299, 300, 301, 303, 304, 306

Larimar, 34, 170, 245, 247, 249, 250, 253, 255, 256, 258, 261, 262, 263, 264, 265, 266, 267, 268, 270, 272, 274, 276, 279,

280, 282, 283, 284, 285, 291, 292, 293, 294, 297, 298, 299
Laryngitis, 273
Larynx, 273
Laser points, 20
Laser Quartz, 284
Lavender Jade, 153, 294, 301
Lavender-Pink Smithsonite, 244, 281
Lavender-Violet Smithsonite, 270, 276, 280, 281, 284, 294
Laxative, 273
Layered crystals, 21
Left-right brain, 273
Legal situations, 273
Legs, 273
Leo, 34
Leopard-skin Jasper, 276
Lepidolite, 21, 34, 88, 171, 244, 245, 252, 253, 256, 257, 258, 259, 260, 261, 262, 263, 268, 269, 270, 272, 276, 277, 278, 280, 281, 282, 284, 289, 290, 291, 293, 296, 297, 299, 300, 301, 304, 305
Leprosy, 273
Lethargy, 273
Leucorrhaea, 273
Leukemia, 273
Libido (loss of), 273
Libra, 34
Life force(enhance), 273
Life Path Quartz, 27
Ligaments, 273

Light body, 274
Light Green Serpentine, 279, 283
Lightheadedness, 274
Lilac Kunzite, 164, 257, 301
Lithium Quartz, 245, 284, 304
Liver, 274
Logic, 274
Loneliness, 274
Longevity, 274
Love, 274, 306
Love and friendship, 306
Lower extremities, 275
Luck, 306
Lumbago, 275
Lungs, 275
Lymphatic system, 275
M.E, 275
Magnesite, 54, 172, 245, 246, 248, 249, 254, 257, 258, 261, 262, 263, 264, 265, 267, 268, 271, 272, 274, 276, 277, 279, 281, 285, 286, 288, 291, 295, 297, 298, 299, 302, 303, 304
Magnetite, 33, 34
Mahogany Obsidian, 34, 181, 243, 251, 266, 283, 296, 297
Malachite, 18, 23, 33, 34, 41, 58, 63, 95, 97, 173, 244, 245, 246, 247, 248, 249, 250, 252, 253, 254, 255, 257, 258, 259, 260, 261, 262, 263, 264, 265, 268, 269, 270, 271, 272, 273, 274, 275, 277, 279, 280, 281, 283, 284, 285, 286, 287, 288, 289,

290, 291, 292, 293, 295, 297, 298, 299, 300, 301, 302, 303, 305, 306, 307

Malaria, 275

Malignant conditions, 275

Manifestation stones, 275

Marcasite, 95, 174

Mastectomy, 275

Measles, 276

Meditation, 276

Melancholy, 276

Memory, 276

Menopause, 276

Menstruation, 276

Mental body, 47

Mental chatter, 277

Mental clarity, 306

Mental imbalance, 277

Mercury poisoning, 277

Metabolism, 277

Miasms, 277

Mica, 178

Mid-life crisis, 277

Migraines, 277

Mind, 278

Minerals, 278

Mistakes, 278

Mohawkite, 95

Mohs Scale, 41

Moldavite, 175, 244, 246, 253, 256, 261, 262, 264, 266, 267, 274, 284, 286, 290, 292, 301

Moodswings, 278

Mookaite, 54, 159, 247, 248, 253, 254, 266, 268, 269, 295, 297, 304, 305

Moonstone, 33, 34, 41, 98, 177, 242, 244, 245, 249, 250, 253, 254, 255, 257, 258, 259, 260, 261, 262, 263, 264, 267, 268, 269, 270, 271, 273, 274, 276, 277, 278, 282, 283, 285, 286, 287, 289, 292, 293, 295, 297, 302, 304, 306

Moss Agate, 33, 54, 58, 98, 103, 243, 244, 245, 247, 249, 254, 255, 256, 257, 258, 259, 260, 262, 263, 264, 265, 268, 269, 270, 272, 273, 274, 275, 276, 282, 283, 286, 287, 290, 291, 293, 294, 295, 297, 299, 300, 301, 304

Mother image problems, 278

Motivation, 278

Mouth, 279

Mucus membranes, 279

Multicoloured Gem Tourmaline, 277

Multiple personality, 279

Mumps, 279

Muscle system, 279

Muscovite, 34, 178, 244, 248, 258, 270, 272

Muscular disorders, 279

Narrow mindedness, 279

Nasal passages, 280

Natural formations, 22

Natural Rainbow, 195, 280

Nausea, 280

Neck, 280
Negativity, 280
Nephritis, 280
Nerves and nervous system, 280
Nervous tic, 281
Nervousness, 281
Neuralgia, 281
Neuritis, 281
Neuroses, 281
Neurotic patterns, 281
Night sweats, 281
Night terrors, 243
Night vision (aid), 281
Nightmares, 281
Nose bleeds, 281
Nose problems, 281
Nurturing stones, 281
Nutrient absorption problems, 282
Obelisk shaped crystal, 22
Obesity, 282
Obsessive thoughts, 282
Obsidian, 33, 34, 41, 63, 90, 179, 242, 243, 244, 245, 246, 252, 254, 255, 256, 257, 258, 259, 261, 262, 265, 266, 267, 270, 272, 274, 279, 280, 283, 284, 285, 286, 287, 291, 292, 294, 297, 301, 304, 306
Obstacles (remove), 282
Occlusions, 22
Odema, 282
Oesophagus, 282
Okenite, 34

Olivine, 185
Onyx, 33, 34, 41, 90, 97, 183, 242, 243, 244, 248, 249, 256, 257, 263, 264, 265, 266, 278, 284, 287, 290, 291, 293, 296, 297, 298, 305, 306, 307
Onyx Marble, 54
Opal, 33, 34, 40, 41, 97, 184, 243, 246, 247, 254, 255, 258, 259, 260, 261, 262, 263, 264, 267, 269, 270, 272, 273, 276, 277, 281, 283, 284, 285, 286, 287, 291, 296, 297, 301, 303, 305, 306
Optic nerve, 282
Optical Calcite, 263
Optimism, 282
Opyrite, 95
Orange, 64
Orange Brown Selenite, 209
Orange Calcite, 34, 54, 124, 247, 252, 258, 260, 263, 265, 271, 272, 286, 289, 305
Orange Carnelian, 252, 295
Orange Jade, 153, 272
Orange Sapphire, 264
Orange Spinel, 33, 216
Orange Sunstone, 307
Orange Zircon, 239
Orbicular Jasper, 258, 285, 289
Osteoporosis, 282
Ovaries, 282
Overactive, 282
Overeating, 282
Overindulgence, 282

Overreacting, 282
Oversensitive, 282
Overstimulation, 282
Overthinking, 282
Overwhelm, 283
Oxygenators, 283
Pain relief, 283
Pancreas, 283
Panic attacks, 283
Paralysis, 283
Paranoia, 283
Parasites, 283
Parathyroid, 283
Parkinsons disease, 283
Past lives, 283
Patience, 285
Peace (inner), 285
Peach Aventurine, 282, 299
Pearl, 33, 40, 41, 306, 307
Perception (enhance), 285
Peridot, 33, 34, 41, 185, 244, 245, 247, 250, 252, 253, 254, 255, 256, 258, 259, 260, 261, 262, 263, 264, 265, 266, 268, 269, 271, 273, 274, 275, 277, 278, 279, 282, 283, 284, 286, 287, 288, 289, 291, 293, 294, 295, 297, 300, 301, 302, 303, 306
Period pains, 285
Perseverance, 285
Personal power, 285
Pessimism, 285
Petalite, 34

Petrified Wood, 55, 186, 246, 257, 260, 262, 266, 267, 268, 270, 273, 277, 282, 284, 289, 293
Phantom crystal, 22
Phantom Quartz, 195, 267, 276, 284
Phobias, 285
Picture Jasper, 156, 244, 247, 257, 260, 262, 266, 269, 273, 274, 275, 284, 289, 302
Pietersite, 187, 262, 264, 266, 268, 271, 273, 274, 275, 277, 278, 282, 284, 285, 289, 292, 295, 297, 299, 301
Pineal gland, 285
Pink Agate, 260, 274, 292
Pink Beryl, 269, 275, 283, 289, 292, 294, 297, 301, 303
Pink Calcite, 124, 244, 265, 266, 274, 276, 277, 281, 290, 291, 292, 301
Pink Carnelian, 260, 292
Pink Chalcedony, 249, 261, 268, 287
Pink Danburite, 137, 252
Pink Opal, 269, 294
Pink Sapphire, 205, 274
Pink Topaz, 228, 274, 289
Pink Tourmaline, 33, 34, 232, 245, 252, 259, 261, 263, 268, 274, 275, 281, 283, 284, 288, 291, 293, 295, 301, 306
Pisces, 33
Pituitary gland, 285

Plutonium poisoning, 285
PMS, 285
Pneumonia, 285
Poison (antidote), 285
Polished Quartz, 22
Pollen allergies, 286
Pollution, 286
Poltergeists, 286
Poppy Jasper, 273
Positivity, 286
Post-natal depression, 286
Potential, 286
Pregnancy, 286
Prehnite, 34, 188, 247, 248, 253, 262, 266, 272, 275, 276, 281, 284, 285, 286, 293, 300, 301, 303, 304
Preseli Bluestone, 189
Productivity, 306
Prolonged illness, 286
Prosperity, 306
Prostate, 286
Protect chakras, 251
Protection, 286, 306
Psiomelan, 95
Psychiatric conditions, paranoia or schizophrenia, 243
Psychic surgery, 287
Psychic vampirism, 287
Psychic abilities, 287
Psychic attack, 287
Psychic vision, 287
Psychometry, 287

Psycho-sexual problems, 287
Psychosomatic dis-ease, 287
Public speaking, 287
Purifiers, 287
Purple, 64
Purple Fluorite, 143, 248, 249, 253, 293
Purple Jasper, 253
Purple Obsidian, 34
Purple Sapphire, 205, 253, 272, 295
Purple Sugilite, 256
Purple Tourmaline, 244, 258, 282, 285
Purple-Violet Tourmaline, 232, 254, 286
Pus, 287
Pyramid shaped crystals, 22
Pyrite, 41, 57
Pyrolusite, 34
Qi (life force), 287
Quartz, 19, 22, 33, 34, 41, 53, 55, 58, 59, 64, 97, 98, 191, 246, 249, 251, 252, 253, 255, 256, 258, 259, 262, 263, 265, 267, 268, 269, 272, 275, 276, 279, 280, 283, 284, 285, 287, 288, 292, 294, 296, 297, 298, 302, 304, 306, 307
Quartz wands, 20
Quinsy, 288
Radiation, 288
Rage, 288
Rainbow Aura Quartz, 289

Rainbow Obsidian, 181, 284, 297
Rashes, 288
Rational thought, 288
Realgar, 95
Re-birthing, 288
Record Keeper Quartz, 27, 305
Recovery (to aid), 288
Recuperation, 288
Red, 64
Red Black Obsidian, 254
Red blood cells, 288
Red Calcite, 125, 243, 248, 252, 257, 268, 272, 273, 302
Red Carnelian, 304
Red Chalcedony, 248, 254, 256, 275, 304
Red Jade, 153, 259, 299
Red Jasper, 63, 89, 98, 159, 244, 245, 250, 252, 254, 257, 259, 265, 266, 268, 272, 274, 277, 279, 288, 290, 294, 295, 303, 304, 305, 306
Red Obsidian, 34, 260, 295
Red Serpentine, 253
Red Spinel, 34, 217, 272, 295, 297
Red Tiger's Eye, 225, 273, 277, 278, 292
Red Tourmaline, 233, 248, 254, 258, 259, 274, 279, 282, 283, 289, 295, 296, 298, 302
Red Zircon, 239
Red-Black Obsidian, 264, 272, 303
Reiki, 288
Rejection, 288
Rejuvenation, 288
Relationships, 288
Relaxation, 288
Reliability, 289
Repression, 289
Reproduction system, 289
Resentmen, 289
Resistance, 289
Respiratory system, 289
Responsibility, 289
Reynaulds disease, 289
Rheumatism, 289
Rhodochrosite, 34, 200, 243, 245, 246, 248, 252, 253, 254, 256, 258, 259, 261, 263, 264, 266, 268, 270, 271, 272, 274, 275, 277, 279, 281, 283, 284, 286, 288, 289, 291, 292, 293, 294, 296, 297, 299, 301, 302, 303
Rhodonite, 18, 33, 55, 90, 201, 243, 245, 246, 248, 250, 251, 252, 253, 255, 256, 257, 258, 259, 260, 261, 264, 265, 266, 267, 268, 269, 270, 271, 272, 273, 274, 276, 279, 281, 284, 285, 286, 288, 289, 290, 291, 292, 295, 297, 298, 299, 301, 302, 304, 305
Rhomboid Calcite, 277, 278, 282
Rhyolite, 55, 202, 244, 260, 269, 270, 272, 279, 284, 286, 288,

290, 291, 293, 297, 300, 302, 303

Rickets, 289

Ringworm, 290

Risk-taking, 290

RNA (stabilise), 290

Rose Aura Quartz, 291

Rose Quartz, 56, 57, 58, 63, 87, 90, 98, 179, 196, 243, 244, 245, 246, 248, 249, 251, 252, 253, 254, 258, 260, 261, 262, 263, 264, 265, 266, 267, 268, 269, 270, 272, 274, 275, 276, 277, 279, 280, 281, 282, 283, 284, 285, 286, 288, 289, 290, 291, 292, 293, 297, 298, 299, 300, 301, 302, 303, 305, 306

Rough/raw chunks, 23

Royal Plume Jasper, 261, 296

Royal Sapphire, 271, 289

Rubelite, 233

Rubellite, 34

Ruby, 33, 34, 41, 56, 63, 89, 203, 242, 243, 244, 245, 247, 249, 252, 254, 256, 257, 258, 262, 263, 264, 266, 267, 268, 269, 270, 272, 273, 274, 275, 276, 278, 279, 280, 281, 282, 283, 284, 285, 286, 287, 288, 289, 290, 292, 294, 295, 297, 298, 302, 303, 304, 305, 306, 307

Ruby Aura Quartz, 292

Ruby in Zoisite, 203

Rutilated Quartz, 33, 34, 197, 245, 248, 253, 258, 262, 264, 265, 266, 267, 269, 277, 280, 283, 284, 285, 287, 289, 291, 292, 293, 294, 298, 299, 300, 302

Sacral chakra, 48, 63

Sacral/navel chakra, 252

Sadness, 290

Sagittarius, 34

Sapphire, 33, 34, 41, 204, 205, 243, 245, 247, 248, 249, 250, 255, 256, 258, 259, 260, 262, 263, 264, 265, 267, 268, 271, 274, 275, 276, 277, 279, 281, 283, 285, 290, 291, 297, 299, 301, 302, 305, 306, 307

Sardonyx, 59, 207, 250, 258, 259, 269, 271, 275, 276, 282, 285, 286, 287, 291, 293, 294, 296, 297, 301, 305

Satin Spa, 208

Scarring, 290

Scattered energy, 243

Scepter Quartz, 305

Sceptre Quartz, 27, 284

Schizophrenia, 290

Schorl, 229

Sciatica, 290

Scorpio, 34

Scrofula, 290

Seasonal affective disorder (SAD), 290

Security, 290

Seer stone, 23

Sefishness, 292

Selenite, 33, 35, 36, 55, 59, 208, 209, 246, 249, 250, 251, 253,

256, 259, 262, 265, 266, 271, 274, 276, 277, 278, 281, 284, 285, 286, 287, 292, 293, 294, 295, 296, 297, 298, 302

Self acceptance, 290

Self analysis, 290

Self awareness, 290

Self belief, 290

Self confidence, 290

Self containment, 290

Self control, 291

Self criticism, 291

Self deceit, 291

Self destructiveness, 291

Self doubt, 291

Self esteem, 291, 307

Self exploration, 291

Self expression, 291

Self hatred (overcoming), 291

Self Healed Quartz, 28

Self healing, 291

Self knowledge, 291

Self limitation, 291

Self love, 291

Self realisation, 291

Self righteousness, 291

Self sabotage, 291

Self sufficiency, 291

Self trust, 292

Self worth, 292

Selflessness, 292

Senile dementia, 292

Sensitivity, 292

Septicemia, 292

Serafina, 211

Seraphinite, 211, 253, 254, 274, 279, 280, 283, 291, 304

Serenity, 307

Serpentine, 33, 55, 92, 212, 246, 247, 250, 257, 258, 259, 260, 261, 264, 265, 268, 272, 274, 275, 276, 277, 282, 283, 284, 287, 297, 300, 305

Sexual, 292

Shadow side, 292

Shingles, 292

Shock, 292

Shoulders, 293

Shungite, 251

Shyness, 293

Siberian Blue Quartz, 280, 287, 296, 297, 298, 299, 301, 302, 303

Siberian Quartz, 297

Sick Building Syndrome, 51, 293

Sighing (excessively), 293

Sight, 293

Silver, 64

Silver, Smoky Quartz, 306

Silver-Sheen Obsidian, 276, 285

Single termination (point), 23

Sinuses, 293

Skeletal system, 293

Skin, 293

Sleep sickness, 294

Sleep walking, 293

Sluggishness, 294

Smell (restore sense of), 294

Smithsonite, 33, 34, 95, 213, 244, 245, 252, 258, 259, 260, 267, 269, 270, 277, 278, 279, 282, 287, 288, 290, 293, 297, 298, 301, 302

Smoking, 294

Smoky Amethyst, 251, 262, 284

Smoky Quartz, 33, 34, 55, 98, 197, 244, 246, 247, 250, 251, 252, 253, 255, 256, 257, 258, 260, 261, 262, 264, 265, 266, 267, 268, 270, 272, 273, 276, 277, 278, 280, 281, 283, 284, 286, 288, 289, 292, 293, 296, 297, 298, 300, 302, 303, 305

Snake bite, 294

Sneezing, 294

Snow Quartz, 198, 289

Snowflake Obsidian, 34, 55, 92, 179, 182, 259, 260, 263, 271, 274, 276, 278, 280, 293, 294, 303

Sodalite, 34, 55, 64, 214, 244, 248, 250, 253, 256, 259, 260, 264, 266, 269, 270, 271, 273, 275, 277, 278, 279, 282, 283, 285, 288, 290, 291, 292, 293, 299, 300, 301, 304

Solar Plexus chakra, 48, 63, 252

Soothing stones, 294

Sore throat, 294

Sores, 294

Sorrows, 294

Soul, 294

Soulmate (attracting), 294

Soulmate Quartz, 28, 294

Spasms, 295

Speech, 295

Spine, 295

Spinel, 34, 215, 249, 258, 270, 272, 286, 288

Spirit Quartz, 284

Spiritual vision, 295

Spite, 295

Spleen, 295

Spleen chakra, 252

Spondulytis, 295

Spontaneity, 296

Square crystal, 23

Stabilising, 296

Stagnant energy, 296

Stamina, 296

Stammering, 296

Static electricity, 296

Steadfastness, 296

Steroids (natural boost), 296

Stibnite, 95

Stiff neck, 296

Stillbite, 218, 249, 258, 260, 271, 273, 275, 285, 298

Stimulating, 296

Stitches (heal), 296

Stomach-abdomen, 296

Strength and confidence, 307

Strengthen chakras, 251

Strengtheners, 297

Streptocal infections, 297

Stress, 297
Subconscious, 297
Sugilite, 34, 64, 219, 246, 249, 250, 257, 258, 260, 262, 264, 265, 266, 267, 275, 277, 279, 280, 281, 283, 284, 286, 287, 290, 292, 294
Suicidal thoughts, 298
Sulphur, 35
Sunburn, 298
Sunshine Aura Quartz, 300, 301
Sunstone, 33, 34, 91, 98, 220, 243, 247, 250, 251, 255, 258, 261, 263, 267, 270, 271, 272, 277, 278, 281, 284, 286, 288, 289, 290, 291, 294, 295, 297, 302
Supporating wounds, 298
Supra-adrenals, 298
Survival instincts, 298
Swelling, 298
Tabular crystals, 23
Tachycardia, 298
Tact, 298
Talents (realising), 298
Tangerine Quartz, 199, 284, 292, 294
Tantric Twin Quartz, 28
Tanzanite, 221, 250, 267, 272, 281, 284, 299, 306
Taste (restore), 298
Taurus, 33
Teeth, 298
Teething pain, 298
Tektite, 222, 250, 254, 255, 256, 264, 266, 287, 298
Telepathy, 298
Temper, 298
Temperature, 299
Tempest Stone, 187
Tenacity, 299
Tendonitis, 299
Tension (release), 299
Testicles, 299
Tests (taking), 299
Third Eye chakra, 48, 64, 253
Throat, 299
Throat chakra, 48, 63, 252
Thrombosis, 299
Thrush (candida), 299
Thulite, 241, 264, 281, 297, 304
Thyroid, 299
Tibetan Quartz, 276
Tibetan Turquoise, 284
Tics, 299
Tiger's Eye, 33, 34, 41, 53, 55, 57, 63, 97, 98, 223, 244, 245, 246, 249, 252, 255, 258, 259, 262, 263, 265, 267, 268, 272, 274, 275, 277, 278, 279, 281, 284, 285, 286, 287, 289, 290, 291, 294, 295, 296, 297, 298, 299, 302, 303, 305
Tiger's Iron, 226, 247, 253, 262, 264, 268, 273, 279, 288, 296, 303
Time Link Quartz, 28
Timidity, 299

Tinnitus, 299
Tiredness, 300
Tissue, 300
Toenails, 300
Toes, 300
Tolerance, 300
Tonic, 300
Tonsilitis, 300
Tonsils, 300
Toothache, 300
Topaz, 33, 34, 41, 227, 243, 245, 247, 249, 250, 252, 253, 257, 258, 259, 262, 265, 266, 268, 269, 270, 272, 275, 276, 277, 278, 279, 280, 281, 287, 288, 290, 291, 293, 294, 295, 296, 298, 299, 301, 302, 303, 304, 305, 306, 307
Tourmaline, 33, 41, 229, 243, 245, 246, 248, 249, 251, 252, 253, 254, 255, 256, 257, 258, 259, 260, 261, 262, 264, 266, 267, 268, 269, 272, 273, 275, 276, 278, 279, 280, 281, 282, 283, 286, 287, 290, 291, 292, 294, 295, 297, 298, 300, 302, 304, 305, 306
Tourmalined Quartz, 33, 199, 266, 268, 291
Toxicity, 300
Toxins, 300
Trance states, 300
TranquillityTranquilliser, 300
Trans-Channeling Quartz, 29
Transformational stones, 301
Transitional stones, 301

Transmitter Quartz, 29
Trapped nerve, 301
Trauma, 301
Trigonic Quartz, 29
Trust, 301
Truth, 301
Tuberculosis, 301
Tumbled (polished) stones, 24
Tumours, 301
Turquoise, 18, 33, 34, 41, 56, 57, 63, 92, 235, 244, 245, 246, 249, 250, 253, 254, 257, 258, 260, 261, 262, 263, 266, 267, 269, 270, 271, 273, 275, 276, 278, 279, 280, 281, 282, 283, 284, 286, 287, 288, 289, 291, 295, 296, 297, 299, 300, 303, 304, 306
Ulcers, 302
Ulexite, 33
Unacceptable thoughts, 302
Unakite, 236, 257, 264, 266, 267, 276, 284, 286, 287, 288, 289, 293, 303, 304
Uncertainty, 302
Unconditional love, 302
Understanding, 302
Ungroundedness, 302
Urinary problems, 302
Uro-genital tract, 302
Uterus, 302
Vagina, 302
Vampirsm, 302
Vanadanite, 95

Variscite, 33, 34, 237, 244, 252, 256, 257, 258, 262, 265, 266, 269, 275, 281, 284, 285, 289, 291, 292, 293, 302, 303

Vascular cramps, 302

Veins, 302

Veneral disease, 303

Venomous bites, 303

Verdelite, 231

Vertebrae, 303

Vertigo, 303

Vigour (increase), 303

Violence (negate), 303

Violet Purple Fluorite, 276, 287

Violet Spinel, 217, 271

Viral infection, 303

Virgo, 34

Virility (increase), 303

Viruses, 303

Vision, 303

Visualisation (enhance), 303

Vitality (increase), 303

Vitamin absorption, 303

Vocal cords, 304

Vogel wands, 20

Voice, 304

Vomiting, 304

Walking (difficulties), 304

Warming stones, 304

Warts, 304

Wasting disease, 304

Water purifiers, 304

Water rentention, 304

Watermelon Tourmaline, 63, 233, 252, 258, 268, 275, 277, 279, 281, 283, 285, 291

Water-salt imbalences, 304

Weakness, 304

Wealth, 304

Weather sensitivity, 304

Weight, 304

Wellbeing (enhance), 304

White, 64

White Jade, 154, 257

White Sapphire, 259, 282, 286

Whitlow, 305

Whooping cough, 305

Will to be healed, 305

Will to live, 305

Willpower, 305

Wisdom, 305, 307

Worry, 305

Wound healers, 305

Wrinkles, 305

Wulfenite, 34, 95

X-ray damage (prevention), 305

Yellow, 64

Yellow Apatite, 254, 256, 258, 259, 265, 274, 275, 300, 304

Yellow Calcite, 125, 305

Yellow Fluorite, 144, 254, 258, 274, 296

Yellow Jade, 154, 259

Yellow Jasper, 63, 160, 255, 259, 262, 271, 272, 274, 295, 297

Yellow Kunzite, 164, 250, 256, 259, 286

Yellow Kyanite, 288

Yellow Labradorite, 168, 244, 255, 265, 270, 274, 278, 282, 285, 295, 297, 300, 303

Yellow Sapphire, 97, 206, 243, 247, 262, 275, 279, 304

Yellow Smithsonite, 261, 282, 293

Yellow Spinel, 34, 217, 261

Yellow Tourmaline, 234, 265, 274, 290, 295, 297

Yellow Zircon, 240

Yin-Yang imbalance, 305

Zeolite, 35

Zircon, 64, 238, 246, 249, 257, 258, 277, 279, 282, 290, 293, 294, 295, 303, 306

Zoisite, 33, 241, 244, 253, 264, 269, 282, 284, 288, 294, 303

www.ingramcontent.com/pod-product-compliance
Lightning Source LLC
Chambersburg PA
CBHW070531010526
44118CB00012B/1096